RACISM

IN COLLEGE ATHLETICS:

The African-American Athlete's Experience

Dana D. Brooks, Ed.D.
West Virginia University

Ronald C. Althouse, Ph.D.
West Virginia University

FITNESS INFORMATION TECHNOLOGY, INC.
MORGANTOWN, WV 26504

Library of Congress Catalog Card Number 92-73667

ISBN 0-9627926-2-4

Cover Design: Brian Caudill
Copy Editor: Sandra R. Woods
Production/Design Editor: Brian Caudill
Printed by: BookCrafters

Printed In The United States of America
10 9 8 7 6 5 4 3 2

Fitness Information Technology, Inc.
P.O. Box 4425, University Avenue
Morgantown, WV 26504 USA
(800) 477-4348
(304) 599-3482

To all student-athletes, especially African-American student-athletes, coaches and administrators. Hopefully, this book will enrich the quality of your lives on and off the playing fields.

Co-Editors: Ronald C. Althouse, Dana D. Brooks

Contents

Contributors

Ronald Althouse is a professor of sociology, Chairperson of the Department of Sociology and Anthropology, and Acting Director of the Survey Research Center at West Virginia University. He received the M.A. and Ph.D. in sociology from the University of Minnesota. Dr. Althouse's research interests and publications have focused on workers' risk and workers' health, health care delivery, and health systems. He has contributed to the literature on athletic participation, and is committed to efforts focused on social justice in sports. He is currently involved in work on a West Virginia Humanities Council Project: The African-American Athlete: From Coal Fields to College. In his leisure time he enjoys bicycling, is an avid science fiction reader, and enjoys jazz.

Audwin Anderson is an assistant professor in the Department of Sociology and Anthropology, University of Southern Alabama. He earned the Ph.D. from Texas A & M University in 1990. He has made numerous presentations at professional meetings. Dr. Anderson's recently co-authored article focuses on "Career Orientations of Male College Basketball Players." From 1986-1990, he was a member of the editorial board, *Journal of Applied Research in Coaching and Athletics*. He is member, and past-president of the Psych-social Committee of the National Sickle Cell Disease Centers. For hobbies, he enjoys all sports, reading, and jazz.

Dana Brooks is a professor and Interim Dean of Physical Education at West Virginia University. He received the B.S. from Towson State University (1973), and M.S. (1976) and Ed.D.(1979) from West Virginia University. He has published and presented nationally and internationally in the areas of sport sociology and sport social psychology. Dr. Brooks served as Chairperson of West Virginia University's Athletic Council, member of a Special Task Force to Review the Feasibility of a Student-Athlete Academic Learning Center, the Black Community Concerns Committee, and the Affirmative Action Committee. In addition, he served as Minority Recruitment, Retention Coordinator in the Office of the Provost. He is Project Administrator for the National Youth Sport Program at West Virginia University. Dr. Brooks is a member of the North American Society for Sport Sociology, North Central Sociological Association, and the American Alliance for Health, Physical Education, Recreation and Dance. He enjoys tennis, whitewater rafting, tole painting, fencing, and photography.

Doris Corbett is an associate professor at Howard University. Since receiving her Ph.D. from the University of Maryland Dr. Corbett has centered her scholarship in the areas of ethics in physical education and sport; comparative and international sport; women in sport; cultural diversity, and mentoring. She is a member of numerous professional organizations including AAHPERD, International Council for Health, Physical Education and Recreation, and International Committee for Sociology of Sport. In her leisure time, Dr. Corbett enjoys tennis, reading, travel, and walking.

Alison Dewar is currently an associate professor of physical education and women's studies affiliate at Miami University, Ohio. She received both the M.PE. and Ed.D. from the University of British Columbia. Dr. Dewar has made presentations nationally and internationally and published articles and book chapters on issues relating to feminist critiques of sport and physical education. Her professional organization memberships include the North American Society for the Sociology of Sport. For recreation she runs, hikes, and reads feminist mystery novels.

D. Stanley Eitzen is a professor of sociology at Colorado State University. He received a B.A. in history from Bethel College in 1956, an M.S. in social science from Emporia State University in 1962, and an M.A. (1966) and Ph.D. (1968) in sociology from the University of Kansas. While an undergraduate, he lettered in three varsity sports: football, basketball, and track. Dr. Eitzen's scholarly interests include the sociology of sport, social problems especially social inequality, elite deviance, and political sociology. He has authored or co-authored 13 books, including 2 in sport: *Sociology of North American Sport*, fifth edition forthcoming in 1993 (with George H. Sage); and *Sport in Contemporary America*, fourth edition forthcoming in 1993. He has published sports articles appearing in at least 15 journals and quarterlies. Dr. Eitzen belongs to the International Sociological Association, the American Sociological Association, the Society for the Study of Social Problems, the Midwest Sociological Society, the Western Social Science Association, the North American Society for the Sociology of Sport, and the International Committee for the Sociology of Sport. His hobbies are recreational running, watching sports, and wood sculpture.

Tina Sloan Green is currently a professor of physical education at Temple University. She received the M.Ed. in Physical Education at Temple University. Since 1973 she has served as head coach of women's lacrosse and women's field hockey. Professor Green has co-authored two books, including *Black Women in Sport*. Her many activities include the founding of the U.S. Field Hockey Association's Inner City Field Hockey Program in 1980. For recreation Ms. Green enjoys travel, tennis, and walking.

Othello Harris is an assistant professor of physical education, health and sport studies at Miami University, Ohio. He received his B.A. (1979), M.A. (1981), and Ph.D. (1989) degrees in sociology from the University of Maryland, College Park. In addition to many publications and presentations, Dr. Harris is a member of the North American Society for the Sociology of Sport, the North Central Sociological Association and an editorial board member for the *Sociology of Sport Journal*. His recreational hobbies include racquetball, basketball, and jogging.

William Johnson is an assistant professor and associate department chairperson in educational administration at Howard University. He received the M.S. from Indiana University and attended George Washington University for further graduate study. During college, he participated in football and track and field. He served as gymnastic coach at Howard University. His academic work has focused on curriculum development in higher education. He is a life member of AAHPERD. His recreational activities are golf, tennis, and fitness.

Carole Oglesby is a professor and Chairperson, Department of Physical Education, Temple University. She received a Ph.D. in physical education from Purdue University. Two teams that she coached at Purdue and the University of Massachusetts attended the College World Series. Dr. Oglesby has authored numerous books and articles. She has served as

ix

context editor of several journals, including *Quest* and the *Journal of Sport and Exercise Psychology*. Her many professional associations include serving as first president of the AIAW and president of the Sport Psychology Academy. She competed and completed the 6th New York City Marathon.

George Sage is currently a professor of kinesiology and sociology at the University of Northern Colorado. He received the Ed.D. from the University of California, Los Angeles in 1962. From 1963 to the present he has served as head basketball coach at Northern Colorado University. Dr. Sage has presented over 50 invited speeches and has been the recipient of numerous honors and awards. His publications include numerous articles, 5 books, and over 12 chapters contributed to edited volumes. His books include *Power and Ideology in American Sport: A Critical Perspective* and *Sociology of North American Sport* (co-authored with D. Stanley Eitzen). In addition to memberships in many professional organizations, Dr. Sage relaxes with travel, running, and reading.

Robert Sellers is currently an assistant professor of psychology at the University of Virginia. He graduated from Howard University, cum laude, in 1985. While at Howard, Dr. Sellers was an All-American football player. In 1990, he completed a Ph.D. in personality psychology at the University of Michigan. His research interests have focused on stress and coping, life experience of student-athletes and racial identity. His publications and presentations reflect this focus. He has served as consultant to the NCAA President's Commissions Study of Life Experiences of Student-Athletes, the NCAA Research Committee, as well as principal investigator of the Student-Athlete Life Stress Project. His recreational interests include softball, basketball, and movies.

Donald South is a professor of sociology at the University of South Alabama. He received the M.A. and Ph.D. from Louisiana State University. He has served on the university athletic-academic committee for 15 years. Dr. South has participated in baseball, basketball, and boxing. He has published extensively, contributing to books and authored monographs. In addition, Dr. South has been active on editorial boards of sociological journals, and served as editor of *Sociological Spectrum*. He has held offices in regional professional organizations. For relaxation, he enjoys gardening and furniture refinishing.

David Wiggins is currently a professor of physical education at George Mason University. He received the A.B. and M.A. from San Diego State University and the Ph.D. from the University of Maryland. While at San Diego, he played varsity baseball and served as assistant baseball coach. Dr. Wiggins' research has focused on the history of American sport, particularly as it relates to the involvement of black athletes, at both the amateur and professional levels. His numerous articles deal with such topics as sport on southern plantations, black participation in the Olympic Games, and the debate over black athletic superiority. Dr. Wiggins is a member of the North American Society for Sport History. His recreational hobbies include racquetball, jogging, and tennis.

Preface

Social justice issues focusing on racism, sexism, classism, economically disadvantaged and concerns about the disabled have gained considerable attention on college campuses. Special task forces, university committees, and administrators have been hired to develop strategies to address these issues. A discernible increase in the number of racial and sexual assaults on college campuses further echo the need for reform and change.

While these and other injustices exist in the larger American society, many people believe sport is immune from these conditions. Sport participation has been described as the great equalizer, bringing together athletes from diverse ethnic backgrounds to compete on a "level playing field." However, there is no evidence to suggest that sport participation and personal contact with individuals from different cultural and ethnic backgrounds bring a positive change in attitudes toward racial tolerance.

This text breaks new ground in race relations applied to college athletic participation. It is not merely concerned with the identification of social injustice in college athletics, but offers clear and constructive strategies for change.

The text is divided into four major sections: (a) Historical Analysis of Racism and Critical Events; (b) Recruitment, Retention, and Mobility in College Athletics; (c) Gender and Race Intersections in College Athletics; and (d) Analyses of Racism and Future Prospects for Change. These four sections have been consistently referred to in the literature as problem areas facing the African-American college athlete.

The essays found under each of the four main sections identify strategies and solutions to eradicate the conditions contributing to racism and oppression directed toward the African-American college athlete. The essay format provides the reader with new perspectives, re-assessments, and redefinitions of racism, sexism, and classism. An introductory sketch of the enclosed essays follows.

Historical Analysis of Racism and Critical Events

Essay 1 identifies critical historical events (e.g., establishment of black baseball's first successful league in 1920, signing of Jackie Robinson by the Brooklyn Dodgers in 1945, *Brown v. Topeka Board of Education* in 1954, Civil Rights Movement of the 1960s, and Proposition 48 in 1986) affecting racism in college athletics.

Essay 2 provides a social and historical overview of factors leading to African-American predominance in college athletics. The consequences of stereotyping, stacking, and academic concerns (graduation rates) are discussed in detail. The essay concludes by offering the reader suggestions to address academic problems faced by African-American student-athletes.

Recruitment, Retention, and Mobility in College Athletics

Essay 3 outlines how the conflict between big-time athletics values and the goals of higher education results in racial differences in recruiting, retention, and graduation rates. Specific strategies are recommended to reduce academic and economic exploitation of African-American athletes.

Essay 4 discusses racial, geographical, structural variables, career background, previous playing position, and occupational demand attributes contributing to racial imbalance in coaching and managerial positions in college athletics.

Essay 5 studies the psychological and sociological problems African-American athletes face when they retire from college athletics. The argument is presented that athletic experience will have a positive effect on the quality of postathletic life.

Gender and Race Intersection in College Athletics

Essay 6 traces the social and historical roots of the African-American female participation in college athletics. Detailed discussion of racial and sexual barriers impeding the involvement of the African-American woman in athletics is presented.

Essay 7 is an extension of Essay 6 and offers the reader new strategies to increase the number of African-American females as participants and coaches.

Essay 8 challenges the reader to examine the nature of intergroup race relations in college athletics. The author discusses ways in which racism, sexism, and classism affect race relations in sport.

Analyses of Racism and Future Prospects for Change

Essay 9 clearly outlines the distinction between prejudice and racism.

The author challenges the dominant white culture to recognize and accept responsibility for establishing antiracist programs.

Essay 10 considers the past, current, and future status of race relations in society and college athletics. The author identifies three major trends (racial composition, unequal distribution of wealth, transformation of the economy) that will shape race relations as we move toward the 21st century. The essay concludes with a discussion of strategies and solutions to reform college sport, thus eliminating racism.

The epilogue highlights many of the key concepts presented in the previous ten essays. It concludes by talking about a vision for change that has to be built on conducting antiracist work, questioning past practices, and developing new strategies and policies as we move to the 21st century.

The target audience for this text is college, high school, and community sport coaches. Students enrolled in upper division undergraduate courses in sport sociology may also find this textbook an important supplement to their course of study.

Numerous individuals have assisted us in editing this text. We are indebted to Rochelle Althouse and Aaron Althouse for their editorial assistance. We would particularly like to thank Ms. Linda Hetrick for her secretarial and managerial contributions to this manuscript.

We are grateful to J. William Douglas, Dean, School of Physical Education, West Virginia University, for his "moral"and financial contributions to this project. The Co-Editors express deep appreciation to Dr. Andrew Ostrow, President, Fitness Information Technology, Inc., for his encouragement and support. Appreciation is extended to Mr. Richard Schultz, Executive Director, NCAA; Mr. Stanley Johnson, Director of Professional Development, NCAA; Members of the NCAA Minorities Opportunities and Interest Committee for their insights and recommendations for addressing the social justice problem: racism in college athletics.

The quality of this document resides primarily with the contributing authors: Dr. George Sage, Dr. David K. Wiggins, Dr. Othello Harris, Dr. Audwin Anderson, Dr. Donald South, Ms. Tina Sloan Green, Dr. Doris Corbett, Mr. William Johnson, Dr. Robert M. Sellers, Dr. Alison Dewar, Dr. Stanley Eitzen, and Dr. Carol Oglesby.

Dana D. Brooks
Ronald C. Althouse
Co-Editors

Introduction

George H. Sage

This book is about racism in American college sport. It is too bad that a book with such a focus is necessary because it is an account of human practices that have heaped injustice upon injustice on African-Americans in a sector of human activity—intercollegiate sport—that is typically admired for its commitment to opportunity and justice. But this is also a book about hope. Deeds of the past need not be visited upon African-Americans in the future. As a matter of fact, the essays in this volume emphatically suggest that opportunities are improving for African-American college athletes, but for full equality and opportunity to be achieved a number of still-unresolved problems must be resolved.

Pursuing this topic requires that we begin by framing our discussion at a level much broader than college athletics. We must situate American sports within the context of our contemporary society as well as come to grips with the pervasive racism that has been systemic to American culture for the past 370 years.

Contemporary Sport in the United States

Among popular cultural practices in American society sport is undoubtedly the most ubiquitous. Over 25 million young boys and girls participate in youth sports programs each year, another 5.5 million high school athletes compete in over 25 different sports annually, and more than 300,000 college athletes toil for their institutions each year. Add to those participants the elite-level athletes that represent the U. S. in international competition as well as professional athletes, and you have an enormous number of athletes engaged in organized sports. But the major form of involvement with sports is not as participants. It is as spectators--the millions who watch sporting events, either by actually attending contests or by viewing them on television.

With sports being such a pervasive activity, Americans devote a great deal of their time and energies to sports: They are knowledgeable about rules (or at least think they are); they are avid followers of their favorite teams, able to recite the teams' strengths and weaknesses and chances for winning the championship of their league, and they are enthusiastic admirers of their favorite athletes. Much of this knowledge and enthusiasm is nurtured and sustained by the mass media, which cover several thousands of hours of sporting events each year.

Study of American Sport

In spite of the various ways in which Americans know and follow sports, they are not encouraged to critically examine the prevalent attitudes, values, myths, and folklore about this cultural practice.[1] Throughout American society there tends to be a blissful ignorance about the social relations that control sport. To a frightening degree there is a naivete to the social context and material conditions underlying sporting practices.

Although sports embody specific and identifiable purposes, values, and meanings, they are typically viewed by both participants and fans as ahistorical and apolitical. This is largely the case because most of the written and broadcast information about sports in American society does not confront us with questions about the larger social issues and political and economic consequences of modern sports. Instead, we are fed a diet of traditional slogans, cliches, and ritualized trivia about sports. Although these can be comforting to the devoted fan, they do not come to grips with the social reality of contemporary sport.

Another obstacle to understanding American sports is that sport and society have traditionally been seen as discrete social phenomena, with sport often thought of as an isolated activity that is (or should be) uncontaminated by problems and issues of the wider society. Americans have tended to cherish the illusion that sports are just "fun and games," and those who have held the power and influence in sports have vigorously fought any attempt to change this image.

Attempting to understand sport as a cultural practice must begin with an assumption that it cannot be examined as a practice isolated from the social, economic, political, and cultural context in which is situated. As a set of social practices and relations that are structured by the culture in which sport exists, any adequate account of sport must be grounded in a knowledge about its location within society. Thus, understanding sport as a cultural practice necessitates studying it as part of a larger political, economic, social, and ideological configuration. The essence of sport is to be found within the nature of its relationship to those broader societal forces of which it is a part. Relevant issues involve the ways in which sport is related to social class, race, gender, and the control, production, and distribution of political, economic, and cultural power.

Intercollegiate Sport: The Beginnings

The elaborate system of intercollegiate sports popular in the United States is a unique phenomenon. In most countries of the world there is very little sport in institutions of higher education. In the United States intercollegiate sports originally developed in the last half of the nineteenth century and began at colleges that were attended mostly by students living on campuses. Games and sports were a diversion from the boredom of classroom work and limited social outlets. During the first half of the nineteenth century, students played a variety of sports, first as unorganized and impromptu games and later as organized intramural and interclass activities. As the number of colleges and their proximity increased, the next logical step was for the students at one college to challenge the students of a nearby school to a sports contest. The first officially recorded intercollegiate sports event was a rowing race between Harvard and Yale in 1852. At the beginning, intercollegiate sports were organized by the students, usually over faculty objection. In time, with increased organization and the proliferation of sports teams, faculties assumed administrative control over sports.

Late-nineteenth-and early-twentieth-century college sports were dominated by white, upper-class, Protestant males. A few African-American athletes did make their presence felt in both predominantly white and all-black colleges, but racism was ominously present from the beginning of intercollegiate sports.

Racism and American Society

The racism that has been a salient part of college athletics throughout its history is only one dimension of an institutional racism that has been a pervasive part of the American experience since its beginnings. To understand the role of racism in college athletics, we cannot perceive it apart from the larger cultural context in which it is situated. Thus, it is important to historically situate and culturally locate American racism.

There are many racial and ethnic minorities in the U. S., but African-Americans are the largest minority population. Currently there are approximately about 32 million blacks, who make up about 12 percent of the total U. S. population. A persisting thread running through the garment of the American experience is discrimination against blacks; racism is rooted deeply in our history. African-Americans are the only racial group that has been subjected to an extended period of slavery, they are the only racial group to have segregation laws passed against them that were supported and fully sanctioned by the Supreme Court, and they are the only group to have to struggle against unbelievable odds for basic civil rights that others have enjoyed as a constitutional right (Watson, 1987).

Black Africans were first brought to colonial America in 1619, only 12 years after the establishment of the first English settlement at Jamestown. By the middle of the seventeenth century a slave system among colonial plantation owners had begun, and by the end of that century enslaved black Africans had become a major source of labor and a fundamental component to colonial agricultural and commercial interests. A racist social structure, with blacks at the bottom, was thus created by slave-owners of the agricultural South, together with northern trading and shipping firms.

When the colonists challenged British rule in the late eighteenth century and finally established independence, a system of racism was incorporated into the basic documents of the newly formed United States. The Declaration of Independence and the U.S. Constitution condoned racial subordination and discrimination against African-Americans. So, in spite of what was considered an enlightened stance toward human rights at that time, the framers of these documents saw no contradiction in espousing a liberal view of liberty for white males while denying it to blacks. Slavery was sanctioned, and blacks were denied all of the rights of citizenship.

It took a civil war and the passage of the 13th amendment to the U. S. Constitution in 1865 to officially end the slavery system. Although slavery was abolished by the 13th amendment, in the latter decades of the nineteenth century many states passed Jim Crow laws mandating racial segregation in almost all areas of public life. In effect, then, Jim Crow laws legalized white domination and thus left racism essentially intact. A "separate- but-equal" system replaced slavery and became an even more efficient instrument of domination and subordination than slavery had been.

It was not until 1954 that the "separate-but-equal" doctrine was successfully challenged. In that year, the U. S. Supreme Court in the *Brown v. Topeka Board of Education* decision ruled that separate schools are inherently unequal, thus setting the stage for desegregation of American schools. This decision also set in motion a series of challenges to discrimination against African-Americans that culminated in sweeping civil rights legislation in the mid-1960s. So it has only been in the past 25 years that the civil rights of black citizens have been protected by law.

Even though laws protecting the civil rights of African- Americans now exist and provide improved conditions in some private and public sectors, domination and subordination of African-Americans is still institutionally systemic in American society. Race is still a fundamental determinant of people's position in the social structure. African-Americans are still defined as racially different by the white majority and singled out for a broad range of individual and institutionalized discrimination (Williams, 1987; Wilson, 1987).

Although that last statement may seem to overstate current conditions, it actually does not. In 1988 a national poll conducted by Media General and the Associated Press revealed that 55% of Americans think our society is racist and 42 percent do not think minorities have the same opportunities as whites ("Poll," 1988). More surprising, perhaps, is that the National Institute Against Prejudice and Violence, an organization that monitors racist acts, documented racial incidents on 130 college campuses in 18 months during 1987-88 (Johnson, 1988). This is tragically ironic because college students are supposed to be the most enlightened sector of the population! But, as a University of California sociologist who has studied race relations noted recently, "We used to assume that prejudice would go away when a more enlightened, higher-educated group of young people replaced a generation of bigots. That doesn't follow any more" (Blauner, cited in Levine, 1990, p. 59).

There are widespread perceptions that things are getting better for African Americans, but in fact the economic gap between whites and blacks has actually been widening in recent years. Among the nation's blacks in 1990 the poverty rate was 33% compared with 10.5% of whites. African-American family income was only 56% that of whites, and it has been declining in the past 10 years. Jobless rates for blacks have consistently been over twice those of whites. Not only are blacks twice as likely to be unemployed, but those who are employed are also overrepresented in jobs whose pay, power, and prestige are low. Only a smattering of African-American managers has moved beyond middle levels of authority and control in the business world. Less than three percent of the nation's physicians, dentist, and pharmacists are African-American. In spite of some economic, political, and social gains during the past two decades, this period has been a time of increasing African-American hardship, with inner-city communities devastated by crime and drugs, and national policies of retreat from efforts to increase opportunities for blacks (Dewart, 1988). So, although some African-Americans have made gains economically, politically, and in educationally, many barriers to social equality remain, and these barriers are rooted in institutional patterns and practices of racial discrimination deeply ingrained in the structure of American society (Wilson, 1987).

Where racism co-exists with class stratification, as it does in the United States, the evidence is convincing that it is more basic to social structure and therefore the ultimate determinant of inequality between racial minorities and the dominant class (Ogbu, 1988). The basic fact is that much inequality and discrimination against African-Americans continues, regardless of whether one uses income, employment rates, educational attainment, or political office-holding as measures. African-Americans remain among the most disadvantaged groups in American society, and it is racial barriers, not merely economic or class barriers, that block black achievement. Martin Luther King's dream that one day racism would end in America has not been fulfilled.

Racism, then, is a salient aspect of the structure of American society. The most important aspect of this form of stratification is that it excludes people of color from equal access to socially valued rewards and resources. These people tend to have less wealth, power, and social prestige than do other Americans. Moreover, racism has built-in policies and practices that systematically discriminate against people in employment, housing, politics, education, health care, and many other areas. These conditions result in fewer human resources and diminished life chances for African-Americans.

Racism and Intercollegiate Sport

Despite pervasive and systematic discrimination against African-Americans throughout their history in North America, they have played a continuing and significant role in every era of American sport history, as David Wiggins and Othello Harris document in Essays 1 and 2. Their analyses suggest that this involvement can be divided roughly into four stages: (a) largely exclusion before the Civil War, (b) breakthroughs immediately following the Civil War, (c) segregation from the last two decades of the nineteenth century until after World War II, and (d) integration after World War II.

Sports relations between whites and African-Americans during the slavery era (1619 to 1865) centered around two sports: boxing and horseracing.[2] Plantation owners frequently selected—and sometimes even trained—one or more of their male slaves and entered them in boxing matches held in conjunction with festive occasions. The black boxers, under such conditions were merely used to entertain their white "masters" and their friends. Horseracing was also a popular colonial sporting event. Horses were, of course, owned by whites, and when training occurred much of it was done by whites, but African-Americans were used as jockeys. There was little status and no significant material rewards for jockeying, because slave labor of any kind was free; jockeying was viewed as basically a mechanical task, so blacks could be trusted with a task that whites did not care to do anyway. Social relations, then, can be seen as distant, with whites in control and African-Americans in subordinate roles, pleasing the dominant white groups (Davis, 1966).

As both Wiggins and Harris note, after the Civil War African-Americans made contributions to the rise of spectator sport as boxers, jockeys, and team players, but they were clearly exceptions. Society and sport remained racially segregated by custom and in some places by law (e.g., Jim Crow laws). Freedom had little effect on the social relations between blacks and whites in sports in the late nineteenth and early twentieth centuries. Although a number of African-Americans played on professional baseball teams in the early years of the National League, Jim Crow gradually raised its ugly head. White players threatened to quit rather than share the diamond with black men. Finally, by 1888 major league club owners made a "gentleman's agreement" not to sign any more African-American players. This unwritten law against hiring black players was not violated until 1945 when Branch Rickey, general manager of the Brooklyn Dodgers, signed Jackie Robinson to a contract (Peterson, 1970). As other professional sports emerged, they too barred African-Americans from participation. Among a number of consequences to excluding blacks from professional sports, one was that it perpetuated privileges for whites because white athletes did not have to compete with an entire segment of the population for sports jobs.

When African-Americans were barred from professional baseball, football, and basketball in the late nineteenth and early twentieth centuries, they formed all-black teams and leagues (Peterson, 1970; Rust, 1976). The Harlem Globetrotters and the famous players of the black baseball leagues such as Satchel Paige and Josh Gibson emerged from this segregated situation. When Jackie Robinson broke the color barrier, first in 1946 in the minor leagues and then in 1947 in the majors, he received much verbal and physical abuse from players and fans who resented a black playing on an equal level with whites. The great major league player Rogers Hornsby expressed a common white attitude at the time: "They've been getting along all right playing together and should stay where they belong in their league" (Cited in Chalk, 1975, p. 78).

African-American athletes were largely absent from intercollegiate sports for most of the nineteenth century. A few Ivy League and other eastern schools had black athletes at an early time, but they were exceptions. In fact, collegiate sports remained segregated, except for isolated instances, until after World War II. At the University of Michigan, for example, from 1882 to 1945 there were only four black lettermen in football and none in basketball. In 1948 only 10% of college basketball teams had one or more blacks on their rosters. This proportion increased to 45% of the teams in 1962 and 92% by 1975. The transition from a segregated program to an integrated one is perhaps best illustrated by the University of Alabama: In 1968 there were no blacks on any of its teams, but its 1975 basketball team had an all-black starting line up (Eitzen & Sage, 1989).

For the most part, though, over the past 100 years most black college athletes have played at historically black colleges in black leagues (they were known as Negro colleges and Negro leagues). Of course, the only reason that all-black colleges existed at all was racial prejudice and discrimination.

Nevertheless, the black colleges fielded teams in all of the popular sports, and they played a leading role in women's sports, especially in track and field—Tuskegee with Wilma Rudolph and Tennessee State with the Tigerbelles of are prominent examples. Although the system was segregated, black colleges provided an avenue to athletic prominence for many black athletes, and these schools have developed more outstanding black athletes than any other agency of higher education, though many of the athletes were never known outside the African-American press and African-American community.

Expanding Opportunities

The impact of World War II, the 1954 Supreme Court decision forbidding separate educational facilities, the massive commercialization of collegiate sports, and the desire by white colleges and universities to benefit from talented African-American athletes in building commercialized athletic programs resulted in more and more schools searching for talented blacks to bolster their teams; consequently, black colleges lost their monopoly on African-American athletic talent. The best black athletes found it advantageous to play at predominantly white schools because of their greater visibility, especially on television. This visibility meant a better chance to sign a professional contract at the conclusion of their eligibility. The result was depleted athletic programs at black colleges, forcing several of them to drastically modify their athletic programs and some black leagues to disband.

African-American, receiving college athletic scholarships in the past two decades at predominantly white schools has been a mixed blessing. On the one hand, a few athletically talented blacks have been given the opportunity to attend and graduate from colleges that would otherwise have been inaccessible to them. This has allowed some to achieve social mobility and monetary success. But, on the other hand, the evidence is clear and abundant that many African-American college athletes have been exploited by their schools. They have been recruited lacking the academic background to succeed in higher education, and they have been advised into courses that keep them eligible but are dead-end courses for acquiring a college diploma (Adler & Adler, 1985, 1991; Leach & Conners, 1984; Purdy, Eitzen, & Hufnagel, 1982). When their eligibility has been used up or they become academically ineligible to compete for the team, they are discarded and ignored by the coaches who recruited them. Lapchick (1988) reported that an estimated 80% of black NCAA Division I football and basketball players do not graduate.

There is little doubt that many opportunities are available in college sport for African-American athletes that were not available a generation ago, but racism in college sport has not been eliminated. Many college sports teams still have very few black participants. These sports tend to be linked to upper- class patronage, but class linkage is not the entire explanation for black underrepresentation in these sports. Dominant classes have the wherewithal to insulate themselves against those with whom they do not wish to associate. Laws that prevent African-Americans from being kept out do not assure that they will get in. Ample evidence exists to demonstrate that those who control some sports have created barriers to black participation in a number of sports, thus reproducing some of the more odious features of racism.

Although racial discrimination has always been incompatible with the ideals of American sports, widespread intercollegiate sports opportunities for African-Americans emerged only when discrimination became incompatible with good financial policy. In those team sports in which "revenue producing" has come to dominate, the contribution of outstanding African-American athletes to winning championships and holding public interest has opened opportunities to African-Americans in college sports. Sports more closely linked to upper-class patronage and with less spectator interest have been slow to attract and integrate blacks.

Sporting opportunities have undoubtedly improved for blacks in the past two decades, but racist attitudes appear to persist, albeit in more subtle forms. African-Americans' success in sport has led many to seek an explanation for this phenomenon, and Harris traces the twists and turns of this controversy. He indicates that while some scientists have claimed that the African-Americans possess physical characteristics that are advantageous for athletic performance, most social scientists are of the opinion that sociological and psychological factors are the primary reason for African-American athletes' rise to eminence. Fundamental to this view is a recognition that most African-American athletes come from the low socioeconomic classes; here recreational outlets for the young are mainly sports, so many hours are spent playing in the streets, at recreation centers, and on playgrounds. Furthermore, excellence in sports provides one of the few opportunities for African-Americans to escape the slums and ghettos in which many of them live. Thus, hours devoted to honing sports skills, combined with the desire to escape their childhood environment, seem to cause many African-American youths to approach sport with greater motivation to excel than is found in middle-class whites.

Academic-Athletic Conflicts

In the evolution of college sports, increasing commercialization and the demands for winning teams to generate more and more revenue has produced what are called "big-time" college athletics. Accompanying this trend toward a form of commercial entertainment sponsored by colleges and universities has been a tension between the goals and integrity of higher education and the economic interests and values of big-time sports. For many who view the mission of higher education as the promotion of scholarship and academic training for careers, there is more than just a tension; there is an inherent incompatibility between an economically driven activity that uses college students as a labor force, which big-time college sport does, and the mission of higher education in promoting scholarship and academic achievement. In Essay 3 Audwin Anderson and Donald South locate their essay within this academic-athletic conflict, with a specific focus on recruiting, retention, and graduate rates of African-American male athletes. They cast their analysis of the issues and problems within a current situation in which nearly twice the percentage of white athletes graduate, compared to African-American athletes. In an attempt to bring some meaning to the statistical data on graduation rates, Anderson and South focus on forces such as the social meaning of African-American maleness, recruitment practices, Proposition 48, and the economic and academic exploitative nature of big-time college sport to questions having to do with graduate rates. Finally, they problemize the meaning of graduate rates.

Limited Opportunities in Leadership

Access to sport for African-American athletes has expanded greatly in the past quarter century, but very few opportunities have been made available in positions in the upper levels of the sport hierarchy. Efforts to eliminate discrimination through the legislative and judicial system tend to produce immediate results, but the results are most noticeable at the lower levels of the social formation. The higher levels, where the greatest power, prestige, and material rewards reside, are more insulated from direct scrutiny, so those who control access to the higher levels tend to employ subtle ways of maintaining discriminatory practices. Thus, the oppressed group typically has a difficult time penetrating the higher paying and more prestigious positions. In the case of intercollegiate athletics, coaching and management jobs are under the control of those who presently have the power for determining who gets selected to these upper-level positions. African-Americans in coaching positions are scarce in intercollegiate athletics. Those who are college coaches are overwhelmingly stacked as assistant coaches, and most coaching staffs have only one African-American.

Managerial positions in intercollegiate sports continue to elude blacks. There is a scandalously low percentage of African-American athletic directors in collegiate sports. Most executive vacancies continue to go to whites, sometimes by thinly disguised ploys that eliminate African-Americans from serious consideration for the positions. Racism and its companion racial stratification are still very much alive and well in college sports. In Essay 4 Dana Brooks and Ronald Althouse examine how several factors appear to have affected the career mobility patterns of African-

American head and assistant college coaches. Although they are unable to identify any models that clearly explain why intercollegiate sport has been so slow in incorporating black coaches and athletic administrators into its system, they emphatically affirm that African-American men and women have been underutilized and underrepresented in college athletic leadership positions.

College Athletics: From Equal Opportunity to Equal Outcome

Participation in college athletics has long been touted as good preparation for life after college, but this notion has been based mostly on faith and public relations. As Robert Sellers notes in Essay 5, there has been little empirical study of college athletes after they leave the campus, and what little exists does not confirm the popular portrayal that college athletes, because of their collegiate sporting experiences, lead happy, contented lives and become successful in their chosen careers. Moreover, there is the possibility that African-American and white student-athletes have quite different post college lives and careers.

After describing the unique characteristics of the African-American student-athlete, Sellers reviews the relevant research about athletic retirement. He then develops a framework for evaluating whether college student-athletes are provided reasonable compensation for their participation. In Sellers' view, African-American student-athletes' postcollege lives are influenced by whether they were provided sound educational opportunities or whether they were merely exploited by the institution. The key to providing educational opportunity, according to Sellers' criteria, is whether the opportunity for a college education is present. Three elements compose the opportunity for a college education: opportunities for developing personal competence, opportunities for upward mobility, and opportunities to earn a college degree. Sellers' assumption is that to the extent to which these educational opportunities exist the athletic experience will have a positive effect on the quality of post athletic life. To the extent that they are absent, athletes are being exploited, and personal and economic problems will plague the athletes in their postathletic life.

Sellers devotes the final pages of his essay to recommending interventions that he believes can enhance the quality of life after student-athletes leave the campus. Recommendations are directed to sport sociologists and psychologists, the NCAA, colleges and universities, and the families of athletes.

Women in Intercollegiate Sport

Essay 6 by Doris R. Corbett and William Johnson and Essay 7 by Tina Sloan Green center attention on the historical and cultural conditions for female African-American athletes. An observation that is frequently made about African-American women is that they suffer "double jeopardy," meaning that they are subject to both sexism and racism. Both of these essays amply confirm this observation. As Corbett and Johnson demonstrate, there is a further twist in the cultural milieu of African-American females—they are viewed and treated differently from white females, and this has had consequences with respect to expectations and treatment of them as athletes. A main theme of Corbett and Johnson is the inadequacy of the literature about female African-American athletes, and, they argue, what little exists largely fails to contextualize and give meaning to African-American women's experiences in sports. Instead, the focus is primarily on describing the achievements of an elite group of African-American female athletes who have achieved international status in their sport. The media has been instrumental in making celebrities of a few female African-American athletes, while reinforcing traditional stereotypes of both female and black athletes.

A useful list of twelve racial and sexual barriers impeding the involvement of African-American female athletes is enumerated by Corbett and Johnson. This list is useful because it could be used by various groups in formulating new policies and procedures for redressing the inequalities that now exist for African-American female athletes.

Tina Sloan Green's speculations about the future of African-American women in sport is largely optimistic portrayal. But she does emphasize that increased opportunities are largely contingent on economic conditions, not only economic prosperity in the societal marketplace but also improved economic status for African-Americans. Even where low-income conditions continue to exist, Green foresees improved access to sports through community-based organizations.

High school and college sports have broadened and expanded over the past 20 years to give greater access to female athletes, but African-American female athletes have benefitted only marginally at this point, mainly due to social and gender-related barriers. Green expects many of these barriers to be overcome in the future. Still, according to Green, careers in sports for African-American women—either as athletes, coaches, administrators, sportscasters, etc.—will be extremely limited and difficult to attain.

Intergroup Race Relations

Although power, control, and privilege, and how they work to oppress and marginalize African-Americans in college sports, are background themes throughout this volume, the system of power and privilege that define and structure intergroup race relations in college sports is foregrounded as the analytic framework of Essay 8 by Alison Dewar. She begins by describing and critiquing the dominant ways of viewing race relations in sport. She then proposes alternatives to what she calls the "distributive research" of race and sport. This is done through the work of feminists, womanists, and feminist sport sociologists who have proposed antiracist theories and practices. Dewar then suggests strategies in which such an analysis may be applied to group relations in intercollegiate sport.

Challenging and changing dominant sporting practices and developing alternatives based on antiracist and antioppressive politics can be a way to protest oppression and unlock the power that exists in sport to bind women of all colors while building alliances across existing differences. Alison concludes with a set of recommendations of what she calls "Possibilities for Change."

What About the Future?

The author of Essay 9, Carole Oglesby, calls on white Americans to end the denial, disregard, and resistance that they have historically used, and still use, to maintain and sustain racism in our society at large and in sports in particular. She insists the whites have the power to make a difference in racial matters, and they must begin with acknowledging and accepting responsibility for white domination. For sports, change must begin, according to Oglesby, by confronting the reluctance of the white sports establishment to acknowledge and confront racism. For too long this has been the tactic for refusing to seriously address the widespread racism in sports. Oglesby employs Hardiman and Jackson's stage theory to illustrate the various levels of white racial identity that have historically impeded whites from eliminating racism in our society.

Oglesby argues that in order to enhance a multiracial future, we all need to commit some of our professional work to antiracist activity. She proposes three types of steps: personal, research oriented, and programmatic. An example of the first would be pursuing historical and cultural understanding through courses in African-American studies. Examples of the second would include engaging in research about African-Americans employing various methodologies. Examples of the third include antiracist action programs designed to counteract and even eliminate institutionalized, cultural, and individual racism. Programs of this kind already exist, and Oglesby identifies and describes several of the most successful ones. These steps can make a difference and can be first steps on the path to personal empowerment for whites as well as for African-Americans.

The final essay, written by D. Stanley Eitzen, is a broad-ranging essay examining race relations in American society and big-time intercollegiate athletics. Eitzen cites recent incidents to show that, unfortunately, there seems to be a growing racial polarization in American society, and acts of bigotry have become common on university campuses. Eitzen characterizes big-time intercollegiate athletics as largely a commercial entertainment industry thriving on the labor of African-American student-athletes from low-income families who often are unprepared for the academic rigors of higher education. They are recruited, admitted, and frequently maintained at universities in bogus courses until their eligibility is exhausted; then they are discarded to fend for themselves without a diploma.

Eitzen's essay includes speculations about trends in race relations in the near future and recommendations for reforming college sport to eliminate racism and the exploitation of African-American athletes. Three major societal trends that will shape race relations in the future are identified and discussed by Eitzen: changing racial composition of the United States, increasing disparity in the already unequal distribution of wealth in society, and the transformation of the economy.

As for trends in universities and intercollegiate sports affecting race relations, Eitzen suggests that there are fewer African-Americans attending colleges and universities, a growing commitment toward greater racial diversity in student bodies and faculties, and an unremitting quest by big-time sports for winning teams and profit from such teams. In the last section of his essay, Eitzen lists 22 recommendations for reforming intercollegiate sports that, if adopted, would help eliminate racism.

Pulling Things Together

In the epilogue Dana Brooks and Ronald Althouse synthesize the major ideas advanced by the authors of the 10 essays. This is followed by an account of recent actions by the NCAA on behalf of addressing racism and sexism within intercollegiate athletics. Special attention is devoted to the actions of the Special Subcommittee to Review Minority Opportunities over the past four years. Especially noteworthy is its recent recommendation to create a NCAA Minority Opportunities and Interest Committee to resolve the issues identified by the Special Subcommittee.

The Unique Contributions of This Book

This volume makes a valuable contribution to the literature on American sports, primarily because there is no other single book that focuses on the African-American athlete in college athletics. Furthermore, each of the essays makes a specific contribution to understanding the structure of intercollegiate athletics and the complex role of African-American student-athletes in that enterprise. Of course, college athletics is only one form of sport in which African-American athletes participate; millions participate in youth and high schools athletics, and a few thousand are professional athletes at any one time. Some of the same issues and problems that African-American athletes encounter in college athletics are also encountered at the other levels of organized sports. But those stories deserve separate treatments.

Footnotes

[1] Parts of this section are drawn from my *Power and Ideology in American Sport: A Critical Perspective*. Champaign, IL: Human Kinetics, 1990.

[2] Parts of this section are drawn from my (co-authored with D. Stanley Eitzen) *Sociology of North American Sport*. (4th ed.) Dubuque, IA: William C. Brown, 1989.

References

Adler, P., & Adler, P. A. (1985). From idealism to pragmatic detachment: The academic performance of college athletes. *Sociology of Education, 58*, 241-250.

Adler, P. A., & Adler, P. (1991). *Backboards & blackboards*. New York: Columbia University Press.

Blauner, B. (1990, 7 May) Quoted in Levine, A. America's youthful bigots, *U. S. News & World Report*, p. 59.

Chalk, O. (1975). *Pioneers of black sport*. New York: Dodd, Mead.

Davis, J. P. (1966). *The Negro in American sports* (The American Negro reference books). Englewood Cliffs, NJ: Prentice-Hall.

Dewart, J. (Ed.) (1988). *The state of black America 1988*. New York: National Urban League.

Eitzen, D. S., & Sage, G. H. (1989). *Sociology of North American sport.*

(4th Ed.) Dubuque, IA: William C. Brown.

Johnson, H. (1988, May 10). Racism still smolders on campus. *USA Today*, p.1D.

Lapchick, R. E. (1988). Discovering fool's gold on the golden horizon. *The World and I*, 3, 603-611.

Leach, B., & Conners, B. (1984). Pygmalion on the gridiron: The black student-athlete in a white university. *New Directions for Student Services, 28*, 31-49.

Ogbu, J. U. (1988). Class stratification, racial stratification, and schooling. In L. Weis (Ed.), *Class, race, and gender in American education* (pp.163-182). Albany, NY: State University of New York Press.

Peterson, R. (1970). *Only the ball was white*. Englewood Cliffs, NJ: Prentice-Hall.

Poll: Minorities remain society's unequal partners. (1988, August 8). *USA Today*, p.5A.

Purdy, D.A., Eitzen, D.S., & Hufnagel, R. (1982). Are athletes also students?: The educational attainment of college students. *Social Problems, 29*, 439-448.

Rust, A., Jr. (1976). *Get that nigger off the field*. New York: Delacorte.

Watson, G. L. (1987). *Dilemmas and contradictions in social theory*. New York: University Press of America.

Williams, B. (1987). *Black workers in an industrial suburb: The struggle against discrimination*. New Brunswick, NJ: Rutgers University Press.

Wilson, W. J. (1987). *The truly disadvantaged: The inner city, the underclass, and public policy*. Chicago: University of Chicago Press.

**Essay 1: Critical Events
Affecting Racism in Athletics**
David K. Wiggins

**Essay 2: African-American
Predominance in Collegiate Sport**
Othello Harris

Section One:
Historical Analysis of
Racism and Critical Events

Section One

Historical Analysis of Racism and Critical Events

Although racial oppression in America today may be an extreme case, a historical review of the African-American athlete's participation in American sport brings focus to a legacy of racial discrimination and prejudice. Broadly scaled, the chronicle of African-American participation in sport can be divided into three periods: (1) Segregation: 1863-1954, (2) Integration: 1954-1968, and (3) Post-Integration: 1968-present.

Until recently, as David Wiggins notes, historical research gave scant attention to African-American athletes' participation in sport, and even when it did trace participation, it seldom explored African-American and white cultural differences, or the effect these differences may have had on sport participation. In this section, sport historian David Wiggins and sport sociologist Othello Harris offer the reader very different, yet parallel, social historical overviews of critical events affecting African-American athletes' involvement in collegiate sports. David Wiggins offers an inclusive account of how rising college sport participation was accompanied by racism and discrimination against the African-American athlete, particularly how Social Darwinism, the civil rights movement, and court decisions negatively affected on African-Americans' aspirations and accomplishments in sport.

Bringing attention to different periods of oppression two court decisions significantly affected the integration of sport in America. The 1896 U.S. Supreme Court decision in the *Plessy v. Ferguson* case institutionalized the "separate-but-equal" doctrine and ensured nearly a century of white supremacy in America. After the *Plessy v. Ferguson* decision, sport was largely color coded, and African-Americans participating on predominantly white teams disappeared. Even more insidious, the lack of playing facilities and opportunities for participation of African-Americans came to be increasingly evident in high school, college, and professional sports.

Fifty-eight years later the 1954 Supreme Court decision in *Brown v. Topeka Board of Education* (1954) was a turning point in educational oppression and triggered a new wave of activism that battled for desegregation and changed race relations in America. Although the Brown decision ruled against school segregation, desegregation progressed slowly for nearly a decade, finally gaining greater impetus after Congress passed the 1964 Civil Rights Act. By the mid-1980s, racism was being contested through debates over black superiority in sports and academic performance of athletes. By this time, the NCAA's rulings had become the arena for new controversies.

Since the 1970s the number of African-American athletes participating at the high school, college and professional sport level has increased dramatically. Othello Harris summarizes social conditions leading to African-American predominance in college sport. His discussion is centered on topics such as "Athletes, Scholars, and Superspades," "Black Pride and Protest," "Racial Stereotypes and Stacking," and "NCAA Reform." Harris argues that African-American athletes are being exploited for their physical prowess and that exploitation fosters poor academic performance, feeds ineligibility, and contributes to low rates of graduation. He offers solutions ranging from curtailing eligibility and curbing athletic practice and performance hours, to reallocating the income from lucrative media and television contracts to assist with academic preparation in high school.

Essay 1

Critical Events Affecting Racism in Athletics

David K. Wiggins

Abstract: This essay examines the involvement of black athletes in American sport from the latter half of the nineteenth century up to the present. Particular attention is paid to the critical events that have influenced the status of black athletes at both the amateur and professional levels of sport. A number of outstanding black athletes distinguished themselves in a variety of different sports during the latter half of the nineteenth century. Hardening racial policies, combined with a number of other societal factors in the late nineteenth century forced blacks to form their own teams and leagues in a number of different sports. Although a few black athletes were able to overcome racial barriers and compete in predominantly white organized sport, the large majority participated in sport behind segregated walls throughout the first half of the twentieth century. The signing of Jackie Robinson by the Brooklyn Dodgers paved the way for black athletes to reenter predominantly white organized sport in increasing numbers. Black athletes shed their traditional conservative approach to racial matters and become involved in the Civil Rights Movement during the latter part of the 1960s and early 1970s. Black athletes eventually received a great deal of attention from academicians and become the source of much debate as they realized increasing amounts of success as participants yet endured frustrations wrought by racial discrimination.

Introduction

The history of the black athletes' involvement in American sport has been marked by a number of major successes interspersed with bitter disappointments. Initially exposed to different sports on southern plantations or larger cities in the eastern half of the United States, a number of outstanding black athletes distinguished themselves in highly organized sport at both the amateur and professional levels of competition in the years immediately following the Civil War. By the latter years of the nineteenth century, the large majority of black athletes were, for various reasons and under different circumstances, excluded from participating in most highly organized sport and forced to establish their own teams and leagues operated without white interference. With the notable exceptions of boxing and international sporting events, black Americans established separate organizations behind segregated walls in such sports as football, basketball, and baseball. These all-black institutions were a source of great pride to America's black community and served as visible examples of black organizational skill and entrepreneurship during the oppressive years of the first half of the twentieth century (Betts, 1974; Henderson, 1939; Lucas & Smith, 1978; Rader, 1983; Somers, 1972). The historic signing of Jackie Robinson by the Brooklyn Dodgers in 1945 was the beginning of the end for many all-black sporting organizations, but it also helped usher in the re-integration of sport in this country. Robinson's signing with the Dodgers, combined with the integrationist policies in post-World War II America, triggered the reentry and gradual acceptance of black athletes into various sports. The following two decades witnessed unprecedented growth in the number of black athletes participating in sport, a growth that proceeded at an uneven rate depending on the particular sport and location (Grundman, 1979; Lowenfish, 1978; Spivey, 1983; Tygiel, 1983; Wiggins, 1983, 1989).

Toward the latter part of the 1960s, many black athletes became involved in the civil rights movement by actively protesting racial discrimination in sport and the larger American society. The two major forums for protest were the Olympic Games and predominantly white university campuses where black athletes staged boycotts and spoke out against the racial discrimination experienced by them and other members of the black community. Although their personal involvement in civil rights issues slowly abated under the weight of the women's rights movement and issues associated with inflation and unemployment, the role of black athletes in organized sport continued to be of great interest to both academicians and lay people. Over the last number of years black athletes have garnered front- page headlines, particularly in regard to their exploitation by educational institutions, inability to assume managerial and upper level administrative positions in sport, and restriction to particular playing positions as well as sports (Coakley, 1990; Edwards, 1973 a, b; Spivey, 1985; Wiggins, 1988).

A Taste of Success in Late Nineteenth Century Sport

The black athlete's first real taste of highly competitive sport took place in the years immediately following the Civil War. Although some black athletes had achieved fame prior to the great war between the states, it was not until the bloody conflict came to an end that large numbers of them would realize national and even international acclaim in a wide range of sports. The newly found freedom following the war and the lasting sporting traditions established during slavery created an atmosphere in which blacks were more readily accepted into horseracing, baseball, and other sports popular during the period. For example, Peter Jackson, the great black boxer from the Virgin Islands by way of Australia, continued the tradition of outstanding black fighters and became a household name among pugilistic fans through his well-known ring battles with such men as James J. Corbett, George Godfrey, and Frank Slavin (Wiggins, 1985). Isaac Murphy and a number of other diminutive blacks dominated the jockey profession, seizing the Kentucky Derby and many of horse racing's other prestigious events (Wiggins, 1979). Marshal "Major" Taylor, the great bicyclist from Indianapolis, seized the imagination of racing fans on both sides of the Atlantic with his amazing feats of speed on the oval track (Ritchie, 1988; Taylor, 1971). Moses "Fleetwood" Walker and his brother Weldy became major league baseball's first black players when they signed contracts with the Toledo Mudhens of the American Association in the mid-1880s (McKinney, 1976; Peterson, 1970).

By the latter years of the nineteenth century, black athletes were being excluded from highly organized sport. Even those black athletes who had achieved great success found themselves being either shunted aside or pressured to drop out of their respective sports. The reasons for their elimination from highly organized sport were varied, including the dominant culture's belief in black inferiority, general deterioration of black rights, and eventual separation of the races in late-nineteenth-century America (Davis, 1966; Lucas & Smith, 1978; Rader, 1983; Somers, 1972). The southern black codes, established shortly after the Civil War to insure legal restrictions against the newly freed slaves, became easier to implement towards the end of the century as northern Republicans abandoned their previous commitment to black rights. Further deterioration of black rights resulted from decisions passed down by the United States Supreme Court toward the latter part of the nineteenth century. In 1883, the Supreme Court affirmed legislation overturning the 14th Amendment, citing that prevention of discrimination against individuals by states did not prohibit discrimination by individual citizens. In 1896, the famous *Plessy v. Ferguson* case legally sanctioned separation of schools by race and upheld "separate-but-equal" accommodations on railroads. In 1898, the Supreme Court kept many blacks out of politics by upholding poll-tax qualifications and literary tests for voting (Logan, 1965; Meier & Rudwick, 1963; Woodward, 1966).

The Supreme Court decisions took place in an increasingly more hostile environment where blacks were being "proven" inferior to whites. The exclusion of black athletes from sport, like the exclusion of blacks from all walks of American life, was given a philosophical rationale that combined of the Social Darwinism, rise of imperialism around the world, and spread of pseudoscientific writings by both academicians and the lay public. Such well-known thinkers as Herbert Spencer and William Graham Sumner, gave support to the belief that blacks were on the lowest rung of the evolutionary ladder, incapable of surviving in a competitive society due to their intellectual and emotional inferiority (Cochran & Miller, 1961; Logan, 1957; Meier & Rudwick, 1963; Woodward, 1966). Social Darwinism was supported in principle by various members of the dominant culture who believed "nonwhite" people of the new territories annexed during imperialist expansion were merely savages in need of education and cultural enlightenment. The belief in black inferiority was further "substantiated" by a number of racist treatises and academic studies completed during the period. Prejudiced whites got all the support they needed from academicians in such divergent fields as history, psychology, sociology, biology, and anthropology who were busily trying to prove black inferiority through their various writings (Cochran & Miller, 1961; Logan, 1957; Meier & Rudwick, 1963; Woodward, 1966).

Striving for an Equal Share in the American Dream

Segregation of highly organized sport did not stop a select number of black athletes from continuing to achieve success in certain kinds of sports at different levels of competition. Throughout the first half of the twentieth century, a number of outstanding black athletes gained prominence in professional boxing rings, on the campuses of predominantly white universities, and in Olympic stadia (Chalk, 1976; Davis, 1966; Fleischer, 1938; Young, 1963).

Involvement of blacks in boxing had a long tradition, extending back to the early years of the nineteenth century when Tom Molineaux, with assistance from Bill Richmond, another famous black pugilist and trainer of boxers, fought for the heavyweight championship against the Englishman, Tom Cribb (Cone, 1982; Goodman, 1980; Rudolph, 1979). A sport that fit nicely into the dominant culture's stereotypical notions of blacks and legendary traditions of gladiatorial combats, boxing provided a better life for some blacks while at once helping delimit the conditions of black identity within American culture and reflecting the racial realities of society in general. Black boxers withstood the segregationist hatchet of the late nineteenth century and continued to engage in matches drawing worldwide attention from audiences attracted to bouts where at least one of the fighters was black (Early, 1989; Sammons, 1988).

The two most prominent black fighters of the first half of the twentieth century were the similarly legendary, yet decidedly different, Jack Johnson and Joe Louis. Johnson, the powerfully built boxer from Galveston, Texas, became the first black fighter to capture the world's heavyweight championship, holding on to the title for some seven years before losing to the Pottawatomie giant, Jess Willard, in 1915. As great as his exploits were in boxing, it was outside the squared ring that Johnson gained most of his attention and caused the greatest controversy. He has often been referred to as "Bad Nigger," a man who played on the worst fears of the dominant culture by marrying three white women and having illicit affairs with a number of others, usually prostitutes whom he treated with an odd mixture of affection and violence. He was absolutely fearless, and attracted to dangerous escapades that challenged white conventions and mores. Although a hero to many members of his race, Johnson drew the wrath of segments of both the black and white communities because of his unwillingness to assume a subservient position and play the role of the grateful black. He was eventually convicted of violating the Mann Act by transporting a white woman across state lines for illicit purposes and was forced to leave the country for a short time before returning home to serve a jail sentence in Leavenworth, Kansas (Gilmore, 1975; Roberts, 1983; Wiggin, 1971).

The bitter aftertaste from Johnson's career, combined with continuing racial discrimination in American society, made it virtually impossible for black boxers to secure championship fights over the next two decades. That all changed in 1937, however, when Joe Louis, the superbly talented boxer from Detroit, became the second black heavyweight champion by defeating James Braddock. Louis was a decidedly different champion than Johnson. Possessing enormous strength and boxing skills, Louis was a quiet, dignified man who assumed the more subservient role whites expected from members of his race. But he became a hero of almost mythical proportions in this country's black community, demolishing white fighters with remarkable regularity and serving as a symbol of possibility for those subjugated by continuing racial discrimination (Capeci & Wilkerson, 1983; Edmonds, 1973; Mead, 1985).

While Louis and Johnson gained fame as possibly America's finest pugilists, a number of outstanding black athletes were competing in intercollegiate sport on predominantly white university campuses across the country. Following in the tradition of William H. Lewis, William Tecumseh Sherman Jackson, and other great college performers of the late nineteenth century, such black athletes as Fritz Pollard of Brown University; Paul Robeson of Rutgers; Jerome "Brud" Holland of Cornell; Eddie Tolan and Willis Ward of Michigan; William Bell, David Albritton, and Jesse Owens of Ohio State; Ralph Metcalfe of Marquette University; and Kenny Washington, Jackie Robinson, and Ralph Bunche of UCLA established lasting reputations for their exploits in intercollegiate sport and, in some cases, Olympic competition. Owens' victories, for example, in the 1936 Olympic Games are legendary, ranking as one of the most significant individual performances in sport history (Behee, 1974; Chalk, 1976; Smith, 1988; Spivey, 1983; Wiggins, 1991).

The great success of black athletes was sometimes overshadowed by insensitivity and various forms of discrimination they experienced on their individual college campus and outside the halls of academia. Black athletes at predominantly white universities invariably faced the loneliness and sense of isolation that comes with being members of a small minority in a largely white setting. A large number of black athletes found white campuses and their environs insensitive to the needs of blacks; not always providing suitable living arrangements, satisfying social and cultural activities, and educational support services necessary for academic success (Miller, 1927; Spivey & Jones, 1975; Wolters, 1975).

Even more traumatic for black athletes than on-campus injustices were the racially discriminatory acts committed against them by white opponents from other institutions. The most noteworthy of these involved the refusal of southern white institutions to compete against northern institutions that had black players on their teams. In 1916, for example, Washington and Lee College of Virginia threatened to withdraw from a football game against Rutgers because Paul Robeson was on the Rutgers team. Rutgers coach George Sanford eventually acceded to Washington and Lee's request, and Robeson was forced to sit out the game without much protest from the Rutgers community (Fishman, 1969; Gilliam, 1976). Approximately 13 years after the Robeson incident, Coach Chuck Meehan of New York University acceded to the demands of the University of Georgia by withholding his star black halfback, Dave Myers, from a football game between the two institutions. This incident resulted in much debate and protest, including protracted negotiations between the (NAACP) National Association for the Advancement of Colored People and university officials (Wolters, 1975). In 1941, New York University complied with the wishes of Catholic University by withholding its three black athletes from a track meet in Washington, DC. In the same year, Harvard University's outstanding black lacrosse player, Lucien Alexis, Jr., was withheld from a match against the Naval Academy because of that institution's refusal to compete against black players. The Alexis decision caused a great deal of protest on Harvard's campus and ultimately resulted in the university's announcing that it would never again "countenance racial discrimination" (Brower, 1941).

Sport Behind Segregated Walls
As a select group of black athletes struggled to realize a measure of success in predominantly white organized sport, America's black community established its own separate sporting organizations behind segregated walls and out of view of most members of the dominant culture. Although remarkably similar to white-controlled institutions, these sporting organizations also reflected special black cultural patterns attested to both the strength and vibrancy of the black community during the oppressive years of the early twentieth century (Ashe, 1988; Henderson, 1939; Peterson, 1990).

Prime examples of all-black sporting organizations were the athletic programs established at historically black colleges. Originally organized during the late nineteenth century, athletic programs at historically black colleges were similar to those at predominantly white institutions in that they began as informal, student-run activities and evolved into highly structured and institutionally controlled phenomena. They were also much like intercollegiate athletic programs on white campuses in that they included a wide variety of sports, were eventually controlled by elaborate bureaucratic organizations, and were rationalized along both educational and social lines. Historically black colleges competed in all the major team sports, including football, which was one of the most popular sports in America's black community. The annual Thanksgiving Day football games between various schools, including the classic match between Howard and Lincoln (PA), drew thousands of spectators from around the country, contributed to a sense of institutional pride and national reputation, and stimulated school spirit by bringing students, faculty, and alumni together to share in the excitement of common pursuits. Organizational structure was first brought to black college sport in 1912 when the Colored Intercollegiate Athletic Association (CIAA) was formed among such well-known black institutions as Howard, Lincoln, and Hampton Institute. Shortly after the creation of the CIAA, similar athletic associations were organized, which led to the further legitimacy of black college sport (Ashe, 1988; Chalk, 1976; Henderson, 1939).

Differences between athletic programs at historically black colleges and predominantly white institutions were almost as great as their similarities. In comparison to their white counterparts, black colleges lacked the funds necessary to hire large coaching staffs, purchase the latest equipment, and build elaborate athletic facilities. The financial circumstances of most black colleges made it impossible for them to outfit the well-equipped teams like those fielded by predominantly white institutions. Sport at historically black schools was also different from athletic programs at predominantly white institutions in that the exploits of many outstanding black college athletes never became known to a larger American audience. Although many of them became household names in the black community, black college athletes were forced to perform behind segregated walls, which obscured their many exploits from public view and minimized the attention they received from the powerful white press. The last major difference between the two forms of intercollegiate sport was that few, if any, athletes from black colleges went on to participate in the Olympic Games or other international sporting events. Athletes from black colleges were left at home while John Taylor, Eddie Tolan, John Woodruff, and other black athletes from predominantly white universities traveled the world competing in international sporting events. Why this occurred is open to speculation, but it probably stemmed from a combination of poor athletic facilities and equipment in black colleges, limited publicity given black college athletes, and the tendency of predominantly white institutions to recruit only the best black athletes (Ashe, 1988; Chalk, 1976; Henderson, 1939).

Holding out as much interest to the black community as college sport were the all-black professional teams and leagues that were organized in early-twentieth-century America. A legacy from the late nineteenth century, a number of all-black teams and leagues were established in the three major sports of football, basketball, and baseball. Of these three, baseball was the most highly organized and popular among members of the black community, enthralling thousands of fans who found the game a meaningful experience and pleasurable counterpoint to the drudgery of everyday life (Peterson, 1970; Rogosin, 1983; Ruck, 1988).

Black baseball's first successful league was formed in 1920 by Rube Foster, the great pitcher and manager of the Chicago American Giants. Foster organized that year the National Negro Baseball League (NNL), an organization patterned along the lines of major league baseball and composed of teams from Chicago, Detroit, St. Louis, Kansas City, and Indianapolis. The NNL collapsed under the weight of financial instability and a host of other problems in 1931, just three years after the rival Eastern Negro League (ENL) seized operation. In 1933, a second NNL was organized and four years later was in competition with the newly created Negro American League (NAL) (Bruce, 1985; Peterson, 1970; Rogosin, 1983).

These two leagues were the cornerstones of black baseball over the next two decades, representing at once some of the worst features of American racism and creative energies of the black community. The NNL and NAL, although quite stable through much of the 1930s and 1940s, were never able to realize their financial potential because clubs lacked ownership of baseball parks and were forced to engage in bidding wars for the services of outstanding players. Clark Griffith and other moguls in major league baseball never allowed black teams to establish significant profit margins because of the high rent white owners charged for the use of their ballparks. This situation caused a myriad of other problems, including inadequate working and living conditions for the league's black players, who already suffered the indignities associated with being members of one of this country's least esteemed minority groups. The players were forced to make long, confined road trips in buses and beat-up old cars, stay in segregated and sometimes dilapidated hotels, and survive on limited meal money. They also had to cope with the frustrations that resulted from being denied service at restaurants, hotels, and other public accommodations (Bruce, 1985; Peterson, 1970; Rogosin, 1983).

Black baseball players, however, overcame the numerous limitations of their separate leagues to carve out meaningful professional careers and more rewarding ways of life. Relative to other members of the black community, players in black baseball enjoyed satisfying lives marked by adulation and pleasurable experiences. The players who participated in black baseball were like most athletes in that they enjoyed the camaraderie of their teammates, matching their skills against other talented performers and traveling to different parts of the country. The more talented black players, who could command relatively high salaries, participated in the greatest spectacle in black baseball, the annual East-West all-star game. First played in 1933, the All-star game pitted the finest players in black baseball against each other, allowing Josh Gibson, Cool Papa Bell, Judy Johnson, Buck Leonard, Satchel Paige, and other legendary performers to showcase their talents to thousands of fans across much of this country (Brashler, 1978; Holway, 1978; Rogosin, 1983).

Campaigns to Re-Integrate Lily-White Sport
Coinciding with the creation of all black sporting organizations were bitter campaigns being waged against the color line in white organized sport. Throughout the first half of the twentieth century, various individuals and groups fought for the re-integration of sport. Of all the groups that hammered away at organized sport for its exclusionary policies, perhaps none were more significant than sportswriters from such well-known black weeklies as the *Baltimore Afro-American, Chicago Defender, New York Amsterdam News*, and *Pittsburgh Courier-Journal*. They led the battle against racism in organized sport, clamoring loudly for an end to discrimination in baseball that symbolically, and in actual practice, was most important to America's black community (Brower, 1940; Simons, 1985; Tygiel, 1983; Weaver, 1979; Wiggins, 1983; Young, 1970).

In the late 1930s, for example, the *Pittsburgh Courier-Journal's* Wendell Smith began a fervent campaign to eliminate the color barrier in major league baseball. From the moment he wrote his first article on baseball's color ban in 1938 to ultimate integration of the sport some nine years later, Smith waged a fierce battle against the bureaucrats in the national game for their exclusion of black players. Like other members of his race, Smith abhorred the discrimination in major league baseball, believing it symbolized the degraded status of blacks in this country. He pointed out, through various means, that blacks could not be considered true American citizens until they gained entry to organized baseball. Although realizing that participation in the national game would not necessarily eradicate political and economic inequality, Smith believed that the desegregation of baseball would help give blacks the sense of dignity and self-esteem essential for the ultimate elimination of racial discrimination in this country (Wiggins, 1983).

Smith's campaign to desegregate organized baseball was remarkably aggressive and took many forms. He was suggesting by the beginning of 1939 that black Americans form a national association for the advancement of colored people (NAACP) on behalf of black players and attack the color line as vigorously as possible. Shortly after announcing his plans to organize an NAACP on behalf of black players, Smith conducted an exclusive interview with the president of the National League, Ford Frick. The interview with Frick, which was characterized by the typical rhetoric voiced for years by leaders in major league baseball, provoked Smith into conducting a series of interviews with 8 managers and 40 players in the National League to determine their views on black players. Culminating in a series of articles in the *Courier-Journal* entitled "What Big Leaguers Think of Negro Baseball Players," the interviews were illuminating in that the only person who believed blacks should be barred from organized baseball was Bill Terry, manager of the New York Giants (Wiggins, 1983).

In the years immediately following the interviews with National League managers and players, Smith became even bolder in his campaign efforts. He admonished Clark Griffith, owner of the Washington Senators, for his blatantly racist view of black ballplayers, called upon President Roosevelt to adopt a "fair employment policy" in baseball just as he had done in war industries and governmental agencies; helped arrange a meeting between the baseball commissioner, Judge Kenesaw Mountain Landis, and the Black Newspaper Publishers' Association; assisted in arranging a tryout for three black players with the Boston Red Sox; and suggested to Branch Rickey that Jackie Robinson would be the ideal player to integrate the national game (Wiggins, 1983).

The Walls Came Tumbling Down

The efforts of Smith, as well as those of others involved in their own campaigns to integrate organized baseball, finally paid off in 1945 when

Rickey signed Robinson to a contract with the Brooklyn Dodgers. The signing of Robinson was received with unabated enthusiasm by America's black community and immediately catapulted the former UCLA and Kansas City Monarch star into the national limelight. Like Jesse Owens and Joe Louis before him, Robinson became a much-needed example of achievement and symbol of possibility for black Americans. He had an uplifting effect on other members of his race by becoming a participant in the sport considered the great leveler in society and America's national pastime (Frommer, 1982; Polner, 1982; Robinson, 1971; Tygiel, 1983).

The most obvious outcome of Robinson's signing was that it paved the way for further desegregation of sport at various levels of competition, a process that would not be completed until the latter half of the 1970s. Five months after obtaining the rights to Robinson, Rickey signed two more black players, Roy Campanella and Don Newcombe, to contracts with the Dodgers; and about a year later Bill Veeck began integration of his Cleveland Indians organization. Other major league teams were slow to follow the examples set by Rickey and Veeck, and integration in organized baseball proceeded very deliberately and at an uneven pace. During the latter part of the 1940s absence of financial incentives coupled with the racism and conservatism of baseball executives limited the number of teams that were willing to take chances with black players. By 1951, however, the pace of integration quickened as more teams were stimulated to seek black talent on account of the impressive performances of Robinson, Campanella, and others. Three years later, 12 of the 16 teams in major league baseball had black players on their rosters. In 1959, the curtain finally dropped on baseball's color line for good when the Boston Red Sox promoted the talented black infielder Pumpsie Green from their minor league affiliate in Minneapolis (Moore, 1988; Tygiel, 1983).

Desegregation of major league baseball would be duplicated in other professional and amateur sports over the next two decades. For example, the year after the signing of Robinson by the Brooklyn Dodgers, the color line was broken in professional football. The Los Angeles Rams of the National Football League, under pressure to field black players and fearful of losing its lease to the LA Coliseum, signed Kenny Washington and Woody Strode to contracts. The two black stars were, ironically enough, former teammates of Robinson's at UCLA. In the same year the NFL was integrated, the Cleveland Browns of the newly organized All-American Football Conference signed two black stars, fullback Marion Motley of the University of Nevada at Reno and lineman Bill Willis of Ohio State

University (Gems, 1988; Smith, 1988). The American Bowling Congress allowed blacks to use its lanes for the first time in 1949 (Lucas & Smith, 1978). A year later, Althea Gibson became the first black to participate at Forest Hills in the United States Tennis Championships, and the color line was broken in the National Basketball Association when the Harlem Globetrotters' Nat "Sweetwater" Clifton signed with the New York Knicks and Chuck Cooper of Duquesne University inked a contract with the Boston Celtics (Gibson, 1958; Salzberg, 1987). Art Dorrington became organized hockey's first black player in America when he signed with the Johnstown Jets in Pennsylvania in 1952. Some 22 years after Dorrington took to the ice with the Johnstown Jets, Lee Elder became the first black golfer to participate in the prestigious Masters Tournament in Augusta, Georgia (Lucas & Smith, 1978).

Perhaps the most significant battles against lily-white sport took place in intercollegiate athletics in the southern part of the United States. For years, blacks who wanted to participate in intercollegiate sport were forced to choose between athletic programs at historically black colleges in the South or predominantly white universities in the North. The chance to compete in intercollegiate athletics for one of the schools in the prestigious Atlantic Coast (ACC), Southwestern (SWC), and Southeastern (SEC) conferences was out of the question for blacks, who found themselves thwarted by southern racial policies and segregation (Ashe, 1988; Chalk, 1976; Henderson, 1939; Wiggins, 1991).

By the early 1960s, however, integration slowly began to take place in southern athletic conferences (Paul, McGhee, & Fant, 1984; Spivey, 1983; Wiggins, 1991). The *Brown v. Topeka Board of Education* school desegregation decision in 1954, combined with the fledgling civil rights movement and desire of educational institutions to achieve prominence in sport, resulted in the gradual integration of athletic programs at schools that had historically refused even to compete against black athletes. The color line was broken in the ACC by football player Darryl Hill of the University of Maryland in 1963 (Spivey, 1983; Wiggins, 1991). Two years later, Texas Christian basketball player James Cash became the first black athlete in the SWC (Pennington, 1987; Spivey, 1983; Wiggins, 1991).

The last major conference to integrate its sports programs was the SEC, a traditional stronghold of both athletic excellence and racial prejudice. Conference schools had received much notoriety for their athletic achievements through the years, but were equally famous for racial intolerance and acts of discrimination committed against blacks. Perhaps nowhere was the color line drawn tighter than in athletic programs of SEC schools, which operated against a backdrop of burning crosses and robed Klansman as well as large stadiums intended for white players only. In spite of these circumstances, segregation in the SEC slowly toppled under the weight of the civil rights struggle just as it had in the ACC and SWC. The University of Kentucky, the northern most school in the conference, led the charge against segregation when football coach Charlie Bradshaw signed black high school stars Nat Northington and Greg Page in 1966. Over the next few years, black athletes began to appear in different sports at other SEC schools, with Vanderbilt basketball coach C.M. Newton being the first person to recruit blacks in significant numbers and the University of Mississippi being the last member of the Conference to integrate in 1971 (Paul et al., 1984).

Black Athletes and the Civil Rights Movement
Integration of southern athletic conferences shared the spotlight with the black athletic disturbances taking place on predominantly white university campuses across the country. By the latter part of the 1960s, young black athletes were creating chaos on college campuses by becoming active participants in the civil rights movement and protesting racial discrimination in sport and American society at large. Inspired by the examples set by such outspoken professional sportsmen as Jim Brown, Bill Russell, and Muhammad Ali, black college athletes shed their traditional conservative approach to racial matters and vehemently protested everything from lack of black studies in the curriculum to the dearth of black coaches and athletic administrators. This path was sometimes paved with dire consequences, many black athletes enduring the wrath of university administrations and jeopardizing their careers for daring to speak out on behalf of themselves and members of their race. The protests also defied easy classification as they took place on different size campuses, in both urban and rural settings, and from one end of the country to the other. Black athletic rebellions occurred, for example, on the campuses of Syracuse University; Oregon State University; Michigan State University; San Francisco State University; University of Washington; University of California Berkeley; University of Kansas; University of Wyoming; University of Texas at El Paso, University of Arizona, and Oklahoma City University (Edwards, 1969, 1970; Scott, 1971; Wiggins, 1988).

Rebellious black athletes sometimes took their protests off campus and into larger settings where they could better publicize their fight for racial equality. Certainly the most celebrated protest of this type was the proposed boycott of the 1968 Olympic Games in Mexico City. In the fall of 1967, Harry Edwards, now a well-known professor of sociology at the University of California, Berkeley, assembled a group of outstanding black athletes who threatened to withdraw from the games in Mexico City unless certain demands were met. The demands included the removal of Avery Brundage as President of the International Olympic Committee, restoration of Muhammad Ali's heavyweight title, exclusion of Rhodesia and South Africa from Olympic competition, appointment of at least two blacks to the United States Olympic Committee, complete desegregation of the New York Athletic Club (NYAC), and addition of at least two black coaches to the men's Olympic track and field team (Edwards, 1969, 1980; Sendler, 1969).

Edwards and his band of black athletes, who termed their movement the Olympic Project for Human Rights (OPHR), got their protest off to a terrific start by successfully organizing a boycott of the NYAC's 100th Anniversary Track Meet in February, 1968. It became increasingly apparent following the NYAC boycott, however, that there would not be enough unanimity of opinion among the disgruntled black athletes to manage a successful boycott of the Mexico City Games. As serious as they were about making a contribution to the civil rights movement and protesting racial discrimination, black athletes found it impossible to forgo Olympic competition and not represent themselves and their country against the best athletes in the world. For most of the black athletes, the Olympic games were the ultimate in athletic competition, representing years of preparation and bringing them potential glory and unmatched worldwide acclaim. To sacrifice all this was extremely difficult, even for the most racially conscious black athletes (Edwards, 1969, 1980; Johnson, 1972; Spivey, 1985).

Academicians and Black Athletic Performance

The protests of black athletes declined in number by the early 1970s. Desegregation resulting from civil rights legislation of the 1960s, coupled with the fledgling women's movement and problems associated with inflation and unemployment, took some steam out of the black athletic revolt just as it had the larger black power movement (Rader, 1983; Roberts & Olson, 1989). Black athletes continued to fight racial discrimination, but they increasingly became the topic of discussion among people of both races who had become sensitized to racial issues emanating from the athletic protests of the previous decade. One of the legacies of the athletic protest movement of the 1960s was that the problems of black athletes were made more visible to the American public. The result was an outpouring of research studies and more popular essays dealing with the various forms of discrimination committed against black athletes, rather than any substantive changes made in sport itself (Johnson & Marple, 1973; Loy & McElvogue, 1970; Pascal & Rapping, 1972; Skully, 1974; Yetman & Eitzen, 1972).

Topics receiving a great deal of attention from academicians and others interested in black athletes were the phenomenon known as stacking, unequal opportunities and inadequate reward structures in sport, and differences in performance between black and white athletes. Of these three topics, perhaps none was as controversial and reflected more clearly the racial stereotypes held by Americans than the discussion of performance differentials between black and white athletes. In 1971, Martin Kane, a senior editor for *Sports Illustrated*, ignited the age-old debate over black athletic superiority by claiming in an article titled "An Assessment of Black Is Best" that "there is an increasing body of scientific opinion which suggests that physical differences in the races might well have enhanced the athletic potential of the negro in certain sports" (p. 72). Drawing on the expertise of sport scientists, coaches, medical doctors, and black athletes themselves, Kane argued that the dominance of black athletes in sport was the result of racially linked psychological, historical, and physiological factors. The outstanding performances of black athletes, in other words, were based on racial characteristics indigenous to the black population.

Kane's essay resulted in an angry response from Harry Edwards. In a series of articles, Edwards claimed that Kane's theories suffered from serious methodological problems and were based on questionable assumptions about racial differences. He refuted Kane's argument that black athletes possessed innate psychological and physiological skills that predisposed them to certain physical activities and accounted for their outstanding performances in sport. Kane's assertions were ludicrous and implied that blacks, while physiologically talented, were intellectually inferior to their white counterparts (Edwards, 1972, 1973 a, b).

To Edwards, the outstanding performances of black athletes in sport stemmed from a variety of societal conditions rather than innate physiological or psychological characteristics. Edwards claimed, among other things, that black youths placed a high value on sport and the result was a channeling of a disproportionate number of skilled blacks into athletics at both the amateur and professional levels. In contrast to their white counterparts, black Americans had less visible prestige role models, fewer job opportunities, and a more limited range of occupational choices. The upshot of all this was that blacks viewed sport, and to a lesser degree entertainment, as their most achievable goals and quickest path to stardom and wealth. This career path, unfortunately, has often been paved with bitter disappointments for aspiring black athletes, the vast majority either ending up back in the ghetto because they lacked the talent to become a superstar or dropping out of sport altogether because they refused to comply with the racist American sport establishment (Edwards, 1972, 1973).

The exchange between Kane and Edwards did not put an end to the debate over black athletic superiority. The increasing number of blacks participating in sport throughout the last two decades has continued to spark much controversy among academicians and lay public alike. In 1972, for instance, black Harvard psychiatrist Alvin F. Poussaint argued in an essay titled "Sex and the Black Male" that the need of black males to display physical power has accounted for their outstanding performances in sport. Stripped of any social power, black males have focused their attention on other symbols of masculinity, particularly on America's playing fields (pp. 115-116). Two years after Poussaint's article appeared, Jesse Owens, the man whose great performances on the cinder track in the 1930s contributed to initial discussions about black athletic superiority, told members of the American Medical Association that desire rather than innate physiological differences accounted for the disproportionate number of blacks in sport ("Byline," 1974).

In 1977, *Time* magazine published an article titled "Black Dominance" in which the opinions of various people, including famous black athletes, were gathered concerning the issue of black athletic superiority. A majority of the black athletes interviewed argued that physical differences accounted for the outstanding performances of black athletes (*Time,* 1974). Academician Legrand Clegg suggested in a 1980 essay in *Sepia* magazine that the superior accomplishments of black athletes resulted from the large amounts of melanin in blacks. Citing the work of several black scholars in the School of Ethnic Studies at San Francisco State University, Clegg believed melanin, rather than simply serving to protect skin from the harmful effects of the sun, was capable of absorbing a great deal of energy that blacks used to achieve great speeds in track (pp. 18-22).

In 1982, sociologist James LeFlore argued in an essay titled "Athleticism Among American Blacks" that the disproportionate number of black athletes in certain sports, although obviously influenced to some degree by genetic, environmental, and economic factors, was determined primarily by the cultural setting in which blacks found themselves and the type of information available to them and their particular subculture (pp. 104-121). Some six years after the publication of LeFlore's article, Jimmy "The Greek" Snyder, the famous sports prognosticator and announcer on CBS's *The N.F.L. Today* show caused an uproar when he told an interviewer at a restaurant in Washington DC that black athletes were superior to their white counterparts because of the way they were bred during slavery (*Fortune*, 1988; Rowe, 1988; *U.S. News & World Report*, 1988). In 1989, Tom Brokaw, partly in response to Snyder's controversial interview, hosted an NBC special devoted to the issue of black athletic superiority. The special, which included guests such as Harry Edwards, Arthur Ashe, anthropologist Robert Malina, and sports activist Richard Lapchick, received widespread coverage in the popular press and resulted in mixed reactions from America's black and white communities (NBC, 1989).

Continued Forms of Discrimination

Just as controversial as the debate over black athletic superiority has been the recent flurry of interest concerning the academic preparation of black college athletes and dearth of blacks in coaching and high-level administrative positions within sport. In 1983, the National Collegiate Athletic Association (NCAA) attempted to remedy the poor academic performance and low graduation rates of college athletes by passing a rule known as Proposition 48 (Coakley, 1990; Figler & Whitaker, 1991). Implemented for the first time in 1986, Proposition 48 declared that all freshman athletes would be ineligible to participate on varsity sports teams if they had not achieved a 2.0 GPA in 11 designated core subjects in high school and either a score of 15 on the American College Test (ACT) or 700 on the Scholastic Aptitude Test (SAT). This rule allowed athletes who satisfied just one of these requirements to be accepted into college and be given athletic aid, but they were not allowed to practice with their team during the freshman year and forfeited a year of athletic eligibility. In 1989, the NCAA toughened its standards even more by passing Proposition 42, which prohibited universities from providing athletic aid to athletes who did not meet both the GPA and test-score requirements (Coakley, 1990;

Figler & Whitaker, 1991).

Propositions 48 and 42 were ultimately designed to encourage high school athletes to commit themselves to academics as well as sports and to insure that universities recruited athletes who were prepared to do the work expected of all students in institutions of higher learning. The two propositions have seemingly had a positive effect at the high school level, encouraging young athletes to take academics more seriously and spurring the development of academic support programs by coaches and sports administrators. Both propositions have been heavily criticized, however, for being unfair to black athletes (Coakley, 1990; Figler & Whitaker, 1991). The passing of Proposition 48 had no sooner taken place than many black educators and civil rights activists began lashing out at the rule for its discriminatory nature. The National Alliance of Black School Educators, National Association for Equality of Opportunity in Higher Education (NAFEA), and such well-known black leaders as Jesse Jackson, Benjamin Hooks, and Joseph Lowery were critical of the rule because they believed it was formulated without black input. They also claimed that the ACT and SAT tests were culturally biased in favor of whites (in actuality the two tests were probably more discriminatory along socioeconomic rather than racial lines). It was their belief that the scores required for both tests were unfair to black athletes because nearly 75% of black students score below 15 on the ACT and more than 50% score below 700 on the SAT (Coakley, 1990; Figler & Whitaker, 1991).

But these charges were countered by an equally sincere cadre of black Americans who argued that the propositions were not racially discriminatory and were a step in the right direction (Edwards, 1983; Hackley, 1983) Harry Edwards was in principle the most outspoken advocate of the rule changes, but there were a fairly substantial number of black academicians who also supported the tougher academic requirements for student-athletes. For instance, Lloyd V. Hackley, Chancellor of the University of Arkansas at Pine Bluff, had great difficulty understanding how people could link Proposition 48 to racism (Hackley, 1983). He implied that critics of the new rule were unintentionally "retarding the progress of deprived peoples" by claiming racism and arguing against higher academic standards (Hackley, 1983, p. 37). He believed the only way to improve the academic performance of black athletes was to support the tougher eligibility requirements included in Proposition 48 rather than decry the unfairness of testing procedures. Anything else was exploitation, and nothing less (Hackley, 1983).

The black community's concern about the academic preparation of black athletes was matched only by its frustration over the lack of blacks in coaching and administrative positions within sport. Serious concern over the limited number of blacks in coaching and administrative positions has been regularly expressed by black Americans since at least the latter half of the 1960s, but has become a cause celebre the last few years. In 1987, Al Campanis, a top executive with the Los Angeles Dodgers, brought sensitive racial issues to the forefront once again when he suggested to Ted Koppel on the *Nightline* television program that the scarcity of blacks in baseball management positions resulted from their lack of abilities. "I truly believe they may not have the necessities to be, let's say, a field manager or perhaps a general manager" (Chass, 1987, p. B14). The public outcry following the interview was so great that Campanis was fired by the Dodgers and Baseball Commissioner Peter Ueberroth hired Harry Edwards to study the problem of racism in major league baseball and increase the number of blacks in management positions (Figler & Whitaker, 1991).

Last Vestiges of Racism in Sport

The Campanis folly, combined with several comments made by Jimmy "The Greek" Snyder in his aforementioned interview in Washington DC, refocused attention on the small number of blacks in coaching and management positions in sport. Perhaps most importantly, however, it made clear that many people in the dominant culture still held to their racist beliefs and deep-seated stereotypical notions about blacks. Although blacks are now disproportionately represented in certain sports and even find themselves in some upper level management positions, the same racist beliefs that resulted in years of segregation in sport are still evident in American society today. The belief that the success of black athletes results from innate physical skills rather than dedication and hard work has been slow to die in this country (Chass, 1987; Wiggins, 1989). And so has the notion that black athletes, like other members of the black community, are either docile, savage, deceptive, childlike, oversexed, or a combination of all the above. The simple truth is that people, both black and white, continue to insist on differentiating between human beings based solely on race (Early, 1989; Wiggins, 1989). Although the scientific literature does not support such claims, people are still convinced that a person's color defines his or her very being and separates the person from others both emotionally and physically. This is what accounts for the attraction of interracial athletic contests, but also explains the racially insensitive remarks uttered by well-known sports prognosticators and top-level baseball executives.

Based on the historical experiences of black athletes, only time will tell when the insensitive remarks will finally cease and the last vestiges of racism be eliminated from sport in this country. The evolution of the black athletes' involvement in American sport has been a turbulent one at best characterized by major successes as well as a host of problems stemming from habitual prejudices and beliefs in the inequality of the races. As has been shown, black athletes during the second half of the nineteenth century realized major successes in the athletic field only to have the door of opportunity closed on them by believers in Jim Crow and white supremacy.

This process was repeated in one form or another throughout much of the first half of this century and beyond. Although great sums of money and adulation were realized by a select number of black athletes, the large majority of them were either forced to endure the racial discrimination evident in white-controlled sport or retreat into all-black sporting organizations where they could find comfort in their own kind. This was unfortunate because black athletes, like their white counterparts, merely wanted the opportunity to compete against the best athletes regardless of color and realize the numerous benefits resulting from successful participation in sport. In many regards, the critical events for black athletes usually took place off the field where their physical abilities were unable to shield them from the racial discrimination in American society.

References

Ashe, A. (1988). *A hard road to glory: A history of the African-American athlete, 1619 - present.* (3 Vols.) New York: Warner Books.

Behee J. (1974). *Hail to the victors!: Black athletes at the University of Michigan.* Ann Arbor, MI: Swink-Tuttle Press.

Betts, J.R. (1974). *America's sporting heritage, 1850-1950.* Reading, MA: Addison-Wesley.

Black athletes: Fact and fiction. (Television Special). New York: NBC, April 25.

Black dominance. *Time* (1977, May), pp. 57-60.

Brashler, W. (1978). *Josh Gibson: A life in the Negro leagues.* New York: Harper & Row.

Brower, W.A. (1940). Has professional football closed the door? *Oppor-*

tunity, 18, 375-377.

Brower, W.A. (1941). Prejudice in sports. *Opportunity, 19,* 260-263.

Bruce, J. (1983). *The Kansas City Monarchs: Champions of black baseball.* Lawrence, KS: University Press of Kansas. Byline. *New York Times,* (1974, December 2).

Capeci, D.J., & Wilkerson, M. (1983). Multifarious hero: Joe Louis, American society and race relations during world crisis, 1935-1945. *Journal of Sport History, 10,* 5-25.

Chalk, O. (1976). *Black college sport.* New York: Dodd & Mead.

Chass, M. (1987, April 9). Campanis is out; Racial remarks cited by Dodgers. *New York Times,* pp. B13-14.

Clegg, L.H. (1980). Why black athletes run faster. *Sepia,* pp. 18-22.

Coakley, J. (1990). *Sport in society: Issues and controversies* (4th ed.). St. Louis, MO: Times Mirror/Mosby.

Cochran, T.C., & Miller, W. (1961). *The age of enterprise.* New York: Harper & Row.

Cone, C.B. (1982). The Molineaux-Cribb Fight, 1810: "Wuz Tom Molineaux robbed?" *Journal of Sport History,* 9, 83-91.

Davis, J.P. (1966). The Negro in American sports. In J.P. Davis (Ed.), *The American Negro Reference Book* (pp. 775-825). Englewood Cliffs, NJ: Prentice-Hall.

Early, G. (1989). *Tuxedo junction: Essays on American culture.* New York: The Ecco Press.

Edmonds, A.O. (1973). The second Louis-Schmeling fight: Sport, symbol and culture *Journal of Popular Culture,* 7, 42-50.

Edwards, H. (1969). *The revolt of the black athlete.* New York: The Free Press.

Edwards, H. (1970). *Black students.* New York: The Free Press.

Edwards, H. (1972). The myth of the racially superior athlete. *Intellectual Digest,* 2, 58-60.

Edwards, H. (1973a). The sources of the black athlete's superiority. *The Black Scholar, 3,* 32-41.

Edwards, H. (1973b, November). 20th Century gladiators for white America. *Psychology Today,* pp. 43-52.

Edwards, H. (1980). *The struggle that must be: An autobiography.* New York: MacMillan.

Edwards, H. (1983, August). Educating black athletes. *The Atlantic Monthly,* pp. 31-38.

Figler, S.K., & Whitaker, G. (1991). *Sport & play in American life: A textbook in the sociology of sport.* (2nd ed.). Dubuque, IA: Wm. C. Brown.

Fishman, G. (1969). Paul Robeson's student days and the fight against racism at Rutgers. *Freedomways, 9*, 221-229.

Fleischer, N.S. (1938). *The story of the Negro in the prize ring from 1782 to 1938.* (3 Vols.). New York: The Ring Book Shop.

Frommer, H. (1982). *Rickey and Robinson: The men who broke baseball's color barrier.* New York: MacMillan Publishing Company.

Gems, G.R. (1988). Shooting stars: The rise and fall of blacks in professional football. *Professional Football Research Association Annual Bulletin,* 1-16.

Gibson, A. (1958). *I always wanted to be somebody.* New York: Harper and Brothers.

Gilliam, D.B. (1976). *Paul Robeson: All-American.* Washington, DC: New Republic Book Company.

Gilmore, A. (1975). *Bad nigger: The national impact of Jack Johnson.* New York: Kennikat Press.

Goodman, M.H. (1980). The Moor vs. Black Diamond. *Virginia Cavalcade, 29*, 164-173.

Grundman, A.H. (1979). Image of intercollegiate sports and the Civil Rights Movement: A historian's view. *Arena Review, 3*, 17-24.

Hackley, L.V. (1983). We need to educate our athletes! *The Black Collegian, 13*, 35-37.

Henderson, E.B. (1939). *The Negro in sports.* Washington, DC: The Associated Publishers.

Henderson, E.B. (1972). Physical education and athletics among Negroes. In B.L. Bennett (Ed.), *The History of Physical Education and Sport* (pp. 67-83). Chicago, IL: The Athletic Institute.

Holway, J. (1978). *Voices from the great black baseball leagues.* New York: Harper and Row.

Johnson, N.R., & Marple, D.P. (1973). Racial discrimination in professional basketball. *Sociological Focus, 6*, 6-18.

Johnson, W.O. (1972). *All that glitters is not gold: The Olympic Game.* New York: Putnam.

Kane, M. (1971, January). An assessment of black is best. *Sports Illustrated,* pp. 72-83.

LeFlore, J. (1982). Athleticism among American blacks. In R.M. Pankin (Ed.), *Social Approaches to Sport.* Toronto: Associated University Press.

Logan, R.W. (1957). *The Negro in the United States.* Princeton: D. Van Nostrand.

Logan, R.W. (1965). *The betrayal of the Negro from Rutherford B. Hayes to Woodrow Wilson.* New York: Collier Books.

Lowenfish, L. (1978). Sport, race, and the baseball business: The Jackie Robinson story revisited. *Arena Review, 2,* 2-16.

Loy, J.W., & McElvogue, J.F. (1970). Racial segregation in American sport. *International Review of Sport Sociology, 5,* 5-23.

Lucas, J.A., & Smith, R.A. (1978). *Saga of American sport.* Philadelphia: Lea & Febiger.

McKinney, G.B. (1976). Negro professional baseball players in the upper south in the gilded age. *Journal of Sport History, 3,* 273-280.

Mead, C. (1985). *Champion Joe Louis: Black hero in white America.* New York: Charles Scribner's Sons.

Meier, A., & Rudwick, E.M. (1963). *From plantation to ghetto.* New York: Hill and Wang.

Miller, L. (1927). The unrest among college students: Kansas University. *Crisis, 34,* 187-188.

Moore, J.T. (1988). *Pride against prejudice: The biography of Larry Doby.* New York: Praeger.

Of fingerprints and other clues. *Fortune* (1988, February), pp. 123-124.

Pascal, A.H., & Rapping. L.A. (1972). The economics of racial discrimination in organized baseball. In A.H. Pascal (Ed.), *Racial Discrimination in Economic Life.* Lexington, MA: Heath Publishing.

Paul, J., McGhee, R.V., & Fant, H. (1984). The arrival and ascendence of black athletes in the southeastern conference, 1966-1980. *Phylon, 45,* 284-297.

Pennington, R. (1987). *Breaking the ice: The racial integration of southwest conference football.* Jefferson, NC: McFarland.

Peterson, R.W. (1990). *Cages to jumpshots: Pro basketball's early years.* New York: Oxford University.

Peterson, R. (1970). *Only the ball was white.* Englewood Cliffs, NJ: Prentice-Hall.

Polner, M. (1982). *Branch Rickey: A biography.* New York: Atheneum Publishing Company.

Poussaint, A.F. (1972, August). Sex and the black male. *Ebony,* pp. 114-120.

Rader, B. (1983). *American sports: From the age of folk games to the age of spectators.* Englewood Cliffs, NJ: Prentice-Hall.

Ritchie, A. (1988). *Major Taylor: The extraordinary career of a champion bicycle racer.* San Francisco, CA: Bicycle Books.

Roberts, R. (1983). *Papa Jack: Jack Johnson and the era of white hopes.* New York: The Free Press.

Roberts, R., & Olson, J. (1989). *Winning is the only thing: Sports in American life since 1945.* Baltimore, MD: The Johns Hopkins University Press.

Robinson, J. (1971). *I never had it made.* New York: G.P. Putnam's Sons.

Rogosin, D. (1983). *Invisible men: Life in baseball's Negro leagues.* New York: Atheneum Publishers.

Rowe, J. (1988, April). The Greek Chorus: Jimmy the Greek got it wrong but so did his critics. *The Washington Monthly,* pp. 31-34.

Ruck, R. (1988). *Sandlot seasons: Sport in black Pittsburgh.* Urbana: University of Illinois Press.

Rudolph, J.W. (1979). Tom Molyneaux--America's 'almost' champion. *American History Illustrated, 14,* 8-14.

Salzberg, C. (1987). *From set shot to slam dunk.* New York: E.P. Dutton.

Sammons, J.T. (1988). *Beyond the ring: The role of boxing in American society.* Urbana, IL: University of Illinois Press.

Scott, J. (1971). *The athletic revolution.* New York: The Free Press.

Sendler, D. (1969). The black athlete — 1968. In P.W. Romero (Ed.), *In Black America, 1968, The Year of Awakening.* New York: Publishers Company.

Simons, W. (1983). Jackie Robinson and the American mind: Journalistic perceptions of the reintegration of baseball. *Journal of Sport History, 12,* 39-64.

Skully, G.W. (1974). Discrimination: The case of baseball. In R.G. Noll (Ed.), *Government and the sport business.* Washington, DC: The Brookings Institute.

Smith, T.G. (1988). Outside the pale: The exclusion of blacks from the National Football League. *Journal of Sport History, 15,* 255-281.

Somers, D.A. (1972). *The rise of sport in New Orleans, 1850-1900.* Baton Rouge, LA: Louisiana State University.

Spivey, D. (1983). The black athlete in big-time intercollegiate sports, 1941-1968. *Phylon, 44,* 116-125.

Spivey, D. (1985). Black consciousness and Olympic protest movement, 1964-1980. In D. Spivey (Ed.), *Sport in America: New historical perspectives* (pp. 239-262). Westport, CT: Greenwood Press.

Spivey, D., & Jones, T. (1975). Intercollegiate athletic servitude: A case study of the black Illinois student-athletes, 1931-1967. *Social Science Quarterly, 55*, 939-947.

Taylor, M.M. (1971). *The fastest bicycle rider in the world.* (Reprint ed.). Battleboro, VT: Green-Stephen Press.

Tygiel, J. (1983). *Baseball's great experiment: Jackie Robinson and his legacy.* New York: Oxford University.

Weaver, B.L. (1979). The black press and the assault on professional baseball's color-line, October 1945-April 1947. *Phylon, 40*, 303-317.

What we say, what we think. *U.S. News & World Report* (1988, February), pp. 27-28.

Wiggins, D.K. (1971). Jack Johnson a bad nigger: The folklore of his life. *Black Scholar, 2*, 4-19.

Wiggins, D.K. (1979). Isaac Murphy: Black hero in nineteenth-century American sport, 1861-1896. *Canadian Journal of History of Sport and Physical Education, 10*, 15-32.

Wiggins, D.K. (1983). Wendell Smith, the *Pittsburgh Courier-Journal* and the campaign to include blacks in organized baseball, 1933-1945. *Journal of Sport History, 10*, 5-29.

Wiggins, D.K. (1985). Peter Jackson and the elusive heavyweight championship: A black athlete's struggle against the late nineteenth century color-line. *Journal of Sport History, 12*, 143-168.

Wiggins, D.K. (1988). The future of college athletics is at stake: Black athletes and racial turmoil on three predominantly white university campuses, 1968-1972. *Journal of Sport History, 15*, 304-333.

Wiggins, D.K. (1989). Great speed but little stamina: The historical debate over black athletic superiority. *Journal of Sport History, 16*, 158-185.

Wiggins, D.K. (1991). Prized performers, but frequently overlooked students: The involvement of black athletes in intercollegiate sports on predominantly white university campuses, 1890-1972. *Research Quarterly for Exercise and Sport, 62*, 164-177.

Wolters, R. (1975). *The new Negro on campus: Black college rebellions of the 1920's.* Princeton: Princeton University.

Woodward, C.V. (1966). *The strange career of Jim Crow.* New York: Oxford University.

Yetman, N.R., & Eitzen, J.D. (1972). Black Americans in sport: Unequal opportunity for equal ability. *Civil Rights Digest, 5*, 20-34.

Young, A.S. (1963). *Negro firsts in sports*. Chicago: Johnson Publishing.
Young, A.S. (1970, October). The black sportswriter. *Ebony*, pp. 56-58+.

Essay 2

African-American Predominance in Collegiate Sport

Othello Harris

Abstract: This essay investigates the involvement of African-Americans in collegiate sport and the attendance problems. The first part examines African-American collegiate sport participation in the early years (the late 1800s until World War II); the post-World War II influx of black athletes into athletic programs; black militancy and the changes that occurred in collegiate sport during the 1960s; and the predominance of African-Americans in Division collegiate programs from the 1970s through the early 1990s.

Today, many revenue-generating collegiate athletic programs, particularly programs in the South, have a preponderance of African-American athletes on their teams (although many of these athletically and academically prestigious colleges enroll few African-American nonathletes). However, this change in the racial composition of teams has not been accompanied by the disappearance of athletic and academic problems faced by African-American athletes in earlier decades. The second part of the essay addresses problems faced by present-day African-American athletes at predominantly white colleges and universities. Among these problems are athletic concerns such as racist perceptions and stereotypes and a continuation of stacking patterns. The essay also addresses academic problems such as poor academic performance and low graduation rates.

Finally, the NCAA's attempts to address the poor academic performance of African-American student-athletes are analyzed.

Introduction

Collegiate sport in America has become a showcase of African-American talent. No longer denied athletic scholarships and opportunities at major colleges and universities, African-Americans dominate the record books. Statistical leaders in categories such as rushing and receiving in football, scoring and rebounding in basketball, and sprinting in track and field are, almost without exception in recent years, African-Americans.

Television highlight films bring us replays of African-Americans receiving passes, running into the end zone for touchdowns, scoring baskets, and anchoring suffocating defenses. Their presence is required, it seems, for teams to compete, not to mention excel, in revenue-generating intercollegiate sports. For example, African-Americans figured prominently in the New Year's Day bowl games that concluded the 1990-91 football season where an estimated $45 million dollars was paid to participating teams for eight collegiate contests. Even at quarterback, a position that appears to have been, in the past, the domain of white players, the presence of African-Americans was felt; the teams that received the AP and UPI polls nominations as the top college team were both led by African-American quarterbacks. (The AP and UPI differed on their choice for the "number one" team.)

In the 1990 balloting for the Heisman Trophy, the oldest and most prestigious of the individual player awards, three of the top four candidates were African-Americans. For only the third time in 17 years the award was won by a white player, Ty Detmer of Brigham Young University. Like the two other white players who have won the award in more than a decade and a half, he played quarterback (Meserole, 1991). (The last white player to win the award, other than a QB, was Penn State's John Cappelletti, a running back). In the professional football draft that followed the 1990-1991 college football season, the top 7 draft choices and 23 of the 27 first-round selections were African-Americans.

In college basketball many of the key players in the 1991 Final Four were African-Americans. The University of Nevada, Las Vegas (UNLV), which was the top-ranked team from preseason until its NCAA Final Four loss, carried an all-black starting five; four of them were taken in a two-round draft by professional teams. The remaining starter was invited to camp by one of the professional franchises.

In short, there is no denying that intercollegiate sport has come to regard the presence of African-American athletes as essential to its goal of presenting an exciting, professional-style game that will attract spectators and network dollars. But it hasn't always been that way. As recently as 40 years ago intercollegiate sport was, on the whole, opposed to, or at best indifferent to, African-American participation.

Athletes, Scholars, and Superspades

According to David Wiggins (1991) during the latter half of the nineteenth century sport was not of primary importance to African-American student-athletes; they were more concerned about academic success. Many of these student-athletes were from upper-middle-class families and had attended private academies, prestigious public schools, or black colleges in the South. Still, few schools, even in the North, accepted them on their athletic teams. The U.S. Military Academy and U.S. Naval Academy (Army and Navy), Catholic schools like Notre Dame, and Ivy League schools like Princeton and Yale all shunned African-American athletes, if not African-Americans altogether. Athletic ability and a predisposition for academic success meant nothing to coaches and administrators if they were not cloaked in a white body.

During the next few decades intercollegiate sport provided a few more opportunities for African-Americans to participate, mostly in football and track and field. A larger number of northern schools had African-Americans on their teams, but segregation still prevailed off the field. In many cases there was only one African-American on the team (and there were few on campus). As Behee (1974) noted, those who made varsity teams were "superspades." That is, they were expected to do more than simply participate in the team's success, they were expected to *carry* the team to victory. Willis Ward is a shining example of a "superspade;" he scored 13 of the University of Michigan's 18 3/4 points to lead them to victory over Illinois in the 1932 Butler Relays. Three years later Jesse Owens scored 40 of Ohio State's 40 1/5 point in a win over UC, Berkeley. Paul Robeson, the lone African-American on campus at Rutgers, was an All-American in 1917 and 1918. They and other African-Americans were expected to provide super performances to justify their presence on athletic teams at predominantly white colleges and universities.

Super performances notwithstanding, African-Americans were often treated shabbily by their schools. Campus housing was off-limits to most of them; they were refused service in restaurants and not allowed to stay at hotels with their white teammates (even in northern cities like Chicago and Buffalo, New York); and probably most humiliating, they were kept out of home and away games against southern teams. (When playing southern teams on the road, northern teams were expected to be *gracious guests* by keeping their African-Americans, who were considered offensive to southern whites, off the field. When northern teams played at home against southern teams they were expected to be *gracious hosts*, again, by keeping their offending players off the field.) The NCAA steered clear of these abominable practices, and the games went on as planned. Men like Robeson, an All-American for two years and Phi Beta Kappa at Rutgers, and Willis Ward had to watch from the sidelines as their football teams sought to uphold the honor of the school without them.

While a few African-Americans (e.g., Robeson, Ward, Fritz Pollard and "Duke" Slater) were found in football programs in the North, most were barred from athletic activities that required interracial contact. Until the 1930s, most of the participation occurred in track and field where, according to Behee (1974), there were 100-200 black athletes competing from major colleges and universities at the time of the 1936 Olympics. Only later would football and basketball programs begin to accept African-Americans in more than token roles.

The Aftermath of World War II

World War II brought about a number of changes in the status of African-Americans. They, like other Americans, had fought in Europe to eliminate Nazism, yet racism pervaded nearly every American institution. Upon their return they (along with black civilians) were prepared to fight for integration at home.

After the war several factors combined to greatly increase the college attendance rates of African-Americans. Congress passed legislation that created the G.I. Bill, which provided funds for the postsecondary education of returning servicemen. This allowed many Americans to attend college who would otherwise have otherwise, lacked the finances to attend. More than one-fourth of the students registered at colleges and universities in 1945-46 were veterans of World War II (Andrews, 1984). Many African-Americans were among the beneficiaries of the G.I. Bill (Green, 1982). And in some cases the veterans were former athletes who, in addition to furthering their education, were interested in participating in collegiate sports.

Also, President Truman appointed an interracial committee to study problems in higher education. It called for an end to discrimination in higher education, including inequalities in educational opportunities (Franklin & Moss, 1988). This recommendation, coming from a committee appointed by the nation's chief executive, made discrimination in colleges and universities a national issue (Wiggins, 1991) and, undoubtedly, made college desegregation a more acceptable, if not expected, practice. Finally, after the war professional sports—baseball, football, and basketball—began to accept more black players on their teams. Collegiate sport was moving in the same direction.

The above factors resulted in the presence of more African-Americans at predominantly white colleges and universities. Consequently, at a time when Americans were more receptive to African-Americans—at least at the level of secondary structural assimilation, there was also a larger pool of potential black athletes available to collegiate athletic teams.

The change in racial attitudes in intercollegiate sport led to a new look in collegiate football. In 1944 two African-Americans were selected to the *Look* magazine All-American team; no others were selected in the decade of the 1940s. However, during the 1950s, 15 African-Americans made the magazine's All-American team (Behee, 1974).

Basketball experienced similar changes. By 1948 10 percent of the basketball programs at predominantly white colleges and universities had African-Americans on their roster; one percent of all players at these schools were black (Berghorn, Yetman, & Hanna, 1988). Although this did not constitute a large number of African-Americans, it was a sizable increase from the pre-World War II figures. No black basketball player was named to Look magazine's All-American team until 1952. Thereafter, African-Americans have been on every Look All-American team; 21 made the team during the 1950s (Behee, 1974). The Associated Press named five African-Americans to the 1958 All-American team, the first of many times that this happened.

As more African-Americans participated in intercollegiate sport the "superspade" requirement was dropped. Still, a disproportionate number of them were rookies of the year, conference most valuable players and All-Americans. They, more than their white peers, were expected to turn in stellar performances in return for their athletic scholarships.[1]

The desegregation of collegiate sport did not mean, however, the integration of sport. African-Americans in the 1940s and 1950s faced many of the same problems their predecessors faced. For example, while their teammates were quartered at prestigious hotels, they were often left to seek lodging at the "black YMCA" or with black families in town. When the University of Cincinnati team traveled to Texas in 1959, Oscar Robertson, the star of the team, had to stay at a black college while the rest of the team was housed in Houston (Ashe, 1988). Even when the entire team stayed at the same hotel, segregation was carried out through racial pairing in the room assignments; black and white players were seldom allowed to room together.

Housing was still a problem for African-Americans because they were often required to seek accommodations away from campus. The isolation from other athletes was magnified away from campus as black athletes found many stores, restaurants, and movie theaters in college towns off-limits to them. To wander too far from campus could be risky, yet they were prohibited from most aspects of campus life.

What makes the opprobrious treatment of African-American athletes described above even more untenable is that it occurred in northern, midwestern and western regions of the country. Southern schools' athletic programs, for the most part, remained segregated during this period. A 1956 legislative act that banned interracial sports in the state of Louisiana and the riots that met Autherine Lucy's attempt to integrate the University of Alabama that same year (see Paul, McGhee & Fant, 1984) were clear signs of a southern aversion to segregation. That this inclination to distance themselves from African-Americans was not confined to intrateam competition can be illustrated by the Mississippi State University basketball team's decision to sit out NCAA tournaments in 1959 and 1961 and the University of Mississippi football team's willingness to forgo a 1961 bowl game rather than compete against integrated teams (Paul et al., 1984).

To the disappointment of African-American athletes, the post-War period did not result in the collapse of discrimination in intercollegiate sport. Nevertheless, there were some changes in the attitudes of whites toward black athletes. Many conferences dropped racial bans (Rader, 1990) and gentleman's agreements (Behee, 1974) that prohibited African-American participation in basketball and football (although schools continued to set quotas on the number of African-Americans permitted on a team). Some schools canceled games with teams that refused to play against their black players. More importantly, African-American athletes were experiencing a change in "attitude" and demeanor; resistance to their maltreatment was growing. Discontent would soon turn into rebellious outbursts.

Black Pride and Protest

During the latter part of the 1950s African-Americans showed their impatience with America's unfulfilled promise of full equality by participating in mass demonstrations. Through peaceful forms of civil disobedience they demanded an end to discriminatory practices such as segregated seating on public transportation and the disenfranchisement of eligible black voters. Participants in the protests were counseled not to retaliate against those who verbally and physically assaulted them as they opposed America's racist practices. Instead, they were advised to "turn the other cheek." Although their nonviolent tactics were often met with violence by angry mobs, police clubs, attack dogs, and the spray of fire hoses—the demonstrators, for the most part, remained nonviolent.

As the decade of the 1960s began, a new weapon of peaceful protest was unleashed on southern businesses: sit-ins. In February of 1960 four African-American students who attended North Carolina A & T were refused coffee at a department store in Greensboro, North Carolina (Morris, 1984). Their response was to sit and wait for service, thereby depriving the store of the opportunity to profit from service to other customers, while bringing attention to their grievance. This movement spread all over the South.

At the same time institutions of higher education in the South found themselves engaged in heated battles over the issue of desegregation. In 1962 it took a court order, deputy marshals, and the National Guard to enroll James Meredith at the University of Mississippi. The next year Governor George C. Wallace, in defiance of a court order, stood in the door of the University of Alabama to prevent African-Americans from enrolling and attending classes. Wallace proclaimed segregation to be a way of life in the South; it was an unstated but widely acknowledged component of most organizations in the nation.

Although discrimination was a way of life in most American institutions, many thought sport, particularly college sport, was exempt from this contemptible treatment of participants; there seemed to be evidence to support this egalitarian notion of college athletics. By 1962 African-American presence in collegiate basketball was comparable to their distribution in the general population (Berghorn et al., 1988). Oscar Robertson was college basketball's player of the year in 1960 (for the third consecutive time); by 1966, when Cazzie Russell was player of the year, the All-America first team was predominantly black. It would remain that way the rest of the decade. In 1963 Loyola of Illinois started four black players, a practice unheard of at that time in college basketball, and won the national championship. The decade ended with Lew Alcindor (later, Kareem Abdul-Jabbar), also a three-time college basketball player of the year, leading UCLA to its third straight national championship.

Similar feats were accomplished by African-Americans in other college sports. Many of the records in track and field, particularly in the sprints, hurdles, relays, and long jump, belonged to African-Americans. Bob Hayes, Jim Hines, and Charlie Greene held the fastest times in the 100-yard dash in the 1960s. Tommie Smith topped the field in the 220-yard dash, and Wyomia Tyus set records in the 100-yard and 100-meter dashes while Wilma Rudolph did the same in the 200-meter dash. Lee Calhoun was the 120-yard hurdles champion, and African-American men owned the records in the 400-meter and 1600-meter relays (Edwards, 1969). Perhaps most impressively, at the 1968 Olympics Bob Beamon set a record in the long jump that lasted for more than 22 years. Moreover, African-Americans were an integral part of many of the top collegiate track and field programs.

African-American presence and stature on the football field were growing as well, as evidenced by the honors these athletes were winning: Syracuse's Ernie Davis, in 1961, became the first African-American to win the Heisman trophy. In the decade of the sixties two others would follow, Mike Garrett and O.J. Simpson, both of USC. Other players like Gale Sayers and Warren McVea accumulated impressive rushing and passing statistics.

By the middle of the 1960s even southern teams had begun to welcome black athletes. The Southeastern Conference (SEC), one of the premier athletic conferences in the South, integrated in 1967; other southern conferences (e.g., the Atlantic Coast and Southwest conferences) had already desegregated. It seemed that programs all over the country sought black athletes. But African-American athletes understood that the attention, adulation, and rewards they received from the athletic department were ephemeral. They felt the sting of prejudice and exclusion that the black athletes who preceded them had experienced. They began to perceive that "once their athletic abilities are impaired by their age or by injury, only the ghetto beckons and they are doomed once again to that faceless, hopeless, ignominious existence they had supposedly forever left behind them" (Edwards, 1969, p. xxvii). Once they left the confines of the athletic field their treatment, like that of nonathletic African-Americans, was at best insensitive and often abominable.

African-American collegiate athletes began to rebel. They called for an end to stacking (intraracial competition for team positions), racial stereo-typing, policing of social activities (including interracial dating) and other forms of discrimination in athletic programs (Spivey, 1985). In some cases they adopted the tactics of the civil rights movement: peaceful demonstrations. Black athletes, and sometimes white athletes, boycotted practices and banquets and refused to compete in events for organizations that discriminated against African-Americans (e.g., the New York Athletic Club, which had discriminatory policies regarding accommodations). In other cases, African-American athletes and activists announced their intention to cancel athletic contests staged by schools that mistreated them as students and/or athletes "by any means necessary" (Edwards, 1969). By 1968 a movement by African-American athletes to boycott the Olympic Games, to be held later that year in Mexico, appeared to be growing. Athletes were using athletics to bring about social change.

The proposed boycott of the 1968 Olympics never materialized; few prominent black athletes declined to participate in the Games. However, the struggle for social equality by African-American athletes and the willingness of some to sacrifice their athletic scholarships[2] for the movement brought about changes in college sport. For example, the Big Ten conference appointed a committee to look into the complaints of black athletes. They found evidence to support the athletes' charges of academic neglect and athletic exploitation. Changes were then instituted to improve academic support and counseling for African-American athletes, and efforts were made to recruit more African-American coaches and other athletic personnel (Wiggins, 1991). Big Ten schools, like many other schools during the late sixties and early seventies, hired black assistant coaches to serve as intermediaries for African-American athletes and white head coaches. Problems of discrimination, social isolation, and ill-treatment by coaches did not disap more inclined to confront coaches and administrators than they had been in earlier years. Their services were needed now more than ever. Some of their demands had to be met.

African-American Predominance
The period since the mid-1970s has been one of increasing interracial participation in revenue-generating collegiate sports. Basketball and football command larger television contracts, and televised games result in more money for participating schools and their conferences. For example, in 1966 the NCAA received $180,000 from television for the basketball tournament. In 1988 the tournament was worth $58 million to

the NCAA; each Final Four team received in excess of one million dollars. The present television contract calls for payments of approximately $115 million per year. As the payoff for successful seasons has soared, the reliance on African-American athletes has ascended (particularly in basketball where one outstanding player can have a dramatic effect on the outcome of a game).

African-Americans constituted more than one-third of all male collegiate basketball players in 1975 (Berghorn et al.,1988). By 1988 over half (56%) the male basketball players and one-third of the female basketball players were black (American Institute for Research, 1989). Southern teams have the highest percentage of African-Americans; 61% of players on Southern teams are black. In many cases they are the majority on the same teams that found them objectionable two or three decades ago. By 1985 95% of NCAA basketball teams had black players, and the average number of black players on integrated squads was 5.7 (Berghorn et al., 1988).

African-Americans have dominated nearly every statistical category in college basketball--scoring, rebounding, assists, etc., especially in the more recent years. They have also garnered most of the player of the year awards (e.g., UPI, AP, U.S. Basketball Writers' Association, Naismith, Rupp, and Wooden awards) and an inordinate number of the all-conference and NCAA all-tournament awards. Furthermore, since 1971 when the All-American first team comprised of only African-Americans, white first team All-Americans have become more rare. In the 1980s only 6 of the 53 All-America selections were white players,[3] and no All-America team in the eighties (or thus far in the nineties) has had more than one white player on the roster.

Similarly in football African-Americans have overshadowed all others in recent years in rushing, receiving, punt return, and kickoff return statistics. In addition to the Heisman Trophy winners mentioned earlier, African-Americans have won a disproportionate share of the other player-of-the-year awards--Maxwell, Camp, and Rockne awards, and the recently inaugurated Thorpe award. Following the 1989 college football season African-Americans virtually swept the offensive and defensive player of the year awards winning the following: the Heisman Trophy and the Maxwell Award (top player); the Camp Award (top back); the O'Brien Award (top quarterback); the Rockne and Lombardi Awards (top lineman); the UPI lineman of the year award; the Butkus Award (top linebacker); and the Thorpe Award (top defensive back).

In track and field African-Americans continued to dominate the sprints, long jump, relays and men's hurdles. However, their presence was felt most in the "money" sports of basketball and football. And although they were no longer plagued by problems of discrimination in public accommodations and housing, they faced some of the same difficulties confronted by African-Americans of earlier generations (e.g., stereotypes and positional segregation) as well as new crises (e.g., poor academic performance and new academic standards for acquiring and maintaining athletic eligibility).

Racist Stereotypes and Stacking

A stereotype is "a largely false belief or set of beliefs concerning the characteristics of the members of a racial or ethnic group" (McLemore, 1991, p. 137). It is a distorted picture of a category of people that the out-group (and even in-group members) accepts as part of the cultural heritage. Furthermore, by ignoring or explaining away contradictory evidence, stereotypes become rectified; overgeneralizations are treated as if they really exist (Davis, 1978). Stereotypes are resistant to change, although contemporary events may alter or weaken beliefs. For much of their history in the United States, people of African descent were believed to be superstitious, lazy, happy-go-lucky, and ignorant (McLemore, 1991). Secondary structural assimilation, the movement of African-Americans into previously segregated schools, occupations, and other institutions, has been accompanied by a diminution in the salience of these stereotypes in many areas of life. However, major American sport, in spite of its inclusion of African-Americans in player positions, has been resistant to the abandonment of racial stereotypes. Athletic excellence is believed to be determined by different sets of traits for African-Americans and whites. (See Edwards, 1973 for a discussion of myths about black superiority in sport.)

African-Americans are thought to possess natural athletic ability in speed, quickness, and jumping ability, traits that many coaches believe cannot be taught; you are either born with these qualities or you do without them. That they excel in sport, then, has little to do with their work ethic or their intellect, according to this perspective. This view allows African-Americans to be outstanding athletes without negating the belief that they are lazy and ignorant; in fact, it reinforces the belief in their indolence and incognizance. This is what I think some sports fans (and fans of black athletes) had in mind when they stated their admiration for the athletic gifts bestowed on African-American athletes and followed that by asking me, "Without inborn talent, where would the black athlete be? What do you think his fate would be if he had to work as hard as the white athlete?"

Whites, on the other hand, are believed to excel at sport because they possess traits that are valued both in and (especially) out of sport: intelligence, industriousness, and other unspecified intangibles. Athletic ability is a limiting but not a deciding factor in their sport participation. According to this view, they rely on other traits to overcome their mediocre endowment. An article entitled, "The Best in College Hoops," which appeared in *Sport Magazine* in January, 1991, illustrates the above. In describing the top four point guards in college basketball the article pointed out the following:

1. Kenny Anderson (Georgia Tech)—"Kenny has superb instincts, unbelievable quickness, and he's also amazingly mature for his age...But...he often shoots when he should pass, a serious indictment for a point guard."

2. Bobby Hurley (Duke)—"So what's the deal here? Hurley's a team genius, the type of kid coaches love to love...From a team point of view—and what other point of view is there for a point guard?—This perceptive penetrator does every bit as much for the Blue Devils as Anderson does for Tech."

3. Chris Corchiani (North Carolina State)—"If he gets the ball on the move, he's almost impossible to stabilize. Still, many experts question CC Rider's quickness and outside shot. Legitimate queries. But with a guy like Chris, his intangibles will always outweigh his ability."

4. Lee Mayberry (Arkansas)—"Mayberry's a brilliant athlete and a great passer, but not a true point guard. He just doesn't *think* like one, says Hamilton. 'More often than not, I disagree with his decision making.'" (Kertes, 1991, p. 70).

Anderson and Mayberry are (of course) African-Americans. The writer gives them credit for their physical ability but has reservations about their mental abilities. The white players—Hurley and Corchiani—lack the physical skill of Anderson and Mayberry, but they make up for it with cognitive abilities and intangibles. Thus, while it appears the writer is honoring Anderson and Mayberry by their inclusion in this exclusive group, he is, in fact, reproducing one of the most pervasive stereotypes of African-Americans: They have the tools, but their intellect is questionable. The real praise is reserved for the white players because they have managed to prevail despite what the writer perceives to be their modest athletic endowment. The persistence of stacking in college football is a product of this stereotype. (Stacking is the practice of assigning individuals to sport positions on the basis of race or ethnicity.) African-Americans are still, primarily, relegated to positions that are said to require speed, quickness, and jumping ability. The rare player, black or white, who occupies a position that deviates from the expectations for members of his group finds that his abilities are (re)defined in ways that are consistent with the race-linked stereotypes. To quote Tom Waddle, a white wide receiver for the Chicago Bears, "When you don't fit into the computer on things like size, speed and vertical jump, you are basically a reject. You are a possession receiver. A possession receiver is a polite term for slow" (Sprout, 1991, p. 3). *Possession receiver* is a term that is used almost exclusively for white receivers.

Even the presence of African-Americans in positions that have been traditionally reserved for whites (e.g., quarterback) tends to support rather than refute stereotypes about athletic ability. Many African-American college quarterbacks are required to gain significant yards by running the ball. They often accumulate as many yards as, if not more than, the halfbacks or tailbacks on their teams. In other cases where they exhibit proficiency as passers they still find it difficult for coaches and profes- *Charlie* sional scouts to take their accomplishments seriously. Perhaps this helps *Ward* explain why in the last four years two African-American quarterbacks who were runners-up for the Heisman Trophy and one Heisman Trophy winner had to watch lower-rated white quarterbacks get drafted ahead of them National Football League teams, although each of the African-Americans was the top-rated quarterback in the Heisman balloting. They probably would have fared better in the draft if they had entered it in "traditionally black" positions.

Intercollegiate sport has made considerable progress in its treatment of African-American athletes. They are found in programs all over the country and in every prominent conference. Few schools would deny athletic scholarships to very talented African-American athletes. The overt racism that characterized earlier periods has dissipated. However, more subtle forms of racism continue to limit opportunities available to players (not to mention coaches and administrators). Racist stereotypes and stacking are examples of the racism collegiate athletes face. The use of African-American student-athletes by schools that value their athletic competency but not their academic potential is another.

Academic Concerns

Perhaps the most critical problems faced by African-American collegiate athletes revolve around academic issues, particularly graduation rates. Consider the following:

1. An annual NCAA survey ("Athletes in Division I," 1990) reported that Division I athletes graduated at a slightly higher rate than did nonathletes at those same institutions, but basketball and football players lagged behind participants in other sports, especially at public universities. Of student-athletes who entered college in 1983, only one-third of all Division I basketball players graduated within five years; less than 25% of those at public universities graduated within five years. For football, slightly more than half the private university athletes, and about one-third of public university athletes graduated in five years.

2. A *USA Today* study of student-athletes recruited between 1980 and 1985 found that most Division I basketball players fail to get their degree five years after enrolling in school. Most consistently competitive programs have lower graduation rates than the less competitive schools. African-American males have the lowest graduation rates' less than one-third received their degrees. Eight schools recruited 10 or more minority male athletes and failed to graduate *even one* during the period studied. A dozen other schools recruited between 10 and 17 minority athletes and graduated *only* one (Brady, 1991).

3. A survey by the Associated Press ("Athletic Notes," 1990) found that nearly two-thirds of Division I athletes who were drafted by professional football and basketball teams in the spring of 1990 failed to graduate. Most of the nongraduates were more than one semester away from earning their degrees. And although some universities graduated most or all of their athletes (e.g., Notre Dame and Michigan State University), others graduated few.[4] For example, Florida State University and the University of Houston graduated none of their (total of 15) drafted athletes.

All of the nongraduating athletes are not African-Americans but a disproportionate number are. For example, football had 410 Proposition 48 casualties[5] in the first two years of the rule's implementation and 346 (84%) of them were African-Americans. Of the 150 basketball players who were Proposition 48 casualties, 138 (92%) were African-Americans (Bannon, 1988). African-Americans are overrepresented among the Proposition 48 "at risk" college student-athletes—in basketball and football.

Academic Performance

Some studies of the academic performance of student-athletes suggest sport and scholastic activities are compatible. For example, Schafer and Armer (1968) found athletes are not poorer students than nonathletes; athletes had a higher mean grade point average. Another study (Picou & Curry, 1974) found a positive relationship between academics and educational aspiration *for boys from lower class backgrounds*. Although they didn't perform well academically, boys from modest backgrounds who played sports expected to attend college more than their peers who did not participate in sports.

However, many scholars (e.g., Edwards, 1979; Meggyesy, 1971; Scott, 1971) contend that sport and academics are incompatible for most student-athletes. Student-athletes, they say, are shielded from demanding academic courses and programs, exempted from academic responsibilities, and often directed toward "Mickey Mouse" courses and programs (Edwards, 1969). This is especially true of "blue-chip" athletes. African-Americans are overrepresented as athletic stars in big-time college sports; they are also less likely than their white peers to do well academically and to graduate from college.

College and university officials have, for some time, recognized the poorer scholastic performance of student-athletes compared to student-nonathletes. NCAA Propositions 48 and 42[6] were developed to address student-athletes' academic performance in colleges. These proposals were met by disapprobation from many African-American educators, administrators, and leaders. Their concern was that the NCAA's reliance on test scores worked to the disadvantage of African-Americans because the standardized tests reflect a cultural bias toward white students and white standards.

In an effort to improve the academic performance of its scholarship holders, the NCAA took the position that the onus was now on student-athletes to better prepare themselves for college (presumably by studying harder, longer, and better while training harder, longer, and better for a college scholarship); it is the fault of the student-athletes that they don't perform better in college. This NCAA position does not give proper attention to other factors that contribute to academic performance.

Marginal Student-Outstanding Athletes

One explanation for the poorer academic performance of African-American compared to that of white American student-athletes is the singular emphasis on sport among African-Americans; the student-athletes and their significant others (e.g., parents) attach more importance to doing well in sport than in school. However, my own research (Harris, 1990), which examined the relationship between sport and scholarship for male black and white high school basketball players indicates that African-American high school student-athletes and their significant others are *more* concerned about academics than are their white peers.

A more plausible explanation would consider the conditions under which many African-American student-athletes are expected to achieve academically. While there are many success stories, a larger proportion of African-Americans than other Americans are still poor or near-poor and attend schools in poor areas that are compromised by inadequate resources. Students from these schools in less privileged areas tend to exhibit poorer academic performances. A recent study (Banas, 1990) that documented the relationship between student achievement and property wealth of school districts found that students from school districts with the highest real estate property values scored substantially higher on standardized tests (e.g., state-mandated reading and mathematics exams and the ACT) than those from poorer districts. This difference is largely attributable to per-pupil spending; rich districts spent 66% more per high school pupil than did poor districts. Many of these property-poor districts are the source for collegiate athletes; some schools in these districts annually send their top athletes to one or more colleges. Although their academic programs are inadequate to prepare a large number of students for Division I colleges, their athletic programs in basketball and football are exceptional in preparing athletes for athletic scholarships. African-Americans who attend private or predominantly white high schools often fare better academically than their public school counterparts (Harris, 1990), but many of them have attended less affluent elementary schools and find themselves behind their high school classmates. When they are "recruited" by academically elite high schools it is often for the same reason they are recruited by colleges—for the rewards they bring to the athletic program.[7] In some cases the students benefit little from the rigorous academic curriculum of the high school. They are there to render athletic services; academic concerns center around keeping them eligible, not preparing them to be scholars.

As a group, African-American male student-athletes enter college with lower GPAs, and lower SATs and ACTs than those of their white student-athlete peers and those of African-American student-nonathletes (American Institute for Research, 1989). In short, they are at a disadvantage when they arrive on campus, and many schools do little to correct this academic deficiency.

When the marginal student-outstanding athlete arrives on campus, especially if he is a football player, he is likely to find that his first activity is not becoming acquainted with the library or the classroom, but getting to know the playing field. In fact, if he or she is like most football or basketball players, the student-athlete will spend more time on sports (about 28 hours per week) than on attending class or labs (12 hours per week) *and* preparing for class or labs (12 hours per week).[8] And he or she will miss, on average during the season, two days per week of classes (American Institutes for Research, 1989); *the athlete will be absent from 40% of the class instruction.* It is small wonder that many of these student-athletes get incompletes and find themselves on academic probation.

Absenteeism from class leads to poorer academic performance and, perhaps, lower academic aspiration: Students who don't perform well in class may sense their academic transcript will undermine their ability to compete with classmates for nonathletic jobs. This sense of academic marginality may combine with the perceived rewards for making a professional roster (perhaps a more likely possibility than academic success in the minds of many student-athletes) to create enormous obstacles to scholarly work for the marginal student-athlete. Therefore, the fact that many athletes do poorly in the classroom may be less a reflection of what they value than of what they see as within their grasp. This is not to say that student-athletes would forsake the "big bucks" of a professional sport career for the modestly paid position of a public servant. Rather, when one road appears to be a dead end they, like others, take an alternative path. For many of them, the road to academic success is not easily accessible. While others go speeding by, they sit idling.

Of course many of them still hope that a professional sport career beckons, but only a small number of collegiate athletes will ever have an opportunity to play even one game of professional ball, and few of those who do will last beyond four or five years. Perhaps this is what led Joe Paterno, the football coach at Pennsylvania State University, to declare:

> For at least the last two decades we've told Black kids who bounce balls, run around tracks and catch touchdown passes that these things are ends unto themselves. We've raped them. We can't afford to do it to another generation. (Cited in Edwards, 1984, p. 14.)

NCAA Reform

As the 1991 annual NCAA meeting neared many expected reform, including academic reform, to be the theme of the assembly. Indeed, a number of proposals concerning academic issues were submitted, but they were rejected by the delegates, who chose to wait until 1992 to address academic reform. However, a measure was adopted that requires athletes to fulfill most of their major requirements by the start of their fourth year to retain their eligibility ("Sidelines," 1991). Other measures were adopted that will limit the time athletes are allowed to spend on their sport to 20 hours per week, shorten the length of the season, and reduce the number of games a team may play in a season ("NCAA overwhelming backs," 1991).

Many of the issues taken up at the meeting concerned cost-cutting measures (e.g., a reduction in the number of scholarships allowed in all sports) and how to spend the $115 million--the first of seven annual payments from the NCAA's television contract with CBS for basketball. The NCAA set aside $45 million to create a fund for needy athletes, to provide catastrophic-injury insurance for athletes, to increase financing for championships, and to more than double the size of traveling parties (e.g., cheerleaders, bands and university officials) for the Division I men's basketball tournament (Lederman, 1991). Only $7.4 million was set aside for programs to enhance the academic performance of athletes. *This means using less than seven percent of the funds to combat the most serious problem facing collegiate athletics today.*

Although there has been much discussion about how teams that make it to the Final Four in the basketball tournament will fare financially,[9] very little attention has been paid to improving the academic performance of student-athletes. It appears that the 1991 NCAA meeting was business as usual: "Let's split up the money and figure out ways to make more." As an afterthought the NCAA may remember that athletes who make the money are deserving of a quality education. In the meantime, the NCAA is helping to perpetuate the problem. It is time to seek solutions.

Suggested Reforms

Two reasons for the poor academic performance of African-American male collegiate athletes are that many come from less privileged school programs and all are expected or required by collegiate athletic programs to spend excessive hours on sports. My first suggestion (one that has been made by many people in and out of college athletics) is to curtail freshman eligibility. The student-athletes will benefit immensely from having their first year to concentrate on academics without the demands of athletics. Spending the first year on campus, instead of on the road, should afford student-athletes more time to spend preparing for classes, and they will not be required to miss an excessive number of classes. It is very difficult to be successful academically when one is required to miss in excess of one-third of the class meetings; it is nearly impossible when one is a marginal student. Perhaps the reason a number of Proposition 48 casualties have been successful academically (Kornheiser, 1989; Wiley, 1991) is that they were required to sit out intercollegiate athletics a year, which gave them time to concentrate on academics.

The suggestion of freshman ineligibility causes tremors in some coaches and athletic directors. They want money and exposure, and they realize a talented athlete, albeit a freshman, can generate both, even if it is at the expense of the student-athlete's education. Other coaches and sports administrators would like to see freshman ineligibility, but they fear they will be at a competitive disadvantage if their schools adopt changes and other schools not. For example, the president of Oklahoma State University reported that he was considering proposals from a faculty panel to bring about changes in the sports program (e.g., raising admissions standards for athletes and barring academically deficient athletes from competition). The men's football coach said, "....if standards are raised for everybody, I have no problem with it. But, I don't want to be in the vanguard because it puts me at a competitive disadvantage." (Lederman, 1990, p. 36) My hope is that if NCAA schools lack the sagacity to keep freshmen from competing in college athletics, some schools will have the courage of their conviction to act alone.

I like the NCAA rule to limit the amount of time spent on sport to 20 hours per week, but it needs to go even farther. Therefore, my second suggestion is to restrict hours spent on sport to no more than the amount of time spent in class. If the mission of universities is to develop scholarship, then less, not more, time should be spent on athletic compared to academic endeavors. Put the emphasis back on academics.

Third, the NCAA should distribute a larger percentage of the money from television contracts to schools for academic enhancement. The NCAA should work with member schools to identify and develop programs that educate, not merely retain, student-athletes. Member schools have to go beyond providing study halls or quiet times and tutors to write papers and take notes for student-athletes. And successful programs should be rewarded and duplicated.

My fourth suggestion is, perhaps, an unpopular one. NCAA schools and the companies that advertise during their games ought to contribute considerable amounts of money to the schools and communities these athletes come from. This would be an important step in aiding poor schools that produce collegiate athletes but have inadequate resources for academic programs. For example, a contribution of $50,000 could be made to the high school of each of the 12 basketball players on each basketball tournament Final Four team. The total amount (about $2.4 million) is less than a number of conferences received for their Final Four appearances in 1991. (A lesser amount could be paid to the high schools of football players whose teams participate in bowl games.) A large portion of the money, perhaps 80% could be earmarked for the academic programs of the recipient schools. Most importantly, perhaps the sponsors of the NCAA telecasts will become as interested in some of the schools as they are in the athletes who come from these schools. (Of course, it doesn't have to stop here. Advertisers who use professional athletes to promote their products could, for philanthropic reasons, support the secondary and primary schools these athletes attended.) Advertisers give thousands of dollars to colleges in the name of "the players of the game" every week. Why not give some of that money to the schools and programs that need it most, the secondary and primary schools these student-athletes come from? Academic enhancement should begin before student-athletes are in secondary schools and continue, as necessary, throughout their college tenure.

Summary

This paper has examined the predominance of African-Americans in revenue-generating collegiate sports. It has traced their involvement on athletic teams from the era of "superspades" to today's "semiprofessional" players. In every era race has played an important part in the acceptance or rejection and expectations of African-American athletes. While some forms of segregation have disappeared (e.g., segregation in public housing) other forms continue to exist (e.g., stacking). Furthermore, racist stereotypes are still prevalent in collegiate sport; virtually no television coverage (and little newspaper coverage) is without them.

African-American collegiate athletes also encounter academic problems, particularly at predominantly white colleges and universities. If we include problems of isolation due to the scarcity of other African-American students, faculty, and staff and problems finding services such as churches and barbershops, it is apparent that these student-athletes have special needs and concerns, many of which are addressed by neither their schools nor the NCAA.

Finally, a number of suggestions have been advanced to address academic problems faced by African-American student-athletes. These suggestions are not expected to obliterate the problems that pervade revenue-generating intercollegiate sports; nothing short of removing interschool sport competition from institutions of higher education is likely to have that effect. However, they are an attempt to offer a corrective to a particular set of problems, those that create and maintain marginal academic performance among the most celebrated group of persons in institutions of higher learning: African-American athletes. I hope this paper makes a contribution to their well-being.

Footnotes

[1] The NCAA did not allow colleges to award scholarships based solely on athletic ability until 1952. Before that schools could award scholarships or jobs to athletes if they demonstrated financial need (Rader, 1990).

[2] Athletes at a number of universities had their athletic scholarships revoked for insubordination. Many others voluntarily gave up their scholarships because of the racism at their school (see Edwards, 1969).

[3] In 1983 seven players were selected to the All-America team whereas the 1985 team consisted of six players (Meserole, 1991).

[4] The low graduation rate of football players is even more problematic when you consider the fact that, as a result of redshirting, many football players are enrolled in college for five years, although they may only compete for four years.

[5] Proposition 48 requires college freshmen to score a minimum of 700 on the SAT or 15 on the ACT and achieve a "C" average in core high school courses to be eligible to participate in athletics at Division I colleges.

[6] Proposition 42 has the same minimum requirements for Division I athletic participation as Proposition 48. However, it would deny financial aid to partial or nonqualifiers. Proposition 48 has been implemented; Proposition 42 has not.

[7] Some high schools use their national exposure, or the potential for national exposure games on television and appearances in tourna-

ments, to induce athletes to play for their school, even if it means the athlete has to change school districts. In this way, some high schools behave much like colleges, offering athletic shoes, clothing, and trips far away and abroad in exchange for student-athletes' services.

[8] This estimate for time spent on sport is low next to Edwards' (1984). He says that during season, major college Division I football players spend 45-49 hours per week on their sport, 60 hours per week if you count travel time.

[9] The NCAA changed its distribution system for the basketball tournament so that performance in the last six tournaments determines a schools take. In 1991 Duke received over $790,000 of the ACC's nearly $4 million tournament pay ("NCAA Line," 1991). Schools in seven conferences received over half the $62.5 million paid out with the rest going to the other 230 Division I schools ("NCAA pays out," 1991). Five conferences received more than $2.4 million dollars from the tournament payout.

References

American Institutes for Research. (1989). *Report No. 3: The experiences of black intercollegiate athletes at NCAA Division I institutions.* Palo, Alto, CA.

Andrews, D.S. (1984). The G.I. Bill and college football. *Journal of Physical Education, Recreation and Dance, 55,* 23-26.

Ashe, A.R., Jr. (1988). *A hard road to glory: A history of African-American athletes since 1946.* New York, NY: Warner Books.

Athletes in Division I found graduating at higher rate than other students. (1990, July 5). *Chronicle of Higher Education,* p. A29.

Athletic notes. (1990, August 1). *Chronicle of Higher Education,* p. A30.

Banas, C. (1990, June 21). Grades tied to school district property values. *Chicago Tribune,* Sec. 1, p. 3.

Bannon, J. (1988, September 30). Proposal 48: Jury still out; foes vocal. *USA Today,* p. C1.

Behee, J. (1974). *Hail to the victors!: Black athletes at the University of Michigan.* Ann Arbor, MI: Swink-Tuttle.

Berghorn, F.J., Yetman, N.R., & Hanna, W.E. (1988). Racial participation and integration in men's and women's intercollegiate basketball: Continuity and change, 1958-1945. *Sociology of Sport Journal 5,* 107-124.

Brady, E. (1991, June 17). Players: 46% earn degrees in five years. *USA*

Today, pp. 1A-2A.

Davis, F. J. (1978). *Minority-dominant relations: A sociological analysis*. Arlington Heights, IL: AHM Publishing.

Edwards, H. (1969). *The revolt of the black athlete*. New York: The Free Press.

Edwards, H. (1973). The myth of the racially superior athlete. *Intellectual Digest, 2,* 58-60.

Edwards, H. (1979). Sport within the veil: The triumphs, tragedies and challenges of Afro-American involvement. *The Annals of the American Academy of Political and Social Science, 445,* 116-127.

Edwards, H. (1984). The collegiate athletic arms race: Origins and implications of the 'Rule 48' controversy. *Journal of Sport and Social Issues, 8,* p. 4-22.

Franklin, J.H., & Moss, A.A., Jr. (1988). *From slavery to freedom: A history of Negro Americans*. (6th ed.). New York: Alfred A. Knopf.

Green, K. (1982). *Government support for minority participation in higher education*. Washington, DC: American Association for Higher Education.

Harris, O. (1990). Athletics and academics: Complementary or contrary activities? In Grant Jarvie (Ed.), *Sport and Ethnicity,* (pp.124-149). London: Falmer Press.

Kertes, T. (1991, January). The best in college hoops. *Sport Magazine*, p. 70.

Kornheiser, T. (1989, April 4). Robinson's A+ final. *Washington Post,* p. D1, D7.

Lederman, D. (1990, May 16). Athlete's academic and off-field troubles push faculties to demand role in sports programs. *Chronicle of Higher Education,* pp. A1, A35, A36.

Lederman, D. (1991, September 25). NCAA revenues. *Chronicle of Higher Education,* p. A43.

McLemore, D.S. (1991). *Racial and ethnic relations in America* (3d ed.). Boston: Allyn and Bacon.

Meggyesy, D. (1971). *Out of their league*. New York: Paperback Library.

Meserole, M.(Ed.), *(1991) The 1991 Sports Almanac*. Boston: Houghton Mifflin Company.

Morris, A.D. (1984). *The origins of the civil rights movement.* New York: Free Press.

NCAA line. *USA Today*. (1991). Tuesday, April 2, p. 4C.

NCAA overwhelmingly backs reform plan: Coaching staffs and cost will be cut. (1991, January 16). *Chronicle of Higher Education,* p. A1, A38.

Paul, J., McGhee, R.V., & Fant, H. (1984). The arrival and ascendance of black athletes in the southeastern conference, 1966-80. *Phylon 45,* p. 284-97.

Picou, J.S., & Curry, E.W. (1974). Residence and the athletic participation-aspiration hypothesis, *Social Science Quarterly, 55,* 768-76.

Rader, B. (1990). *American sports* (2d ed.). Englewood Cliffs, NJ: Prentice Hall.

Shafer, W.E., & Armer, M. (1968). Athletes are not inferior students, *Transaction, 6(1),* 21-26, 61-62.

Scott, J. (1971). *The athletic revolution.* New York: Free Press.

Sidelines. (1991, January 16). *Chronicle of Higher Education,* p. A37.

Spivey, D. (1985). Black consciousness and Olympic protest movement, 1964-1980. In Donald Spivey (Ed.), *Sport in America,* (pp. 239-262). Westport, CT: Greenwood Press.

Sprout, G. (Ed.). (1991, September 16). Openers. *The Sporting News,* p. 3.

Wiggins, D. (1991). Prized performers, but frequently overlooked students: The involvement of black athletes in intercollegiate sports on predominantly white university campuses, 1890-1972. *Research Quarterly for Exercise and Sport 62*(2): 164-177.

Wiley, R. (1991, August 12). A daunting proposition. *Sports Illustrated,* 27-45.

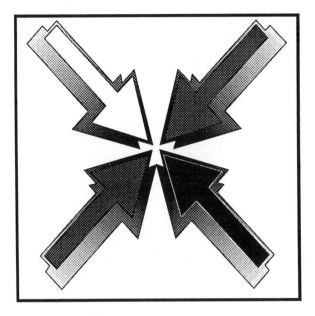

Section Two: Recruitment, Retention, and Mobility In College Athletics

Section Two

Recruitment, Retention, and Mobility in College Athletics

More African-American athletes than ever before are now participating in school, college, and professional sports leading to a belief among some observers that racial discrimination has been steadily drained from American sports. But the sheer magnitude of participation in games is neither an adequate measure of the degree of discrimination nor a viable proxy for collective justice within the African-American community. In balance against the archetypal media image of the high-paid athlete, magically packaged, reproduced, and consumed as goods offered by the sports industry, is the American experience of failure with civil rights, of injustice, discrimination, and inequality encountered among African-Americans.

One of the most hotly debated arguments, says Robert Sellers (sport psychologist) in an essay included in this section, is the value of sports to the overall welfare of the black community. Sport may be viewed as one of the few meritocracies in the country, but there are negative consequences from increased athletic participation in college and professional sport. Audwin Anderson (sociologist) and Donald South's (sociologist) essay is centered on differences in sport experiences by African-American athletes in big time college sports, to an extent that they even question the social meaning of being a "black student-athlete." Noting that African-Americans were absent from big-time college sports in the first half of the twentieth century and forced to attend historically black colleges (HBCUs), Anderson and South examine how the changes in this trend affected the legal and economic factors of participation, and the academic and economic exploitation of athletes. Anderson and South provide a detailed analysis and suggest solutions for those factors leading to social differences in collegiate recruiting, retention, and graduation rates. Specific attention is devoted to describing conditions leading to the adoption of Proposition 48 by the NCAA, particularly how these rulings affected black colleges and universities.

The essay "Racial Imbalance in Coaching and Managerial Positions," by Dana Brooks (sport sociologist) and Ron Althouse (sociologist), reexamines the relationship between sport participation and structural barriers, and explores racial issues such as coaches mobility and career patterns, the lack of minority female and male head coaches, and the underrepresentation of African-Americans in sport leadership positions. Students will find useful the discussion on career mobility that traces across playing position, college assistant- coaching positions, as well as college alma mater, suggesting that institutional prestige may facilitate one's getting preferred coaching positions.

The initial premise in Robert Sellers' essay is that the experiences of the athlete after college sports are affected by "the quality of their experiences in college which is a function of the education that they received." Any reform dealing with the performance of the black student athletes will be better served, Sellers estimates, by enhancing their educational experience on campus. Following up with a series of concerns aimed at improving educational outcomes for those athletes in college, Sellers addresses a set of recommendations to sports sociology and psychology, to the NCAA, to the colleges, as well as to the black athlete and his or her family. Sellers asks, "Who advocates for the student in these various relationships?"

Essay 3

Racial Differences in Collegiate Recruiting, Retention, and Graduation Rates

Audwin Anderson and Donald South

Abstract: Among the rationales for intercollegiate sports is the belief that participation will provide individuals with educational and status-enhancement opportunities. For many athletes, and African-American athletes in particular, this is not necessarily the case. Over the past 15 years, sociology and sport literature has documented racial differences in educational outcomes for college athletes. In fact, recent NCAA disclosures of graduation rates revealed that nearly twice the percentage of white athletes compared to the African-American athletes graduated from college over the past year. This work focuses on some of the circumstances that have not been favorable for the purpose of education for African-American athletes. Our analysis starts by looking at the social meaning of African-American maleness followed by a section on recruitment and Proposition 48. Final discussion addresses the issues of economic and academic exploitation of African-American athletes and the issue of differential graduation rates.

Introduction

Sport in American society has a long history of development (Eitzen and Sage, 1986). Despite some early resistance from religious interests, sport rapidly became an integral part of American culture. Sport and higher education likewise had a sometimes uneasy relationship in earlier years, but that relationship was cemented and intensified over the years as the relationship between sport and the larger society (Chu, 1989). In fact, the collegiate-sports contexts have become so interrelated that aspiring professional athletes in football and basketball have little recourse except to prepare for a sports career by attending college, whether or not they are "college material." In effect, this means that a number of athletes are in college with little enthusiasm for academic work. Thus, there are obvious implications for scholarship and subsequent graduation.

To appreciate the problem experiences of African-Americans in big-time collegiate athletics more fully some issues of athletics and education must be addressed. A basic tension between big-time athletic values and goals and those of higher education has been widely recognized (Asher, 1986; Chu, 1989; Lawry, 1991). Traditional goals of higher education are to promote a high level of academic achievement and integrity. The overriding goal of big-time sports is to win--which translates into high-level entertainment and big revenues. It has been the task of the National Collegiate Athletic Association to promote and enhance the marketability of collegiate sports and simultaneously to maintain the sense of amateurism and academic integrity. The more successful the NCAA is in achieving one of these goals, the more difficult it becomes to achieve the other. The trend among NCAA institutions has been toward promoting entertainment. As a result, such a vast array of rules has been promulgated to regulate collegiate sports recruiting and participation that athletic programs and individual athletes are in constant peril of infractions. This context is applicable for athletes in general, but it is experienced variously by different categories.

Sociological analysis often focuses on differences among various social categories within a population. The act of using categories as a basis for analysis does not assume that such categories are necessarily different because of inherent biological or intellectual traits. Rather, the causal emphasis focuses on differential experiences by given categories. Among the more consistently important categorical differences are those of race, gender, class, and age.

Persons forming major social categories are likely to develop different world-views and to experience different opportunities. In addition, individuals will be accorded different identities, and statuses, and will exhibit different behaviors. In short, the authors acknowledge that race categories are not discrete biological entities. Yet social notions of race categories do have meaning and consequences for those who are assigned to these categories by themselves or others. This essay will focus on differences in collegiate sports experiences of African-American males. More specifically, it will investigate racial differences in collegiate recruiting, retention, and graduation rates.

If there is a position that we take in this work it is one supporting education. Our wish is that this work will become part of the debate and dialogue of college athletes, coaches, counselors, and athletic directors. Our goal is to facilitate changes that will make circumstances favorable for the purpose of education for the African-American athlete.

The Problem

Sport participation in American society has long been viewed as a vehicle for the assimilation of newcomers. As a conduit into mainstream American life, sport has been viewed as teaching the values of hard work, teamwork, and discipline. Proponents of sports developed a number of rationales for sport in society, its inclusion in higher education, and in the character development of individual participants (Schendel, 1965; and Webb, 1969). Detractors have pointed to excesses, dysfunctions, and conflicts of interest in sport (Edwards, 1969; Eitzen, 1989). Among the rationales for intercollegiate sports is the belief that participation in intercollegiate sports will provide the athlete with educational opportunities (Naison & Mangum, 1983). For many athletes, and African-American athletes in particular, this is not necessarily the case. Over the past 15 years, sociology and sport literature has documented racial differences in educational outcomes for college athletes (Naison & Mangum, 1983; Raney, Knapp, & Small, 1986; Spivey & Jones, 1975; and Warfield, 1986). In fact, recent disclosures by the NCAA of graduation rates revealed that nearly twice the percentage of white athletes compared to African-American athletes graduated from college between 1990 and 1991 (Brady, 1991). The numbers showed that African-Americans graduated at a 26.6% rate compared to 52.2% for whites.

African-Americans were absent from big-time college sport for most of the twentieth century. In the first half of this century, African-American college students attended historically black colleges and universities

(Willie & Cunnigen, 1981). This trend began to reverse itself in the years following World War II. At the beginning of World War II, of the approximately 45,000 African-American students enrolled in higher education, only about 10% were enrolled in predominantly white colleges or universities (Mingle, 1981). Presently, most African-American college students attend predominantly white institutions.

Several conditions were responsible for the above-mentioned trend, not the least of which was the 1954 *Brown* decision, which outlawed separate educational facilities. Another important factor was the establishment of federal financial-aid programs for students and institutions. In the 1950s, the National Scholarship Service and Fund for Negro Students (NSSFNS) was established (Mingle, 1981). Legal and economic factors provided the foundation leading to the migration of African-American students to predominantly white universities. This migration pattern also included African-American student athletes.[1]

Harry Edwards has been an important voice in bringing to the forefront the unique social and political situation of the African-American athlete (Edwards, 1969). According to Edwards, the manpower vacuum created by World War II, the 1954 Supreme Court decision, and the urge by whites to further exploit African-Americans economically resulted in African-Americans' being allowed to venture into big-time college athletics (Edwards, 1969). African-American athletes also found it to their advantage to play for predominantly white schools (Edwards, 1969; Eitzen, 1989).

College Athletics and Issues of Race

In *The Souls of Black Folk* (1969), renowned scholar W.E.B. DuBois proclaimed that the prevailing issue of twentieth-century Americans would be the problem of the "color line" (p. XI). Conservative thought in the latter half of the twentieth century presents us with an interesting version of "colorblindness." The suggestion is made that our society does not have a race problem because we judge people on the basis of character and merit, not skin color. Although disputed (Marger, 1985; Takaki, 1987), this view was held to be true, especially in the area of sports. There is much evidence that in reality, skin color continues to have a dramatic impact on one's life chances and opportunities for improved mobility and success. To say that our society is colorblind at this moment in history amounts to aversion to, and neglect of, real problems and issues.

If our society is ever going to "solve" problems of race (assuming they are not insurmountable problems), it must face, in an honest and humane manner, the issues and implications of race. Likewise, if big-time college athletics is going to solve its much publicized problems and dilemmas, it also must face honestly the issues and implications of race and race relations.

In the spring of 1991, the Knight Foundation's Commission on Intercollegiate Athletics released a report on abuses in college athletics.[2] The Commission expressed concern that "abuses in athletics had reached proportions threatening the very integrity of higher education" (Knight Foundation, 1991, p. 1). The report highlighted some of the problems of college athletics and proposed some change and remedies. Yet the report (about 40 pages) makes only four indirect references to the issue of race in college athletics. In the first chapter of the report on page 3 appears the statement "Sports have helped break down bigotry and prejudice in American life" (Knight Foundation, 1991, p. 3). On page 8 in a section entitled "Focus on Students" appears: "Intercollegiate athletics exists first and foremost for the student athletes who participate whether male or female, majority or minority..." (Knight Foundation, 1991, p. 8). On page 19, it is recommended that grants-in-aid for low-income athletes be expanded to the "full cost of attendance; including personal and miscellaneous expenses" (Knight Foundation, 1991, p. 19). And finally on page 31 in the Statement of Principles, "Every student-athlete--male and female, majority and minority, in all sports--will receive equitable and fair treatment" (Knight Foundation, 1991, p. 31).

The egalitarian principles put forth by the Commission are to be commended, and there is no intention here to question the sincerity of their effort. Yet the issue of race and the educational condition of the African-American athlete are not directly addressed.

We take the position that there is a considerable amount of exploitation or victimization of student-athletes in big-time collegiate sports. Further, we contend that African-American youth is especially vulnerable. We are aware of inherent difficulties in making the case for exploitation. Exploitation involves both an objective condition and subjective evaluations. Some in observing a situation will emphasize the former; others, the latter. We will argue that a number of structural conditions are favorable for outcomes that lend themselves to interpretations of exploitation.

Through socialization, by emulation of esteemed role models, and as a consequence of subcultural values African-American youths are highly oriented to the goal of a sports career. Interacting with this condition is the fact of relatively few career options. The colleges need African-American youth to help provide high-level entertainment to match large-scale revenue opportunities. There is virtually no avenue to professional sport careers, especially in football and basketball, except through college participation. Colleges are faced with a paradox of maintaining academic integrity while providing entertainment with youth who are often academically ill pre-pared. The athletes may not be particularly devoted to scholastic pursuit but have few options for gaining social mobility in American society.

The differential in power for these two interests is immense. Colleges can dictate that youth must be capable of generating big-time entertain-ment to generate big dollars in exchange for rather small amounts of compensation and the hope of securing a professional sports position. Intense competition results because the number of positions is small and the number of the players, numerous. To gain one of the scarce positions the athletes, especially those with less talent, must single-mindedly pursue that goal to the exclusion of academic interests. Therefore, the result for many is little monetary reward, little education, and an accumulation of debilitating injuries.

It seems that the issue that most needs to be addressed is the educational experiences of African-American athletics in revenue- producing sports (i.e., football and basketball) at our nation's universities. We currently are witnessing declining university enrollment rates for African-American students, especially African-American males (Marden, Meyer, & Engle, 1992). This is occurring at a time when we are also witnessing conflicts over multiculturalism in university curricula, a backlash against affirma-tive action policy, cutbacks in student financial aid, "race" politics, political correctness, and questions the appropriateness of quotas in hiring. In light of this, an argument can be made that the recruitment by universities of African-American athletes provides these athletes with an increasingly unique *opportunity* for an education. We wish to bring particular attention to the word *opportunity*. *Webster's New World Dictionary* defines *opportunity* as "a combination of circumstances favorable for the purpose" (Webster's, 1988, p. 950).

For the remainder of this work we will focus on some of the circum-stances that have not been favorable for the purpose of education for African-American athletes. We will start by looking at the social meaning of African-American maleness followed by a section on recruitment and Proposition 48. We will then speak to issues of economic and academic exploitation of African-American athletes and the issue of graduation rates.

Social Meaning of African-American Maleness

In a very important piece of work by Fordham and Ogbu (1986), it was found that many inner-city African-American youth define academic success as "acting white." The implication of this position is that academic success is the domain of whites. This perception leads Fordham and Ogbu to suggest that many African-Americans discourage their peers, perhaps unconsciously, from emulating white academic striving and achievement. As a result, African-American students who are academically able do not put forth the necessary effort in schoolwork and, consequently, perform poorly in educational settings. To the extent that this is true, what does it mean, to use the opposite term, to "act black."

In recent history, we have witnessed the label used to describe persons of African descent change from *Negro* to *black* to *Afro-American* to *African-American*. What do these changes connote? Does each label connote a different set of behaviors, attitudes, dispositions, life-styles, which define and delineate? The view held here is that the changes connote an ongoing search for identity, a search for a home on America's cultural landscape, a quest for a self-generated definition of what it *means* to be of African descent and a native-born American.

Sports have been held up in our society as an activity in which African-Americans, particularly males, could compete and achieve without the bane of discrimination, an activity where merit was rewarded and achievement was unambiguous and evident to all. For the African-American male, sport has provided an activity in which to forge an identity. But, one must ask, what of this identity? Where did it come from? Is it self-generated? Why does it involve such physicalness? Why was this identity not forged through medicine or law?

It seems plausible to argue that the aforementioned labels connote a different way of interpreting experiences during this ongoing quest for identity. Certainly the "angry black man" of the 1960s interpreted his experiences differently than did the "docile Negro" of previous times. In this vein the label *African-American* has the potential for eliciting a new interpretation, broader and fuller interpretation of maleness than is proffered by the American stereotype.

Since the Moynihan Report (Moynihan, 1965) there has been increased attention paid to the so-called "absent father" in the African-American family. For Moynihan, one of the factors that directly led to the "deterioration" of the African-American family was the high proportion of African-American families headed by females.

Karenga (1980) took a different view, particularly as it applied to the African-American male. He contended that the major problem in the African-American community was the lack of a cultural base or cultural identity. He concluded with the contention that the media's influence on African-Americans, in particular males, was maximized in the absence of a strong cultural base and identity. Karenga maintained that African-Americans possessed a "popular culture" rather than a "national culture." Popular culture is defined as the "societal perception and stereotypes of your group" (Karenga, 1980, p. 18), whereas national culture is more of a self generated (group-based) definition. The first is externally generated and imposed; the latter is a self-definition by the subject group.

Marable (1986) presents a similar position by suggesting that the essential tragedy of being African-American and male is the inability of African-American men to define themselves apart from the stereotypes that the larger society imposes on them. Marable contends that through various institutional means these stereotypes are perpetuated and that they permeated our entire culture. Marable's position is that the stereotypes have not only informed the larger cultural image of the African-American male but have also had a long-standing influence on how the African-American male develops a definition of self.

The historical stereotypes of the African-American male have been very narrow and usually physical. The image has been of a "laborer," "super athlete," or "sexual stud." The major point to be made here is that these are not self-generated definitions, even though they may be in part accepted by African-American males.

Another argument given for the cultural identity of African-American males is that within the African-American community there is a lack of role models for youth outside the fields of entertainment and sport (Edwards, 1973). The argument is that our society fails to highlight the African-American doctor, lawyer, and other professionals. As a result many African-American youth see their only opportunity for social success in terms of the narrow fields of entertainment and sport. As Edwards states: "Young blacks are encouraged toward attempts at 'making it' through athletic participation, rather than pursuit of other occupations that hold greater potential for meeting the real political and material needs of both themselves and their people" (Edwards, 1973, p. 44). Others have pointed out that the large number of African-Americans in certain sports does not so much indicate a freedom from discrimination as much as it reflects the lack of opportunities in other areas (Castine & Roberts, 1974). In a similar view, Lawson (1979), commenting on African-Americans in sport, points out, "The successes of a few have served to conceal the limited opportunities for the majority" (Lawson, 1979, p. 190).

If the label *African-American* does have the potential for eliciting a new interpretation of identity, it must allow for a more multidimensional identity. Certainly it must include an educational dimension. The term African-American suggests some cultural continuity between West Africa and America; the bringing forth of an emergent cultural legacy to the present; a cultural legacy that defines the male in broader and fuller terms than the American stereotype; a tradition that speaks to intellectual contributions, such as those made in the arts, sciences, and literature. A conscious awareness of these contributions by African-Americans and others is critical if a transformation in meaning and identity is to take place.

Recruitment and Proposition 48

For fifteen years we have had a race problem. We have raped a generation and a half of young black athletes. We have taken kids and sold them on bouncing a ball and running with a football and that being able to do things athletically was going to be an end in itself. (Joe Paterno, cited in Coakley, 1986, p. 143). Head Coach at Penn State to '96

The above remark by Pennsylvania State University head football coach Joe Paterno, spoken from the floor of the 1983 NCAA Convention, is said to have provided the emphasis that lead to passage of Proposition 48 [By-law 5-l (J)]. This proposition was proposed by the American Council on Education and implemented for the 1986-87 academic year. The bylaw establishes the academic requirements that high school seniors must meet in order to be eligible for participation as freshmen in NCAA-sanctioned Division I sports. The requirements are:

1. High school seniors must maintain a 2.0 grade point average in a curriculum that contains at least three English credits, two math, two natural or physical science and two social science courses. At least 11 academic courses in high school must have been taken by a prospective athlete.

2. High school seniors must achieve a combined score of 700 (out of 1600) on the Scholastic Aptitude Test, or a score of 15 (out of 36) on the American College Testing Exam .

More stringent revisions of these standards were passed by the NCAA in 1992, to go into effect for athletes entering college in August 1995 or thereafter. The number of "core" courses will increase to 13 from the current 11. With a high school grade point average of 2.00 (C) the student will need a minimum score of either 900 on the Scholastic Aptitude Test (SAT) or 21 on the American College Test (ACT) to gain full admission status. With higher grade point averages a decreasing scale of SAT or ACT scores will be required.

From its inception, Proposition 48 has been one of the most controversial proposals ever adopted by the NCAA (Picou, 1986). According to Sage (1989), Proposition 48 is a classic example of "blaming the victim." Sage contends that the NCAA places the blame on the student-athlete for being academically ill-prepared for college work. Yet the cause of the problem is that university officials have been willing to admit academically ill-prepared students for reasons of competitive sports success. Sage sees the NCAA's call for higher academic standards as a "charade" that has moved attention away from the "commercialized structure of major college athletic programs and focused it on the athlete" (Sage, 1989, p. 169).

Sage's points are well taken here. Clearly one of the major antecedents of the condition that led to Proposition 48 was the recruitment of academically marginal students and the employment of various methods to keep them eligible. Also, the admission of academically marginal students is primarily a problem of revenue sports (football and basketball).

One of the fallouts or latent functions of the bylaw is that it created a situation whereby the nation's junior colleges, which are not governed by the bylaw, act as "feeders" to Division I schools. Division I schools are in some cases only accountable for the education of the student-athlete for two years and in some cases for a shorter period of time. It is likely that in some colleges and universities the junior college transfer in football could exhaust athletic eligibility by maintaining academic eligibility for only two semesters. This situation does not facilitate education and creates a structural situation that lends itself to exploitation.

The major fallout of the bylaw has been its racial consequences. Reports show that 85% of those losing eligibility under Proposition 48 have been African-American (Cross & Koball, 1991; Johnson, 1988). In addition, Proposition 48 disqualified a sizable percentage of African-American athletes who might have graduated. According to Grambling State University president Joseph Johnson (1988), 40% of the athletes who have graduated in the past would be ineligible under present rules. Chu

(1989) gives figures which show that if Proposition 48 standards had been applied in the years 1977-1980, they would have disqualified 69% of the African-American and 54% of the white athletes who went on to graduate.

Proposition 48 was also met by direct charges of racism by presidents of the nation's historically black colleges. Joseph Johnson, who was Chairman of the National Association of Equal Opportunity in Higher Education Athletic Committee at the time Proposition 48 was passed, speaking on behalf of 114 black institutions, stated:

It was our collective view that Proposition 48 was a very poorly thoughtout proposal. We were concerned because we knew that the rule would impact most severely on black athletes. It was thrust upon us; none of us were included in any of the debates about the proposition. That was the thing. We thought it was unfair because we are members of the NCAA, and the Proposition was brought to the floor by the American Council on Education without our input. (Johnson, 1988, p. 4)

Proposition 48 has a particularly negative effect on historically black institutions, which have a long tradition of remediating the academic shortcomings of African-American students. It has exacerbated the financial difficulties faced by athletic programs at these institutions (Edwards, 1989). As pointed out by Johnson, traditionally black institutions do not have the economic resources to finance the education of students made ineligible by Proposition 48 until they are eligible. Some black college presidents have even proposed that black institutions be exempt from Proposition 48 standards or be allowed to establish their own standards (Edwards, 1989).

Harry Edwards is the most visible and well-known spokesperson on the plight of the African-American athlete in American sports. His activist position on improving the academic condition and image of the African-American athlete is well documented. His work in the area is so important and persuasive that one cannot speak to the social condition of the African-American athlete without recognizing the contributions of Edwards. He has taken a position (see Edwards 1984, 1985) that is at odds with the position of many African-American educators and coaches. Edwards sees the establishment of Proposition 48 as a method of stemming the exploitation of African-American athletes in collegiate athletics. Edwards even goes as far as to argue that the cutoffs for ACT and SAT scores should be higher, which would result in less exploitation. Lowering the standard would send the message to African-American athletes that they are not intellectually capable of achieving these standards. Edwards also contends (as do the authors here) that African-American athletes themselves must take a hand against their own exploitation. They must have an interest in getting an education.

The idea of a universal academic standard seems to us a bit problematic. It seems to ignore the fact that some universities are more academically challenging and rigorous than others. A counterproposal that has some potential for remediating the problem of admissions and low graduation rates would hold universities responsible for not recruiting athletes who do not have a reasonable chance of performing up to that university's standards, whatever those standards may be.

Economic and Academic Exploitation

"The most reprehensible feature of College football today is that many universities engage in what amounts to professional football, but hold fast to the illusion that their athletes are amateurs" (Sack, 1988, p. 165).

Many authors have recently spoken about the influence of the profit-making ideology of corporate business on college sports (Eitzen, 1989; Sack, 1988; Warfield, 1986). The NCAA can be viewed as a business enterprise whose primary function is the production of competitive sporting events (Sack, 1988). Without question the primary labor force for the NCAA is the student athlete. Much debate has centered around the appropriateness of the label amateur applied to football and basketball players at universities that realize high profits from these sports (see Sack 1988 and 1991).

Of the 45 universities placed on NCAA probation between January 1988 and November 1989, 34 cases dealt with improper benefits to athletes (Sack, 1991). Presently, of the 34 schools under NCAA sanctions, 27 involve improper benefits (Lederman, 1991a).

Collegiate sport has a long history of abuses of the standard of amateurism (Sack, 1988; Sage, 1989). A case can be made that the athletic scholarship (grant-in-aid) is in fact a form of payment for athletic ability (Sack, 1988). Given the time demands as well as the physical and mental stress, college athletes rank as some of the most underpaid workers in the economy.

In a recent study of college basketball players, Sack (1988) reports that African-American athletes are far more likely than their white counter-parts to think they deserve workman's compensation, the right to form unions, and the right to share TV revenue. Eighty percent of the lower class

African-American males in the sample felt they deserved a share of the revenue. It was also reported that 55% of lower class athletes, regardless of race, see nothing wrong with accepting illegal payments.

A large number of the athletes who participate in big-time collegiate football and basketball are African-American youth from working-class and lower class backgrounds. It seems that if the NCAA is to remedy the problems of intercollegiate sports it must address not only the economic exploitation of collegiate athletes but also the racial nature of the exploitation.

Given the corporate structure of intercollegiate athletics and the huge profits realized from television contracts, the perpetuation of the notion of college athletes as amateurs appears questionable. The interests of universities and athletic departments are served by labeling as amateur the primary labor force of a multimillion-dollar-a-year industry.

It is not surprising that those who benefit most economically from collegiate sports resist the idea of paying college athletes. In rejecting the idea of paying athletes we often hear the argument that scholarship athletes are being paid in a most meaningful manner: with a free education. This notion begs not only the question of what is meant by "free," but also more importantly what is the nature of the education.

Academics

Our previously stated goal in this work was to facilitate changes that will make circumstances favorable for the purpose of education for the African-American athlete. African-American athletes at predominantly white institutions continue to be faced with a particular set of problems. One of these problems is overcoming the stereotype of being intellectually inferior while possessing innate athletic superiority. Often the message given to African-American athletes is, "You are inferior intellectually. We do not expect you to achieve academically. You are here because of your athletic ability."

In a study by Kiger and Lorentzen (1987) it was found that type of sport and race were negatively related to university academic performance for males. Minority male athletes and revenue-producing sport athletes tend to do less well. Adler and Adler (1989) found that student-athletes enter college with high expectations, then over the course of their college careers make a pragmatic adjustment and resign themselves to inferior academic performance. This adjustment on the part of the students was due to time demands of sport and the coaches' steering them to manageable athletic-related majors such as physical education and recreation. The athletes received greater reinforcement for athletics than for academics.

The above-mentioned studies point to some very serious problems for the educational experiences of athletes. In order to improve the situation we feel the following issues must become part of discourse on college athletes and education. These issues address problems faced by all student-athletes. However, in the context of this essay, it is important to note that African-American athletes are more vulnerable to these conditions.

1. Except under unusual circumstances the athlete's academic schedule should not be made out by the athletic department with little or no student participation. The responsibility for academic careers must be the responsibility of the individual athletes. To treat them otherwise retards the opportunity for intellectual development. If the experience of attending college is to provide preparation for life, the athlete's dependency on the athletic department to "take care of things" retards maturation and provides no preparation.

2. The notion that sports is a fertile avenue of upward social mobility for African-American males must be dispelled. Educational attainment provides far more upward social mobility for African-American males than does sport. The emphasis should therefore be on education as the most fertile avenue of upward social mobility.

3. The one-year renewable grant-in-aid sends out an anti-educational message. It says that you are an athlete first, and your opportunity to get an education is dependent on your athletic achievements. The grant-in-aid should be for five years and should be terminated only for academic reasons, not for athletic incompetence.

4. Given the time demands of collegiate football and basketball it is difficult to stay on schedule for graduation. Some of the revenue generated by intercollegiate sport could be put into a fund that would provide financial resources for the completion of education once a player's eligibility ends.

Graduation Rates

The issue of graduation rates among college athletes has recently been given much scholarly as well as popular attention (Brady, 1991; Lederman, 1991a, 1991b). It has also resulted in proposed federal legislation (HR 1454) better known as the Student-Athlete Right-to-Know Act. This act would require federally funded colleges and universities to report annually the graduation rates of student-athletes by sport,

Table 1. Academic Outcomes of Division I Athletes Entering College, 1984-85

Academic Standing	All	White	Black
Graduated within five years	45.7%	52.2%	26.6%
Left in good standing	29.0%	28.2%	30.9%
Left in bad standing	25.3%	19.6%	42.5%
Remained in college after five years	4.4%	4.0%	5.4%

Graduation Rates	Number	Number graduated	Percentage
All athletes	3,288	1,504	45.7%
White	2,453	1,282	52.3%
Men	1,646	819	49.8%
Women	807	463	57.4%
Black	835	222	26.6%
Men	686	170	24.8%
Women	149	52	34.9%

Lederman, D. (1991b, July 10). Black athletes who entered colleges in mid-80's had much weaker records than whites, study finds. *Chronicle of Higher Education*, p. A31. Reprinted with permission.

race, and gender. These data are to be supplied to high school officials and made available to families so that more informed decisions may be made in choosing college options. This proposal has spurred action by the NCAA to collect data from its member institutions beginning October, 1991 to implement the intent of the congressional bill. Findings from preliminary survey data are given Table 1.

In evaluating graduation rates for athletes, several considerations are in order:

1. How do athlete graduation rates compare with nonathlete rates?
2. How do categories of athletes compare with similar categories of nonathletes--namely, African-American, male athletes with African-American, male nonathletes?
3. Should graduation rates be accepted uncritically as a measure of institutional responsibility?
4. Do graduation rates reveal much, if anything, about academic counseling programs? Do the high graduation rates at Duke and Georgetown, for example, mean they have superior academic supports for their athletes in comparison with schools having lower rates?
5. It is not only a matter of whether a degree is obtained but also a matter of what type degree.
6. Issues of uniformity in how graduation rates are compiled and defined must be addressed and solved.

Collectively, the research on student athlete graduation rates has reached the following conclusions among many:

1. The graduation rates of all college athletes (46%) are about the same as the graduation rates of all nonathletes (48%) five years after entering college. However, there are great variations by school, race, gender, and type of sport.
2. Minority athletes graduated at slightly higher rates (36%) than did their nonathlete counterparts (31%).
3. Generally, but with a few exceptions, the most competitive basketball program schools have graduation rates lower than those schools that do not make it to the NCAA tournaments.
4. Female basketball recruits have an appreciably higher graduation rate (60%) than does the general student population (48%). However, most of the big-time women's programs do not have such favorable rates.
5. African-American male student athletes in basketball had the lowest graduation rates of any category.

Critical Appraisal of Use of Graduation Rates

It is acknowledged that systematic attention to graduation rates may function to sensitize universities and some prospective students to the degree to which universities are adhering to academic goals, yet it would be a mistake to accept uncritically the position that such emphases are all positive.

A labeling-theory perspective would project some unwanted or unintended consequences of the Student-Athlete Right-to-Know Act. Schools labeled as nonacademic through this procedure would likely be avoided by academically interested students and/or parents. Those students wishing a nonacademic athletic experience would have an officially recognized list of schools that would offer a nonacademic athletic experience. Thus, the effect would be to continue or even exacerbate the problem of low graduation rates for some schools.

Another, equally disturbing, prospect is that the pressure for standard graduation rates could result in "special athletes curricula" or the awarding of meaningless degrees. The athletes' interest has not been served by granting a degree that has little or no marketability or potential for other rewards.

Meaning of Graduation Rates

What does a low graduation rate mean? As some wags have indicated it could mean that while we have lowered standards to let some athletes in, we have not yet gone the next step of according unearned degrees. It might mean that, but almost certainly it does not mean that schools with the highest graduation rates are expending the most effort on behalf of the athletes whom they admit. Rather, it is much more likely that high graduation rates reflect selectivity in admissions. There is a finite number of blue-chip athletes who are also blue-chip scholars. Traditional programs are able to recruit these few. If other programs are to compete athletically they must accept good athletes with less scholastic potential. Finally, there are programs that will have to settle for athletes with still greater scholastic deficits. It seems unreasonable to expect similar admission standards and graduation rates in each of these situations.

Rather than promoting a national standard for admissions and graduation rates, perhaps it would be more reasonable to assess these measures against the mission of the school, its own admission standards, and graduation rates. Perhaps it would be more meaningful to try to evaluate what a school does to advance the scope and skills of those athletes whom they do admit. A case study approach might yield some remarkable incidents of scholastic progress on the part of students who could never enter one of the more traditional programs.

Summary and Recommendations

The marriage between education and athletics is likely to endure for the foreseeable future. There will be occasional spats, mediated by the NCAA and the Council of Presidents, but academic interests have become so interwoven with those of sport entertainment that dissolution is unlikely. Indeed, without well-planned policies it is likely that the economic potential of big-time sports will result in the sports partner dominating the union.

African-Americans, particularly inner-city African-Americans, have been socialized to expect sports careers all out of proportion to realities (Edwards, 1973). Given this condition, coupled with the relative lack of alternative occupational opportunities and virtually no other avenues to the pro game, African-Americans are particularly vulnerable to exploitation. The colleges need manpower to produce an exciting spectacle in order to enhance revenue. African-Americans want the experience and exposure necessary to get to the pros.

These basic facts are unlikely to change to any considerable degree; thus, they must be taken as a given in proposing any solutions.

1. If more effective minor league or other preparatory arrangements were provided by the system, then there would be fewer athletes in academia who do not want to be there. In no other industrialized world power is the college expected to train for professional sports.

2. We should continue or develop policies which assure that the athlete can participate in a meaningful educational experience, once admitted.

3. Once in the collegiate setting the athlete should be paid in a manner somewhat more commensurate with his or her economic productivity.

4. The income from collegiate sports should be distributed among colleges more equitably than currently, thus removing some of the emphasis on winning at all costs.

5. The tenure of coaches should be determined in part by considerations other than winning, thus allowing them to be more responsive to academic and character building concerns.

6. Universities should be prepared to spend some of the money generated by sports in assuring counseling, tutoring and related services to those athletes in need because of time and energy expenditure on behalf of the school.

The issues that we raise and our proposals for solution certainly do not exhaust the possibilities. Some of our proposals would no doubt raise additional issues and problems of their own. Our views are shaped by the nature of our discipline and a combined experience of some 40 years of working with athletes in the academic setting. It is our sincere hope that the promise of higher education and status attainment will become a more universal reality for the African-American student-athlete. We pledge our efforts to that end and trust that student-athletes will assume their individual responsibilities in this collective endeavor.

Footnotes

[1] Our discussion will be concerned primarily with the African-American male athlete. This is in no way meant to disparage the experience of the African-American female athlete. There are two fine chapters on African-American female athletes in this volume which do more justice to that experience than space permits here.

[2] It should be noted that the Knight Commission is an independent organization and is not a part of the NCAA.

References

Adler, P., & Adler, P.A. (1989). From idealism to pragmatic detachment: The academic performance of college athletes. In D.S. Eitzen (Ed.), *Sport in contemporary society: An anthology* (pp. 142-157). New York: St. Martin's Press.

Asher, M. (1986). Abuses in college athletics. In R. Lapchick (Ed.), *Fractured Focus* (pp. 5-20). Lexington, MA: D.C. Heath and Company.

Brady, E. (1991, June 17). Players: 46% earn degree in five years. *USA Today*, Sec. A., pp. 1-2, 7-8.

Castine, S., & Roberts, G. (1974). Modeling in the socialization process of the black athlete. *International Review of Sport Sociology, 9,* 59-73.

Chu, D. (1989). *The character of American higher education and intercollegiate sport.* New York: State University of New York Press.

Coakley, J.J. (1986). *Sport in society: Issues and Controversies.* (3rd ed.). St. Louis: Times Mirror/Mosby.

Cross, L.H., & Koball, E.G. (1991). Public opinion and the NCAA Proposal 42. *Journal of Negro Education, 60,* 181-194.

Dubois, W.E.B. (1969). *The souls of black folk.* New York: Signet.

Edwards, H. (1969). *The revolt of the black athlete.* New York: The Free Press.

Edwards, H. (1973). *Sociology of sport.* Homewood, Illinois: Dorsey Press.

Edwards, H. (1984). The collegiate athletic arms race: Origins and implications of the "Rule 48" controversy. *Journal of Sport and*

Social Issues, 8, 4-22.

Edwards, H. (1985). Beyond symptoms: Unethical behavior in American collegiate sport and the problem of the color line. *Journal of Sport and Social Issues, 9,* 3-13.

Edwards, H. (1989). The black "dumb jock": An American sports tragedy. In D.S. Eitzen (Ed.), *Sport in contemporary society. An anthology.* (3rd ed.) (pp. 158-166). New York: St. Martin's Press.

Eitzen, D.S. (1989). Ethical dilemmas in sport. In D.S. Eitzen (Ed.), *Sport in contemporary society: An anthology.* (3rd ed.) (pp. 300-312). New York: St. Martin's Press.

Eitzen, D.S., & Sage, G.H. (1986). *Sociology of North American sport.* (3rd Ed). Dubuque, Iowa: William C. Brown.

Fordham, C., & Ogbu, J. (1986). Black student's school success:Coping with the burden of "acting white." *The Urban Review. 18,* 176-206.

Johnson, J. (1988). Personal interview. *New Perspectives, 19,* 4, 10-12.

Karenga, M. (1980). *Kawaida theory: An introductory outline.* Englewood, CA: Kawaida.

Kiger, G., & Lorentzen, D. (1987). Gender, academic performance and university athletics. *Sociological Spectrum, 7,* 209-222.

Knight Foundation Commission on Intercollegiate Athletics (1991, March). *Keeping faith with the student-athlete: A new model for intercollegiate athletics.* Charlotte, NC.

Lawry, E.G. (1991, May 1). Conflicting interests make reform of college sports impossible. *Chronicle of Higher Education,* A44.

Lawson, H. A. (1979). Physical education and sport in the black community: The hidden perspective. *The Journal of Negro Education, 48,* 187-194.

Lederman, D. (1991a, March 27). College athletes graduate at higher rate than other students, but men's basketball players lag far behind, a survey finds. *Chronicle of Higher Education,* p. A1.

Lederman, D. (1991b, July 10). Black athletes who entered colleges in mid-80's had much weaker records than whites, study finds. *Chronicle of Higher Education,* p. A31.

Marable, M. (1986). The black male: Searching beyond stereotypes. In R. Staples (Ed.), *The Black Family: Essays and Studies* (pp. 64-68). Belmont, CA: Wadsworth.

Marden, C. F., Meyer, G., & Engel, M. H. (1992). *Minorities in American society* (6th Ed.). New York: Harper Collins.

Marger, M.N. (1985). *Race and ethnic relations: American and global perspectives*. Belmont, CA: Wadsworth.

Mingle, J. (1981).The opening of white colleges and universities to black students. In G. Thomas (Ed.), *Black Students in Higher Education* (pp. 18-29). Westport, CT: Greenwood Press.

Moynihan, D.P. (1965). *The Negro family: Case for national action.* Washington, DC: Labor Department, Office of Policy Planning and Research.

Naison, M., & Mangum, C. (1983). Protecting the educational opportunities of black college athletics: A case study based on experiences of Fordham University. *Journal of Ethnic Studies, 4,* 119-125.

Picou, J.S. (1986). Propositions 48, 49-B and 56: Implications for student-athletes, coaches and universities. *The Journal of Applied Research in Coaching and Athletics, 1,* 135-147.

Raney, J., Knapp, T., & Small, M. (1986). Pass one for the Gipper: Student athletes and university coursework. In R. Lapchick (Ed.), *Fractured focus* (pp. 53-60). Lexington, MA: D.C.Heath and Company.

Sack, A.L. (1988). Are "improper benefits" really improper? A study of college athletes' views concerning amateurism. *Journal of Sport and Social Issues, 12,* 1-16.

Sack, A.L. (1991).The underground economy of college football. *Sociology of Sport Journal* (8) 1-15.

Sage, G.H. (1989). Blaming the victim: NCAA responses to calls for reform in major college sports. In D.S. Eitzen (Ed.), *Sport in contemporary society: An anthology.* (3rd ed.). New York: St. Martin's Press. (pp. 167-173)

Schendel, J. (1965). Psychological differences between athletes and non-participants in athletics at three educational levels. *Research Quarterly, 36,* 52-67.

Spivey, D., & Jones, T.A. (1975). Intercollegiate athletic servitude: A case study of the black ethnic student athlete, 1931-1967. *Social Science Quarterly, 55,* 939-947.

Takaki, R. (1987). *From different shores: Perspectives on race and ethnicity in America.* New York: Oxford University Press.

Warfield, J. (1986). Corporate collegiate sport and the rule of race issues for counseling. *Debate and understanding* (pp. 30-36). Boston: Boston University Press.

Webb, H. (1969). Professionalization of attitudes toward play among adolescents. In G.S. Kenyon, (Ed.), *Aspects of contemporary sport sociology* (pp. 161-188). Chicago: The Athletic Institute.

Webster's *New World Dictionary of American English*. (3rd College Edition) (1988). New York: Simon and Schuster.

Willie, C., & Cunnigen, D. (1981). Black students in higher education. *Annual Review of Sociology*, *7*, 177-198.

Essay 4
Racial Imbalance in Coaching and Managerial Positions

Dana Brooks and Ronald Althouse

Abstract: Since 1968 the involvement of African-American head and assistant college coaches has increased slowly. Yet, African-American male and female coaches and administrators have not attained parity and remain underrepresented in college athletics. As recently as 1992 no African-American occupied a NCAA Division IA football head coaching position, and there were only two African-American athletic directors. Throughout this essay the authors identify and describe conditions leading to racial imbalance in coaching and administrative positions among NCAA member institutions. Racial issues of opportunity and discrimination focus on stacking, structural barriers, coaching mobility patterns, media publicity and "old boy networks." The authors maintain that strategies to increase the number of African-Americans in coaching and leadership positions must begin with an understanding of the organization of college athletics and multiculturalism and pluralism.

Introduction

When *Sports Illustrated* (August, 1991) ran a recent series on the "black athlete" (Johnson, 1991), the articles compared the African-American athletes' present experience with conditions 23 years ago. In canvassing African-American and white male athletes from the NFL, NBA and big-league baseball teams about their professional experiences the writers asked the athletes how their sport treated them: how "blacks" were treated by coaches and management, what their chances were of moving into management, and how communities accepted "blacks." Results suggested that "black athletes" believed they were treated worse than "white athletes"; they received lower pay and had to be better athletes to succeed professionally.

About four months later, *USA Today* published a four-part series dealing with race and sport ("Black Access," 1991; "Money and Fame," 1991; "Stacking," 1991; *"USA Today Poll,"* 1991) that asked: "What makes a great athlete?" The series then described the extent of stacking practices; the culture of playground "hoops"; NBA minority hiring, and black access/white flight. These articles were sensational, once again provoking awareness about racial discrimination in American sport.

A prominent theme in both series was the continuing conspicuous absence of more minorities in coaching or management positions. In virtually all these reports minority attention is concentrated almost exclusively on men. In 1991 a *USA Today* survey of 63 Division I college programs found only 12.5% of 3,083 athletic department positions were held by blacks, Hispanics, Native Americans and Asians. Only 2 minority members were athletic directors; 10 were sport information directors; and some 43 held the head coaching position (Boeck & Shuster, 1991).

In less than one year after the survey, the number of African-American head football coaches among the 105 big-time Division I-A teams had declined to zero. Ron Dickerson, assistant football coach at Clemson University and President of the Black Coaches Association said, "It is truly frightening that this is 1992 and we don't seem to have progressed at all" ("And Then There Were None," 1992, A36).

What conditions feed this racial imbalance in coaching and administrative positions among NCAA member institutions? This essay will focus on the relationships among five primary factors: race, college athletic participation, the ability to mobilize resources, the impact of structural barriers, and subsequent career mobility to the ranks of coaching. The lack of African-American men and women in head coaching positions and other leadership positions in college athletics may be a result of one or more of the following conditions:

(1) Overt discrimination on the part of the NCAA Athletic Directors;

(2) African-Americans not playing "central positions" during their collegiate careers;

(3) African-Americans not having the same professional pathways

available to them as white coaches;

(4) African-American coaches not having access to existing head-coach recruiting networks (Brooks, Althouse, King, & Brown, 1989).

Throughout this essay we will examine how these factors can affect career mobility patterns of college coaches, particularly African-American head and assistant college coaches. At the end, we will focus on some strategies and recommendations that might increase the opportunities of African-American men to attain new avenues of access to coaching and managerial positions, and, reduce barriers organized along gender lines.

Sport Participation and Subsequent Mobility

It is a long-held belief in American society that athletic participation provides African-Americans the opportunity to gain social mobility. Braddock (1980) stated that it is apparent that athletic achievement has a positive impact on orienting black males toward college. The focus of this section of the essay is to summarize the literature regarding the effects of athletic participation on educational attainment of high school and college athletes. Scholars have not studied the relationship between race, athletic participation, and social mobility.

The literature written on this issue can be divided into two categories: (a) sport participation enhancing mobility (Braddock, 1980; Leonard & Reyman, 1988) and (b) sport participation limiting mobility (Edwards, 1973). John Loy (1969) identified four avenues of sport participation that enhanced upward mobility:

(1) Development of selected physical skills and abilities which could then lead to direct entry into professional sports;

(2) Facilitation of educational attainment through a college scholarship;

(3) Lead to occupational sponsorship;

(4) Fostering of attitudes and behavior patterns valued in the wider occupational world.

A major research question addressed by scholars was the relationship between athletic participation (high school and college) and future educational and occupational goals, aspirations, and attainment (Buhrmann, 1971; Coleman, 1961; Hanks & Eckland, 1976; Otto & Alwin, 1977; Picou, 1978; Rehberg and Schafer, 1968; Schafer & Armer, 1968; Snyder & Spreitzer, 1977; Spady, 1970; Stevenson, 1975). Findings from finished studies promoted conflicting results. However, consensus was reached with regard to high school and college athletic participation increasing the student-athletes' educational and occupational aspirations and attainment leading to social mobility.

According to Braddock (1980), it is important to differentiate between direct and indirect mobility. Direct mobility occurs when a lower class youth acquires wealth and status and becomes a coach or personnel director. Indirect mobility takes place when formerly successful athletes are given the opportunity to occupy prestigious positions in the nonsport sector (Braddock, 1980).

Since the 1960s, studies investigating mobility of athletes through educational opportunities have been widely discussed. However, relatively few researchers have studied the career mobility patterns of college coaches and administrators. What literature does exist, supports the position that sport participation does increase both direct and indirect social mobility. It would also hold true, then, that sport participation would provide former athletes with the opportunity to become head coaches and athletic administrators.

Miller and Form (1964) organized career mobility patterns into four stages: (a) preparatory stage— the individual is influenced by "significant others" to choose his/her occupations, (b) initial stage— individual takes his/her first job, (c) trial stage— individual begins full-time employment— changing jobs three or four times, and (d) retirement— disengagement from work.

Rosenberg (1980) argued that Miller and Form's (1964) stages of career mobility may be acceptable for the study of professional athletes. The application of their model to the study of career-mobility patterns of college coaches and other administrators may also be appropriate. American college sport has become a big business, generating millions of dollars annually for the various colleges or universities. Yet the role and responsibilities of coaches within these institutions have not been clearly defined.

Career Path or Dead End for African-American Athletes?

Coakley (1986) believed that obtaining sport-related career alternatives (i.e., coaching) requires skill in interpersonal relations, education, knowledge of training, good strategies, sport organization, and connection with individuals who provide job recommendations. These requisite skills are important, because sport, as a social institution, reflects the basic values within society. Having these skills is no insurance of being hired as a head coach. Edwards (1979b) contends that racism exists in American sport and has an impact on hiring decisions and subsequent mobility. Racism throughout the larger society accounts for the disproportionately high percentage of black athletes in some sports.

Oliver's (1980) review of existing literature concluded that both race and social class standing have a very important impact on determining social mobility via sport. The following hypotheses were developed to test the relationship between these two variables:

1. The lower the social class background, the more likely people are to believe in the notion of upward social mobility through sports participation.
2. Members of minority groups, particularly blacks, are more likely than whites to believe in the notion of upward social mobility through participation (Oliver, 1980, p. 66).

The data gathered on 9- to 11-year-old African-American children and their parents revealed that African-American families were more likely than white families to associate with a potential career in professional sport. Earlier research conducted by Rosenblatt (1967) suggested that African-American youth assign high self-esteem to participation in professional sport.

McPherson (1975) suggested that for African-American males, professional athletes provide a visible, high-prestige role model. Young African-American children are socialized by their parents, friends, and relatives to emulate successful professional athletes. At a wider level, there is a general belief among the American population that sports participation provides the African-American with the opportunity to gain upward mobility. For example, the *Miller Lite Report* (1983) found approximately 50% of the respondents (white and African-American) reported that athletics is one of the best ways for African-Americans to advance their social status. However, according to Snyder and Spreitzer (1989) few African-American athletes have an opportunity to become professional athletes. A coaching career is a channel for social mobility and may provide an alternative career path.

Position Discrimination

During the decades of the 1970s and '80s, social scientists investigated the relationships between athletic playing position and social discrimination in sport (Best, 1987; Chu & Segrave, 1981; Curtis & Loy, 1978 a, b; Eitzen & Sanford, 1975; Eitzen & Tessendorf, 1978; Massengale & Farrington, 1977; Medoff, 1977). Initial research focused on participation and racial discrimination in professional college and high school sports.

Blalock's (1962) research remains a significant piece of work providing insights into occupational discrimination, particularly into positional racial segregation in sports. Blalock proposed a set of organizational principles, arguing that the importance of individual performance affected the degree of minority discrimination (Blalock, 1962). Athletes know that the performance appropriate at various playing positions is much the same from one team to another, but player performances cannot be completely measured or summarized. This uncertainty allows for a quality of control by employers, for the factor of race to influence the playing life of the athlete. If uncertainties about assessing performance can affect a player, then uncertainty will affect hiring and careers of coaches and managers. Measurements of performance are less reliable, allowing a greater influence of the racial factor.

Blalock recognized that African-American players had not attained parity with white coaches and faced discrimination, and eventually African-Americans would encounter more severe difficulties in obtaining coaching and managerial positions.

Grusky (1963) added to Blalock's (1962) work by investigating the relationship between an individual's position in the social structure and subsequent career mobility patterns. He argued that

"All else being equal, the more control of one's spatial location:

(1) the greater the likelihood dependent or coordinative tasks will be performed;

(2) the greater the rate of interaction with the occupants of other positions; and

(3) performance of dependent tasks is positively related to frequency of interaction. (p. 346)"

This spatial model was applied to the study of professional baseball teams. Findings suggested that major league managers were primarily selected from high-interaction positions. Numerous researchers immediately began to investigate these conclusions.

Segregation by Playing Position: The Outcome of Stacking

Loy and McElvogue (1970) applied Blalock's (1962) theoretical proposition and Grusky's (1963) theory of formal structure to the analysis of professional baseball and football. The researchers hypothesized that African-Americans would more likely occupy noncentral positions than central positions. The results showed that African-American athletes were underrepresented in central positions (positions that require a high degree of interaction) and overrepresented in noncentral peripheral positions. The researchers concluded that social segregation in professional sport was positively associated with centrality of playing position. The term *stacking* is the disproportional allocation of persons to central and noncentral athletic positions on the basis of race or ethnicity (Jones, Leonard, Schmitt, Smith, & Tolone, 1987).

Stacking and Leadership Recruitment

Over the past 20 years, the study of stacking and racial discrimination in high school, college, and professional sports has received considerable attention. The stacking and leadership recruitment studies all ask the same basic question: How are positions and award structures allocated? (Leonard, 1977, 1986, 1987). More recently, researchers have begun to integrate the two areas to better understand the relationship between position occupation and future career mobility in sports.

The stereotype explanation of stacking concludes that African-Americans are excluded from occupying central positions (quarterback, linebacker) because coaches hold stereotypes that African-Americans lack the leadership abilities necessary to occupy these positions (Edwards, 1973; Eitzen & David, 1975; Eitzen & Yetman, 1977; Williams & Youssef, 1975). The stereotypical beliefs that whites hold about African-American athletes still exist today.

A survey of 159 blacks and 395 whites conducted by *USA Today* (*"USA Today Poll,"* 1991) measured attitudes about athletic abilities. The results indicated a belief that blacks are more physically gifted and that whites possess intellect and leadership. Of particular note, 64% (605 adults; 159 blacks and 395 whites) of blacks questioned said, "Coaches tend to put whites at certain positions and blacks at others because they stereotype athletes by race" (p. 1).

Eitzen and Sanford (1975) initially reviewed the career patterns of African-American athletes and found that as they move from high school to college to professional sports, they move from central to noncentral positions. Steve Weiberg (1991), a reporter for *USA Today* claims that stacking is seen when a high school football player goes on to play college football. Black quarterbacks become wide receivers and running backs. The researchers concluded that discrimination is the source of racial segregation by position, and African-American positions (noncentral) are not considered to be leadership or thinking positions. Consequently, playing noncentral positions is inadequate training for a career in coaching (Eitzen & Sanford, 1974, p. 950).

Table 1. Distribution of Managers by Their Past Playing Positions

Type of Position	Grusky 1921-41 1951-88	1951-80	1980
Infield (1b,2b,3b,ss)	48.8% (52)	46.2% (66.5)	53.1% (17)
Catcher	26.2% (28)	17.0% (24.5)	10.9% (3.5)
Outfield	15.9% (17)	14.6% (21)	10.9% (3.5)
Pitcher	6.5% (7)	5.6% (8)	9.4% (3)
No Experience	2.8% (3)	16.7% (24)	15.6% (5)
Total *N*	107	144	32

Fabianic, (1984). Minority managers in professional baseball. *Sociology of Sport Journal, 1*(2), 163-171. Table p.168 Copyright 1988 by Human Kinetics Publishers, Inc. Reprinted with permission.

This finding was further supported by Fabianic (1984) who studied the absence of minority managers in professional baseball. (See Table 1.)

Between 1921 and 1980 a larger percentage of professional baseball managers were recruited from the infield positions. It was concluded that minority managers would have been expected to appear more frequently in the managerial ranks in 1980 than they actually did.

Similarly, Massengale and Farrington (1977) were interested in determining the relationship between centrality and the recruitment of college coaches. During the 1975 season, press guides from NCAA Division I head and assistant football coaches were used to determine previous playing positions. Massengale and Farrington concluded that playing central positions positively related to upward career mobility in college football.

Finally, Chu and Segrave's (1981) analysis of college and professional basketball players found that African-American athletes were overrepresented (stacked) at the forward position and less prevalent at the guard position (leadership position). This is interesting to note because whites who played at the guard position in college basketball dominate the college and professional coaching ranks. This study further supported the segregation-by-playing position hypothesis and tied coaching mobility to previous playing position.

Eitzen and Tessendorf (1978) also applied the stereotypes hypothesis to basketball. They found that African-Americans were overrepresented at the forward position. This position required speed, quickness, strength, and rebounding ability. African-Americans were underrepresented at the guard and center positions (leadership positions). These findings further supported the segregation-by-playing-position hypothesis.

Berghorn, Yetman, and Hanna's (1988) results conflicted with Eitzen and Tessendorf's (1978) findings. They concluded that stacking at the guard and forward positions was in existence in 1970 but was eliminated by 1975. Berghorn et al. (1988) also observed that stacking in basketball no longer exists. Berghorn et al. (1988) argued that the elimination of stacking in college basketball was associated with the increase in minority participation in basketball. With more minority players it was more difficult to exclude them from central positions through sheer force of numbers.

Best (1987), however, contended that positional segregation is still prevalent in professional football and that African-American career earnings, postcareer earnings and postcareer opportunities are negatively affected. This ties into the existence of a racial wage discrimination in professional sports, documented by Christiano (1986, 1988), Leonard (1989), and Mogull (1975). Basically, African-American athletes were paid less when compared to their white counterparts.

More recently, the economic factors tied to positional segregation have received considerable attention (Yetman, 1987). Medoff (1977) suggested that positional segregation was a result of differential training and development costs associated with playing specific sports. Medoff (1986) extended his argument by concluding that stacking results from free choice by the African-American athlete. These athletes choose to play noncentral positions on their own and are not coerced by coaching staffs to play these positions.

As an alternative to the stereotyping and economic hypotheses of stacking, McPherson (1975) supported role modeling as the foundation to position segregation. He hypothesized that African-Americans segregate themselves in specific positions because they wish to emulate successful African-American athletes who previously played the same positions. Edwards (1973) advocated the outcome-control hypothesis and argued that blacks were excluded from those sports and positions that have the greatest opportunity for influencing the outcome of the contest (quarterback, tennis, golf).

Edwards (1987) reached the conclusion that cultural and social explanations provided the explanation of African-American success and overrepresentation in the athletic role. The following explanations were offered:

1. African-American community tends to reward athletic achievement.
2. The overwhelming majority of aspiring African-American athletes emulate established African-American role models and seek careers in basketball, football, baseball, boxing and track.
3. The American media have increased the visibility of the African-American athlete.

Numerous theories (stereotyping, economic, and role modeling) have been suggested to address the relationship between race, playing positions, and subsequent sport mobility career patterns. The majority of these studies focused on African-American and white male athlete comparisons. Emphasis is placed upon a neglect to evaluate social mobility patterns of Chicanos, Asian-Americans, Jews, and Native Americans (Birrell, 1989) as well as those of African-American female athletes.

The focus on stacking has been treated within the context of racism and specifically racism directed toward the African-American males. One of the initial studies to investigate the relationship between stacking and racism among women was conducted by Eitzen and Furst (1989). They studied the extent to which stacking was evident in women's collegiate volleyball. White female athletes were found to dominate the setter position (leadership and high degree of interaction required) whereas African-American females were occupying the hitter and blocker position. These positions require quickness, agility, and jumping ability. This finding suggests there may be less opportunity for African-American females to gain access to coaching and other managerial positions in volleyball and by extension in other sports.

According to Schneider and Eitzen (1979), stacking research can be summarized into the following topical areas: interaction and organizational centrality (Grusky, 1963; Loy & McElvogue, 1970), responsibility for outcome control (Edwards, 1973), role model socialization (McPherson, 1975), and stereotypes or social class (Edwards, 1973; Eitzen & David, 1975; Eitzen & Tessendorf, 1978; Eitzen & Yetman, 1977).

One of the major points to be drawn from all of this literature is that

African-Americans were not considered for coaching or managerial positions in college or professional sport because during their playing careers, they did not occupy positions requiring leadership and decision-making. None of the theories presented in this section can explain how African-Americans who played noncentral positions became coaches or managers. Clearly, the positional segregation and career mobility model literature cannot fully explain career mobility patterns of coaches. Additional models and explanations must be explored.

Coaching Mobility Models
In contrast to investigating the relationship between position segregation in sport and future mobility opportunities, researchers have begun to develop alternative models to explain career mobility in sport. Scholars are now interested in identifying how geographical patterns, career patterns, managerial changes, organizational effectiveness, and personal attributes for coaches explain, describe, and predict the developmental pathways.

In dealing with coaching mobility Eitzen and Yetman (1977) applied Grusky's (1963) earlier hypothesis of the relationship between the roles of administrative succession and the degree of organizational effectiveness. They systematically studied male college basketball team records between 1930 and 1970 to determine the relationship between coaching tenure (number of years covered in the period divided by the number of coaching changes) and team effectiveness (winning percentages). The results of this study provided support for Grusky's model. Turnover rates and organizational effectiveness were negatively related. Coaching changes had no effect on team performance during the following year. However, the longer a basketball coach remained at an institution, the more successful he tended to be. Beyond a tenure of 13 years, coaching effectiveness began to decline. Coaches who left the profession after 8 or 9 years tended to have higher win/loss percentages at the end of their careers than in their earlier years of coaching.

Eitzen and Yetman's study was significant because the researchers challenged the beliefs that a turnover in coaching would result in immediate changes in team performance. It has also been an accepted belief that managerial change is dysfunctional to the organization. Too often the coach is given responsibility for the success or failure of the team. Historically, head-coaching mobility patterns have been tied to the success or failure of the team.

Table 2. Institutional Level of First Coaching Position

Institutional Level of First Coaching Position	Basketball Coaches		Football Coaches	
	n(349)	%	n(272)	%
Junior High School	18	5.1	4	1.4
Senior High School	207	59.3	162	58.7
Junior College	7	2.0	6	2.2
Small College	70	20.0	29	10.5
University	37	10.6	51	18.5
Top 25 Universities	10	2.8	20	7.2

Sage, G.H., & Loy, J. W., (1978). Geographical mobility patterns of college coaches. *Urban Life, 7*(2), 253-280. Table p. 267. Copyright 1978 by Sage Publications. Reprinted with permission.

Career Mobility Patterns

Sage and Loy (1978) were two of the first researchers to investigate systematically the career patterns of college athletic coaches. Initially, they applied Rooney's (1974) concepts of spatial organization and migration patterns to analyze the geographical movement of college head basketball and football coaches. Sage and Loy found that the majority of basketball (43%) and football (36%) coaches attended small private or public colleges. California, Illinois, New York, Ohio, and Pennsylvania were identified as the five leading states in producing college football and basketball coaches.

One of the most significant findings obtained by Sage and Loy was that most coaches attended colleges in their home state or bordering states (81%). In addition, a majority of coaches obtained their first coaching positions at senior high schools near their undergraduate institutions. (See Table 2.)

The Sage and Loy (1978) data clearly identify the regional nature of college coaching career-mobility patterns. That is, coaches often remained in the same NCAA district. Coaches often changed coaching assignments as much as four or five times prior to obtaining their current head coaching position. Sage and Loy concluded that the athletic prestige of the college from which the coaches graduated was a factor influencing their current coaching position. Further strengthening their ties to their alma mater, basketball and football coaches were first employed by their alma mater as graduate assistants or assistant coaches. The "internship" program provides the new coaches with experience and visibility.

Loy and Sage (1978) adapted Turner's (1960) concepts of elite status and mobility. Links were found between serving as a head coach and assistant coach at a high-prestige university and moving between institutions. High-prestige organizations provided more than their fair share of assistant coaches.

Data obtained from the head basketball and football coaches in 1979 provided support for the sponsored-mobility model. For example, the athletic prestige of undergraduate colleges had more influence on the career mobility patterns of football coaches, and the athletic prestige associated with coaching apprenticeship had greater influence on those patterns for basketball coaches. Surprisingly, variables such as educational status, athletic achievement, coaching experience, and coaching success had very little effect on the athletic prestige of the coaches' first or present job.

The authors concluded by pointing out that the relationship between coaching career patterns and institutional prestige does not fully explain the mobility patterns of college coaches. Additional factors such as "old-boy networks," athletic farm systems, publicity offered by the mass media, and the extent to which social exchange exists in the coaching profession must be analyzed. One must also realize that racism and discrimination may negatively affect coaching career patterns of minorities.

Social, Educational, Athletic, and Career Backgrounds

Early research focused primarily on the coaching mobility patterns of white coaches. Comparatively we have not seen significant career paths for African-American males. By and large, most studies have centered on coaches at the end-point positions (head coaching role). To better understand the coaching career process we need to look at social mobility and organizational structure within these organizations.

Latimer and Mathes' study (1985) represents one of the first attempts to investigate the relationship between social, educational, athletic, and career background of African-American football coaches (1 head, 79

Table 3. Blacks as a Percentage of all Basketball Players by Region and Gender 1970-1985

| | Men | | | | No Change | Women |
	1970	1975	1980	1985	1970-1985	1985
Northeast	17%	29%	35%	38%	+21	16%
South	22%	41%	51%	61%	+39	40%
Midwest	25%	32%	37%	44%	+19	16%
West	29%	35%	48%	49%	+20	20%

Berghorn, F. J., Yetman, N., & Hanna, W. C. (1988). Racial participation and integration in men's and women's intercollegiate basketball: Continuity and change 1958-1985. *Sociology of Sport Journal, 5*(20), 107-124. Table 3, p. 111. Copyright 1988 by Human Kinetics Publishers, Inc. Adapted and reprinted by permission.

assistant). Data from this study permit researchers to begin to understand similarities and differences in the coaching career mobility patterns of white and African-American coaches.

Latimer and Mathes' data revealed that 66% of the African-American coaches attended colleges and obtained their first coaching position in their home NCAA district. This is about the same level that Loy and Sage (1978) found in their study of white coaches (57% of the white coaches initially began their coaching career at the high school level). Apparently, half of the coaches began their career as high school coaches. Similarly about 50% of the African-American coaches began their first coaching assignment at the college level.

Over the past two decades there has been a gradual increase in the number of African-American head coaches. Berghorn et al. (1988) found the number and percentage among black males participating in college basketball from 1970 to 1985 increased dramatically. (See Table 3.)

According to these researchers, in 1985, 61% of male and 30% of female players in Division I were African-American. The greatest increase in the number of African-Americans participating in college athletics was found in the South. Although there has been a significant increase in the number of African-Americans participating in college athletics, there has not been a correspondent increase in the number of African-American head coaches.

The apparent lack of African-Americans in integrated coaching positions was also noted at the high school level. According to Eitzen and Yetman (1977), African-Americans historically obtained coaching positions at predominantly African-American high schools, especially in the South.

One consequence of integrating schools in the South during the 1960s resulted in eliminating African-Americans from head coaching positions. Unfortunately, many of the former African-American head coaches were not hired at the predominantly white schools. This finding led the researchers to conclude that two forms of discrimination existed that prevented African-Americans from becoming head coaches at the professional sport level: (a) overt discrimination when owners ignore qualified African-Americans for available head coaching positions because of prejudice, and (b) a fear that white fans will react negatively if an African-American is the coach or manager.

More recently, research has focused upon coaching success and career mobility paths by identifying relationships between personal attributes and job responsibilities of successful coaches. Banks (1979) surveyed black football coaches to identify the significant attributes a head coach at a major college looks for in selecting a black assistant coach. The coaches identified knowledge of the game, implementation of methods on the field, recruiting skills, personality, ability to get along with others, ability to communicate with both white and black student athletes, and the personal appearance as important selection criteria.

The results of this study showed that approximately one-half of the African-American assistant coaches served as graduate assistants before assuming assistant coach duties. In addition to the selection attributes, the data revealed that at least three-fourths of the black coaches agreed that the college or university at which they played had an influence on securing a major college coaching position. This finding further supports the relationships between college prestige and career mobility indicated by Loy and Sage (1978) and Latimer and Mathes (1985).

Occupational Demands

Grenfell and Freischlag (1989) recognized that the career mobility paths for men may differ from those for women. In consideration of these differences, the researchers hypothesized that a complex set of personal and professional attributes was related to successful coaching. Grenfell and Freischlag (1989) developed a model representing role responsibilities of coaches (Freischlag and Jacob, 1988) through use of questionnaires solicited from 84 men's and 81 women's NCAA Division I basketball coaches. The results included the identification of five factors contributing to coaching success: communication skills, administrative support, public image, dress, and NABC membership in the professional coaches associations (NABC, WABC).

Based upon data found in their study, the researchers outlined the attributes of a typical head coach, because they found both successful male and female college basketball coaches exhibit some career path similarities. The ability to identify the typical coach with certain attributes tends to support the idea that there is a set of minimal competencies that successful coaches are expected to have. Among these competencies are experience, membership in professional associations, clinic attendance, participation in summer camps, and holding of at least a master's degree.

In 1980, Sage identified the need to analyze the occupational demands of the coaching position. His work provides the reader with an excellent review of the literature covering such issues as personality of the coach, leadership styles, social and political attitudes, and value orientation. The literature in 1980 could not clearly differentiate between successful and unsuccessful coaches. During the decades of the 1960s and 1970s articles appearing in local newspapers, magazines, and books were very critical of the role of the coach. Sage (1980) concluded that a majority of these attacks focused upon the personal attributes of coaches. Clearly, the role of the coach and the ultimate success or failure of the athletic program is influenced by more factors than merely the personality of the coach. Indications are that by the time people apply for head or assistant coaching positions, few attributes will distinguish African-American coaches from white coaches. Selection will be based on some other criteria.

Coaching Subculture

Massengale (1974) agreed that an understanding of coaching as an occupational subculture might provide additional insights into the coaching role. Coaches display distinctive ways of thinking, feeling, and acting in a given environment. Coaches are promoted upward through the system, and Massengale pointed out that young coaches learn what is expected behavior within the profession. Subcultures are relatively closed systems, and coaches learn that obtaining a coaching position may be tied to the amount of support that other members of the coaching profession are willing to offer. He also stated that "the subculture can become a referral system to vested interest groups such as alumni organizations or athletic booster clubs, or it can become an acceptable sponsor and offer unsolicited firsthand personal recommendation" (Massengale, 1974, p. 141).

The extent to which African-American coaches are recruited and become members of the dominant white subculture of college coaching is not clearly understood. The application of Massengale's (1974) "favored models" argues that members of the subculture value the credentials of coaches who have similar values, beliefs, and behaviors of recognized successful coaches. African-American coaches who serve as assistant coaches under very successful head coaches learn these values and begin to imitate their mentors. As a result, the African-American coaches become part of an informal recruiting-and-referral coaching system operating in college athletics. To date, there are no formal, structured recruiting systems in the NCAA that have been established to identify potential college coaches.

"Basically, there is no feeder system for athletic departments. An athletic program is so small there aren't enough positions to really work your way up and cultivate young and new managers. The system is self-fulfilling" (Krasnow, 1988, p. 11). John Chaney (men's basketball, Temple University) voiced similar concern and advocated that the NCAA become more proactive and begin to give access to African-American members for coaching positions (Farrell, 1987a).

Network Structure, Mobilization of Resources, and Coaching Mobility

Brooks et al. (1989) wanted to begin to lay a foundation investigating the political economy of college sport related to the African-American coaching experience. The primary goal of their study was to explore various models in an attempt to explain why few African-Americans occupy head coaching positions. Their research represented new alternatives to analyzing coaching career mobility patterns.

In the initial stage of the research, they conducted telephone interviews with members of the Board of Directors of the Black Coaches Association (1988-89) ($n=8$), Regional Directors of the Black Coaches Association ($n=4$) and two members of the Black Coaches Association recommended by the Executive Director. The researchers asked the following questions:

What were the "stand-out" qualifications that must be shown on the resume in order to achieve a "real shot" at head coaching positions; what did they perceive to be their strongest attributes as coaches, did they have a desire to become head coaches; what benefits versus cost are associated with assistant coaching versus head coaching; and who does one have to talk to in order to be recruited as a head coach?

The interviews permitted the researchers to confirm the existence of four coaching avenues. The avenues are: (a) Blalock Talent Avenue, (b) Personal Attribute Avenue, (c) Internal Mobility Career Avenue, and (d) Coaching Mobility Network Avenue.

Blalock Talent Avenue

Blalock (1967) argued that sport creates an opportunity for African-Americans to gain mobility by making individual skill the most important determinant to success. Blalock's statement is based on the following arguments: (a) the lower the degree of purely social interaction on the job, the lower the degree of racial discrimination; (b) to the extent that performance level is relatively independent of skill in interpersonal relations, the degree of racial discrimination is lower; and (c) the greater the importance of high individual performance to the productivity of the work group, the lower the degree of minority discrimination by employers.

Blalock also believed that African-Americans did not attain parity in athletics and that they would encounter difficulties in obtaining coaching and managerial positions. It was argued that African-Americans would require special training and that vague standards for evaluating leadership effectiveness would serve to discriminate against these individuals getting coaching positions.

In addition, Blalock contended that African-American coaches who demonstrate excellence in coaching can be expected to be recruited for additional coaching responsibilities. Some scholars, most notably Harry Edwards, take exception to this assumption. Edwards (1973) argued that blacks do not gain upward mobility via sport and that in fact very few blacks gain access to participate in professional sports.

Blalock's Talent Avenue deserves further investigation. College athletic programs, like many other highly structured organizations, have been established to recognize and reward talent. Coaching talent may be rewarded in the form of extended coaching contracts, higher salaries, or upward mobility into directorships.

Personal Attribute Avenue

The Personal Attribute Avenue suggested that coaches gained upward mobility as they acquired the attributes necessary to perform the functions of head coach. Brooks et al. (1989) showed that coaches perceived they had the following attributes: (a) communication skills, (b) motivation, (c) listening (supportive) skills, (d) job experience, (e) honesty, and (f) ability to relate to students. These coaches believed that certain personal attributes were associated with coaching success. The researchers were unable to explain the fact that the majority of these coaches perceived they had the necessary personal attributes yet remained assistant coaches. Additional factors such as the ability to fit into the institution and compatibility with other coaches, alumni, and the athletic directors must be considered.

Internal Mobility Careers Avenue

This idea suggests that coaching mobility depends heavily on recruiting network ties and communication links with individuals in decision-making positions. Interpretation relies on Collins' (1975) examination of the relationship between individual success and social mobility. Basically, the ability of an assistant coach to achieve upward mobility is tied directly to the success of the head coach. If the head coach is labeled as unsuccessful, his or her assistant coach is also labeled unsuccessful. Negative labeling by those in power (athletic directors, college presidents) makes upward mobility for assistant coaches nearly impossible. The assistant coaches lack power and influence in the decision-making process (Brooks et al, 1989). It is important for upwardly mobile assistant coaches to build acquaintance networks with athletic directors and other head coaches to assist them in acquiring head coaching positions.

Coaching Mobility Network Avenue

Coaching mobility networks or ties are related to the Internal Mobility Careers Avenue. Some evidence indicates successful coaches function as key links in networks that generate other successful coaches. Such "recruiting trees" are affected by an organization's level of success with its athletic program as well as its conference affiliation. Comments made by members of the Black Coaches Association such as "people who have been associated with successful programs become head coaches," and "being associated with 'big-time' institution increases your chances of being hired" pointed to the existence of perceived structural opportunities to career coaching mobility (Brooks et al., 1989).

Brooks et al. (1989) were unable to account adequately for the relatively low upward mobility and the fairly slow development of African-American assistant coaches promoted to head coaching positions. Most of the assistant coaches who were identified remained assistant coaches or left the coaching ranks. Those who became head coaches appeared to take years to get there. This suggests that different factors may be influencing features of recruitment and that both levels (micro and macro) will be important if we are going to understand the recruitment and career mobility coaching patterns.

Friendship networks, professional contacts, and acquaintances are important influences on the upward mobility of African-American coaches. Network relationships appear to tie together coaching mobility and head coaching positions. Coaching careers are considered to be unique for each individual, but networks represent the way in which organizations allocate and mobilize the opportunities for mobility.

Brooks, Althouse, and Brown (1990) also looked at structures of the mobility exhibited in the career paths of 28 African-American head coaches in Division I basketball who held positions in 1989. Notable coaches such as Lefty Driesell, Denny Crum, and Digger Phelps were recruiting "gatekeepers" (mentors, who hired African-American assistant coaches). Career path sponsorship also appears to have depended on the success of athletic programs, conference affiliation, and type of institution (public or private). Evidence suggested that the process can work for African-American assistant coaches as African-American head coaches begin to hire more African-Americans as assistant coaches. In some measure, as African-American head coaches establish their own recruiting system they can increase the potential pool of available coaches. The expanded network may result in increased access to coaching openings. Some evidence (e.g., formation of the Black Coaches Association) suggests that African-American assistants have begun to expand their occupational network, both in their own professional associations and through employment in sports and related commercial jobs. These assistant coaches may be keenly aware of "power brokers" (i.e., alumni, presidents) within the recruiting and hiring structures, and indications are that failure to identify their influence in decision making will result in token interview sessions.

A better understanding of the career mobility is likely to await a more thorough investigation of the network relationships among the career resources acquired by coaches and the rate of organizational turnover and change in mobility among coaches. Turnover among head coaching positions at NCAA levels I, II, and III will vary, but probably amounts to no more than 10%. This results in only a few head positions available before the next season. This rate of coaching turnover among NCAA division institutions has not been documented, and the NCAA has only recently started to monitor this situation.

Brooks et al. (1990) were able to identify four mobility career paths characterizing experiences among African-American basketball coaches: (a) professional road (previous college playing experience; professional playing experience; assistant coach under successful head coach), (b) internship (previous college playing experience; assistant coach (served under two or more head coaches); head coaching position), (c) stepping stone (previous college playing experience; head coach (small college, low student enrollment); head coach Division I level, and (d) mentorship (previous college playing experience; assistant coach (serving under successful head coach) at College X; head coach at College Y.

Further investigation suggested that an individual may experience more than one coaching career path. We simply need to recognize that a good deal of coaching ends at the assistant coach level and that coaching jobs are a source of alternative careers. Sometimes an early job involves a secondary school or prep school position; the individual may again later move into a mobility path at a new entry point. The young, upwardly mobile African-American coach may travel more than one of these paths. However, differences in league structure, league ranking of the college, prestige of the college, athletic program cost, and type of sport (individual/team) may affect the path followed by African-American coaches. Thus, each career path represents potential opportunity and vulnerability to achieve success.

Study of these career patterns can and must focus on internal factors affecting the allocation and distribution of organizational resources. Specifically, we suggest study of the relationships between coaching networks and cycles of athletic participation, coaching schedules and loads, of the schemes and mobilization of alumni support, as well as administration support and future coaching career mobility.

Different career paths in basketball appear to extract different costs of success; many African-Americans may drop out as well as be "forced out" of coaching. Understanding the standardized, but differentiated, career paths of coaches may depend on seeing how assistant coaches are tied together by their occupational level and the chances for coaching mobility from different segments of that labor force. Research is needed to determine whether similar careers exist for men or women, and among revenue or nonrevenue sports.

Persistent Discrimination or Progress?

During the past 15 years, more African-Americans have won jobs as head coaches, and the number of assistant coaches in the NCAA also appears to increase, especially in the sport of basketball. Popular magazines such as *Ebony* and *Jet* applaud these achievements, but also reflect on continuing aspects of discrimination. *Jet*'s 1979 article "NCAA's First Black Head Football Coach is Ready to Tackle the Pressure" traced the career of Willie Jeffries, the first African-American coach of a major white institution (Wichita State). Prior to accepting the position at Wichita State, Jeffries declined interview offers from predominantly white institutions because he felt these institutions were "interviewing Black coaches (only) to fill one kind of criteria" (NCAA, 1979, p. 48).

In 1981, before moving to the 49ers, then Stanford, and recently to the Minnesota Viking head office, Dennis Green was the only head African-American football coach in the Big 10 Conference. He coached at Northwestern University, where his teams had limited success. Two years later, Tony Yates and George Raveling accepted head basketball coaching positions at the University of Cincinnati and Iowa, respectively. Nolan Richardson, previously the head basketball coach at Tulsa University, accepted a head coaching position at Arkansas. Richardson became the first African-American head coach of any men's sport in the Southwest Conference ("Black Head Coaches," 1982). Perhaps a more notable hiring was that of Kenneth Gibson as head track coach at the University of Mississippi in 1985, the first African-American coach of any sport in the school's history. The Southeastern Conference had been the last major college conference to integrate its sports teams, not having done so until the late '60s. Finally when the University of Tennessee hired Wade Houston as the head basketball coach in 1989, Tennessee became the first college in the Southeastern Athletic Conference to hire an African-American head basketball coach (Oberlander, 1989).

Ebony saw some new balance as African-Americans won these positions ("Black Head Coaches," 1982). Although the number of head coaches at the college level was few, the number was slowly increasing. Of the 276 Division I colleges, 13 had hired head African-American basketball coaches. The majority of the coaches being hired for college positions were in basketball, track and field, and football. The magazine's interviews with these African-American coaches revealed that tokenism and decreased support by the alumni still seemed to weigh heavily in accounting for the persistently low percentage of African-American head coaches.

Reports suggest that since 1986, there has been a notable increase of head African-American college basketball coaches. The following prominent African-American men's and women's head basketball coaches were noted by *Ebony* during that year ("A Boom," 1986):

Name	College/University
Walt Hazzard	UCLA
Tony Yates	Cincinnati
George Raveling	Iowa (Men's)
Vivian Stringer	Iowa (Women's)
Larry Farmer	Weber State
Nolan Richardson	Arkansas
David Gaines	San Diego State
John Chaney	Temple
Clem Haskins	Western Kentucky
Bob LeGrand	University of Texas-Arlington
Charles Coles	Central Michigan
Vernon Payne	Western Michigan
Wilkes Rittle	University of Illinois-Chicago
John Thompson	Georgetown

By 1991, 34 African-Americans had head basketball coaching assignments. This amounts to a 500% increase from the 1978-79 season when only 7 African-Americans were head coaches (Keegan & Towle, 1991). By now, coaching experience includes some notable veterans: coaches' tenure ranges from 1 to 19 years. John Chaney, George Raveling, and John Thompson had the longest tenure of head coaches. (See Table 4.)

Dealing only with basketball (football is a totally different power game) the listing shows the following: (a) only 13 of the 35 African-American head basketball coaches occupy positions in major conferences; (b) the majority of coaches have little head coaching experience; and (c) half of the 34 coaches were hired within the past three years.

As a major long-time advocate for social justice and the rights of the African-American athlete, Harry Edwards contends that the revolt of the

Table 4. 1990-91 Division I African-American Basketball Coaches*

Coaching Experience	Coach	Current College
1-3 years	Mike Brown	Central Conn. State
	Ricky Byrdsong	Detroit
	Rudy Keeling	Maine
	Oliver Purnell	Radford
	Al Skinner	Rhode Island
	Randy Ayers	Ohio State
	Perry Clark	Tulane
	Coleman Crawford	Akron
	Wade Houston	Tennessee
	Jerry Lloyd	Louisiana Tech
	Mike Boyd	Cleveland State
	Dwight Freeman	Marshall
	John Wade	Eastern Washington
	Rudy Washington	Drake
	Herb Williams	Idaho State
	John Wright	Miami (Ohio)
4-8 years	Reggie Minton	Air Force Academy
	Jarrett Durham	Robert Morris
	Mike Jarvis	George Washington
	Peter Roby	Harvard
	John Shumate	Southern Methodist
	Gary Brokaw	Iowa
	Larry Finch	Memphis State
	Jimmy Gales	North Texas
	Leonard Hamilton	Miami (Fla.)
	Frankie Allen	Virginia Tech
	Harold Merritt	Northern Arizona
11-19 years	John Chaney	Temple
	George Raveling	USC
	John Thompson	Georgetown
	Clem Haskins	Minnesota

Adapted from Eliopolous, E., Brown, R., & Rebach, R. L.(1991, January 17). Black coaches on the rise. *The National Sports Daily.*

black athletes in the 1960s was a major factor influencing the increase in black coaches (Edwards, 1969; Edwards, 1979b; Edwards, 1982a, b). The black assistant coaches' core activities have changed since the 1960s. Determined specifically by the existing exigencies of each college/ university, assistant coaches serve as recruiters, scouts, academic advisors, and public relation officers. Yet today, it is generally acknowledged that one of the major tasks of the African-American coach is to recruit African-American players (Lederman, 1988; Wulf, 1987). Edwards believed many African-American coaches fill dead-end jobs with no chance for promotion (Dent, 1987).

African-American Female Coaches

Not uncommonly, observers attribute the greater representation of African-American head coaches to an increase in the number of African-Americans participating in college sport. According to Yetman, Berghorn and Thomas (1982) racial participation rates in men's and women's college basketball changed dramatically. In 1948 only 1% of all players at predominantly white institutions were African-American. Participation increased to 45% in 1975 and 49% in 1985, and the greatest increases were found in colleges located in the southeastern United States. Although participation improved for African-American women athletes, as late as 1985, fewer than one-fourth of all women players were African-American (Berghorn et al., 1988).

Between 1948 and 1985 the number of African-American assistant coaches increased more and more rapidly than the number of head coaches. It is disturbing to note that only 3% of all NCAA women's teams had African-American head coaches. Acosta and Carpenter's (1990b) longitudinal study of women in intercollegiate sport showed a dramatic increase in participation rates by African-Americans but also reported a significant decline in female coaches and administrators. Acosta and Carpenter (1990a) argued convincingly that the decline of female leadership in athletics is a result of (a) success of the old-boy network, (b) the weakness of the old-girls' network, and (c) lack of support systems for females. Opportunities for women to gain upward mobility to coaching, officiating, and administration have been limited, especially for the African-American women. Racism, sexism, and structural barriers make it very difficult to gain access to high-quality programs (Eitzen & Sage, 1989).

Discrimination: Underrepresentation

The representation of African-American males coaching in college basketball has been hotly debated in college ranks, and the NCAA has been credited with taking positive steps to reduce disparities in recruitment and correct inequalities found in association with the head coaching position. But reviews of the NCAA initiatives yield mixed results. In interviews of college coaches and administrators, Charles Farrell (1987a) found disparity with the NCAA's efforts to hire more African-American coaches. For example, hiring data showed:

1. Only two athletic directors in the 105-member Division I-A are black.
2. No major college athletic conference, except those composed of black colleges, have black commissioners.
3. Three head football coaches in Division I-A are black.
4. About 25 of the head basketball coaches at the 273 predominantly white institutions in Division I are black. (Farrell, 1987a, p. A40).

Surveying the employment efforts of the NCAA, Wulf (1987) concluded that the NCAA had a poor record in minority hiring. Dent (1987) maintained that the NCAA's poor record is tied to racism. Dent reported on an interview with Peay (a former offensive lineman for the Kansas City Chiefs), "You've got influential people in booster clubs and alumni organizations, and it's very hard for an athletic director to go to them and recommend that an assistant coach be promoted to head coach to fill a vacancy" (Dent, 1987, p. 34). These institutional barriers prevent African-American assistant coaches from becoming head coaches.

The view from the top is a little different. Charles Harris, athletic director at Arizona State, does not believe the lack of head African-American head coaches is due to racism. In his estimate employment opportunities are tied to previous coaching success and the ability to establish network ties among other professionals that would be used to establish career paths that currently do not exist for African-Americans (Farrell, 1987b). Charlie Harris and Rudy Washington (first executive director of the Black Coaches Association) reiterated the belief that the problem is "getting to the mainstream" and "there are no feeder systems for athletic departments" (Krasnow, 1988, p. 11). In effect, slow turnover in the college coaching ranks makes it very difficult for African-Americans work their way up the coaching mobility ladder. Thus, the lasting effects of racism and oppression still produce discrimination and barriers to success, whether the discrimination is regarded as intentional or not.

The NCAA claims to be taking positive steps to identify and establish policy and guidelines to deal with the underrepresentation of African-Americans in NCAA coaching and managerial positions. An action has been to establish an NCAA subcommittee in 1988 to review and promote minority opportunities in college athletics. For the first time this subcommittee surveyed the current status of minorities in the NCAA across Divisions I, II, and III. The data (NCAA, 1988) collected from 74 Division I-A institutions, 51 institutions from Division I-AA, and 54 I-AAA schools revealed that African-Americans hold six percent of full-time administrative positions (athletic directors, sport information directors, ticket managers, equipment managers, business managers), that two percent of full-time administrators at the conference level are African-American, and that African-Americans hold approximately five percent of the full-time men's head coaching positions and about five percent of full-time head coaching positions of women's teams.

The minorities' report shows a different pattern for African-Americans in the assistant coaching ranks, especially in men's basketball. Across NCAA Divisions I, II, and III African-American men hold 29% of all assistant coaching positions in basketball, and 47% of the full-time assistant coaching positions in cross country in Division IA.

The survey concludes on a discouraging note, suggesting that mechanisms to promote minority participation in college athletics will be getting worse. The survey showed that very few African-American graduate and undergraduate students are involved in any of the athletic administrative positions that would be essential to building the basis for leadership in college and universities: "The only identifiable pool of talent from which to draw minority applicants within collegiate athletics administration is composed of the student-athlete themselves" (NCAA, 1988, p. 1).

Strategies for Change

The Black Coaches Association (BCA) recognized the paucity of African-Americans in head coaching and other managerial positions in the NCAA. Rudy Washington, first Executive Director of the Black Coaches Association and currently head basketball coach at Drake University, said,

> What initially motivated me to form an association was 15 years of frustration. I've been in the game in various capacities on different levels: as a head coach, as an assistant, and as an administrator. I've watched my (white) colleagues obtain jobs that I know and know I'm qualified for, and I don't even get a phone call for an interview...and still haven't after a year of success with

the association. Sharing these thoughts with other frustrated black coaches became the basis for the BCA creation. (Ivey, 1988, p. 1)

The Black Coaches Association was primarily created to deal directly with minority issues in sports. Issues included the stereotyping of minority coaches and administrators and the lack of minorities in key decision-making roles. In 1987, members of the BCA met with the NCAA executive director to request a review of minority opportunities in college athletics. The association leadership took the position that if the NCAA is committed to increasing the number of black coaches, institutions have to get away from the buddy system and use affirmative action plans. Membership in the BCA has grown from over 2,000 in 1988 to over 3,000 in 1991, and the Association has been able to establish lines of communication with the NCAA to establish a job-line assisting with the identification of potential head coaches.

Through interviews with the Board of Directors of the BCA, Brooks et al. (1989) concluded that the association was meeting stated objectives. The issues identified by the coaches were

1. Using the BCA's as a vehicle to show the need for black head coaches.
2. Making institutions aware that blacks are more than just performers on the field, and have head coaching ability.

Several of the coaches interviewed in this study realized that changes may not happen overnight even with the creation of the BCA. Change is on the horizon, though, as the political base of the Association has expanded to include Division II, III, junior colleges, and high school coaches (African-American and white). The BCA is gaining recognition as a major advocate for social justice issues in intercollegiate athletics, and it has the potential to affect policy decision-making and implementation affecting the future status of African-Americans in college sport.

The role of advocate for social justice in college athletics goes beyond that of the Black Coaches Association. The Center for the Study of Sport in Society has assumed a major leadership role in this area. Richard Lapchick (1989), Director, has also recognized the lack of African-Americans in head coaching and other administrative positions as an issue facing African-American athletes in the 1990s. He offered the following suggestions and recommendations to increase the number of African-American head coaches:

1. more blacks must become college presidents and athletic directors;
2. black head coaches should be represented in all sports;
3. the number of black assistant coaches must be increased;

4. support for the Black Coaches Association must continue;

5. NCAA vita bank for minorities and women must be supported; and

6. sport information directors should be more aware of stereotypes of minorities (Lapchick, 1989).

Lapchick does not offer the reader a detailed plan on how to implement his six recommendations to increase the number of African-American head coaches. We suggest there are two fundamental issues, internal organization of college sport and multiculturalism/pluralism, that must be understood and addressed if Lapchick's recommendations are going to be realized:

1. How is the organization of college sport tied to wealth (revenue vs. non-revenue sport status), career, and professional achievement? Teachers, coaches, and administrators must gain insights into where African-American players and coaches came from. One could argue that classism, manifested in the form of the amount of resources spent on revenue sport as compared to non-revenue sport, exists in college sport. This is of particular importance because a significant number of African-American male athletes are recruited to play for revenue (football, basketball) teams.

2. Broader base for understanding racism in college athletics must include all ethnic minorities and not be limited to discussion of the African-American athlete. Over the next several decades, more and more ethnic minorities will be seeking and gaining access to colleges and universities. These individuals will be competing with African-Americans for playing and coaching positions.

The United States is becoming a nation of diverse cultures, and as a consequence no real study of racism and dominance can be undertaken without including the various groups who participate on the various NCAA teams. Unfortunately, the experiences and achievements of individuals found within the various ethnic groups are missing from the sport sociology and history literature. A multicultural approach to critiquing racism in college sport would lead to a better understanding and appreciation of cultural diversity. In summary, the African-American experience in college sport has been and will continue to be shaped by the structure of the NCAA. As people of color, African-Americans share opportunities and potential liabilities for participating in college sport.

Expand Personal Acquaintances

Strategies to increase the number of African-Americans in college leadership positions must first begin with an understanding of the political economy of college athletics. The ability of an assistant coach to achieve upward mobility is tied directly to the success of the head coach. If assistant coaches are going to achieve upward mobility they must begin to develop acquaintance networks to help them gain head coaching positions. Athletic directors need to be in the network of personal acquaintances for assistant coaches. Athletic directors are a very important part of the recruiting process, and they ultimately make the decision to hire the head coach.

Future strategies and innovations must also take into consideration the plight of the African-American female. Very few women occupy leadership positions at the high school or college level.

Green, Oglesby, Alexander, and Franke (1981) took a futuristic look at the role of the African-American female athletes in the year 2000. They believed that African-American females will find it necessary to create jobs in the African-American community to gain the necessary skills to compete in the national market, and they advocated the establishment of coaching camps and clinics in the African-American community. These camps would serve as internship programs and training camps to develop leadership skills.

Given the data and information presented in this essay, we do not believe we are going to see a significant increase in the number of African-Americans (men and women) in leadership positions until we begin to address the social issues facing African-Americans and other low socio-economic families. Our school systems must develop and enhance programs to increase the high school graduation rate and college entrance and graduation rates of ethnic minorities. Once on campus, we must begin to address the "chilly climate" faced by African-Americans and women. African-American students in predominantly white institutions are apt to feel different from other students, feel isolated from other students, and feel racial isolation and discrimination (American Institute for Research, 1989).

A historical overview from 1972 to the present suggests that African-Americans and other persons of color have experienced an unequal path through the education system, especially higher education. In 1972 African-American students constituted 8.4% of the full-time undergraduate enrollment, but four years later they received only 6.4% of the baccalaureate degrees (Watson, 1979). The data relative to high school graduation rates and going-to-college rate are very disturbing. From 1976 to 1988 the high school graduation rates for African-Americans increased; however, the college participation rate dropped from 40% to 30% for low-income African-American high school graduates and from 53% to 36% for middle-income African-Americans (Carter & Wilson, 1989). The decrease in college participation may be due to the following factors: a reduction in available financial aid from the federal government, the high number of African-Americans who fail to graduate, and weak educational foundations (Allen, 1988).

Increasing the high school and college graduation rates for African-Americans should be a high priority. One of the many possible outcomes of this action would be a potential larger recruiting pool from which to identify sport leaders.

Currently, there are several unique programs throughout the United States that could be modified to assist with the identification and development of coaching ability.

Partners for Success--Community College

The Office of Bilingual Education and Minority Language Affairs in the U.S. Department of Education established a program at Wayne State University to prepare teacher's aides in Michigan to become teachers. This program can be extended to train teacher's aides to become physical education teachers and coaches. Initiating this program on the community college campus has some advantages particularly because 43% of all African-American undergraduate students were enrolled in two-year colleges (Nettles, 1988). Junior- or community-college coaches and administrators would become role models for the African-American students enrolled in this program. Mentoring and follow-up meetings would be conducted in an effort to ensure that students enrolled in this program graduate and enroll in four year institutions. It is hoped that these students will pursue degrees in sport-related fields.

National Youth Sport Program

The National Youth Sport Program was organized in 1979 to provide economically disadvantaged youngsters, between the ages 10-16, sport skills, drug awareness, and career advising. In 1990, over 60,000 students throughout America were served by this program.

Project directors and activities coordinators of these programs are encouraged to invite sport leaders (coaches, athletic directors) to their camps addressing career opportunities in college sport. As a followup, the

NCAA and the State High School Athletic Federations would host regional conferences/workshop, invite nationally known sport figures, and further explore career opportunities in college athletics. This particular recommendation builds on the existing National Youth Sport network structure.

NCAA Minority Scholarship

After reviewing the data, the NCAA Subcommittee to Review Minority Opportunities concluded that the NCAA's member institutions need to address the lack of minorities in leadership positions. The NCAA Minority Enhancement Scholarship and Internship Programs were established by the NCAA to increase the pool of potential NCAA leaders.

The Postgraduate Scholarship Program was designed to increase the potential pool of minorities pursuing and graduating with degrees in the field of sport administration. Ten scholarships are awarded annually to women and ethnic minorities. The Internship Program provides minorities the opportunity to gain on-the-job training at the NCAA national headquarters. Finally, the NCAA Ethnic Minority and Women's Vita Bank assist colleges and the private sector to identify candidates to fill job vacancies.

Role of College Presidents

College presidents and athletic directors have a major role to perform in increasing the number of African-Americans in leadership positions in college athletics. They can establish affirmative action goals and establish policies and procedures to enhance opportunities for African-Americans. A recommended change in existing policy would require that all Division I NCAA institutions have a senior-level minority athletic administrator and staff member. Select colleges have already employed this strategy to increase the number of African-American faculty on their staffs.

Summary

College and high school sport are often viewed as two of the most responsive of many integrating mechanisms now active in American society. Yet from 1947 (when Jackie Robinson played for the Dodgers) until 1967, few African-Americans participated or coached at the college level. After 1968, the increase in participation rates of African-Americans can be attributed to a change in social climate, the Civil Rights Movement, and recruitment policies (which view college athletics as big business). Sport provided an avenue for mobility for African-Americans both socially and economically. The route followed by many African-American athletes has been the early development of physical skills in order to get out of the ghetto and succeed professionally.

In this essay, the authors chose to identify and describe factors that explain the absence of African-Americans in head coaching positions. Race, athletic participation, the ability to mobilize resources, the impact of structural barriers (i.e., conference affiliation, type of institution, and success of the program), and career mobility patterns were identified as variables influencing the coaching mobility process at the college level.

During the 1960s and 1970s, a large volume of research was conducted to determine the relationship between athletic playing position and racial discrimination. The early research papers utilized sociological theory as the conceptual basis for understanding segregation in American sport.

Literature revealed that coaching and managerial positions in college sports organizations are for the most part exclusively in the white domain. The absence of African-Americans in head coaching positions, especially at NCAA Division I institutions, may be related to discrimination in recruiting at the college ranks, known as stacking. Stacking refers to situations in which African-Americans are relegated to specific team positions (such as wide receiver and defensive back) and excluded from competing for others (quarterback). As a result, African-Americans compete against other African-Americans for a limited number of team positions. A number of theories (psychological and sociological) have been postulated in an attempt to explain this phenomenon.

The stereotype hypothesis has been one of the most widely accepted explanations for stacking in American college sport. The hypothesis states that white coaches believe that African-Americans lack the leadership ability necessary to occupy control or leadership positions. One of the consequences of positional segregation, or stacking, is the relationship found between subsequent coaching mobility and previous position played. A high percentage of college coaches and administrators were recruited from central positions.

This finding suggests that white and African-American coaches were thrust along different career paths to achieve coaching success. Coaching career mobility avenues were also developed in an attempt to describe these differential paths.

The Personal Attribute Avenue holds that coaches gain upward mobility to the head coaching ranks as they acquire the attributes necessary to perform the duties of head coach. Communication skills, cultural values, administrative support, experience, and public image were identified as important characteristics of coaches. African-American coaches also held the notion that selected personal attributes were directly associated with coaching success.

The Personal Attribute Avenue could not explain that the majority of the African-American coaches perceived they had the necessary personal attributes to become head coach, yet remained an assistant coach. A possible explanation was that African-Americans were hired primarily to recruit other African-American athletes. The role of recruiter does not permit assistant coaches to gain the knowledge and experience necessary to become head coaches.

Career coaching mobility patterns of college coaches demonstrated specific geographical movement patterns. The majority of white coaches attended colleges in their home states or bordering states. Likewise, African-American coaches attended colleges in their home NCAA district. The vast majority of the African-American coaches came from the southeastern United States.

The demographic explanation viewed coaching mobility in terms of spatial production and consumption. Understanding geographical movement patterns of coaches was useful because it first specified sport regions and then identified such factors as the proportion of coaches recruited to various colleges and universities. Nonetheless, demographic analysis represented a somewhat simplistic causal relationship between coaching mobility and geographical regions.

None of the avenues presented in this essay could clearly explain the coaching mobility patterns of coaches (white or African-American). The career coaching paths followed by individual head coaches were unique. It is impossible to conclude that the ability to negotiate various career stages successfully will lead to head coaching career.

The essay does conclude that since 1954, the number of head African-American coaches and assistant coaches in the NCAA did increase. This was especially true for NCAA basketball. The increase in the number of African-American head coaches has been associated with the number of African-Americans participating in college sport. Member institutions of the NCAA have taken steps to identify and establish policies to address the lack of African-Americans in NCAA coaching positions.

Since 1986, African-American head coaches have begun moving into positions of coaching and building their own recruiting and ''stem-and-branch'' structures. African-American head coaches are strongly encouraged to hire other African-American assistant coaches. This practice should result in increasing the pool of available African-American coaches.

Throughout this essay we have documented that African-American males and females have been underemployed and underrepresented in college athletic leadership positions. We do not believe America will witness a significant increase in the number of African-Americans in leadership positions until we address the low high school graduation, college entrance and graduation rates of African-Americans. Further, we must address the chilly climate faced by many African-American students who attend predominantly white institutions.

Establishment of affirmative action policies and procedures has not been successful in changing the hiring practices of NCAA member institutions. College presidents, athletic directors, coaches, athletes, and faculty must engage in a program of social justice and equity if we are going to see changes in hiring and promotion practices as we look towards the next century.

We may be witnessing a redefinition in the display and control of collegiate sports and be on the edge of an NCAA athletic transformation: a rejection of old solutions and advocacy of those who have the most to gain (administrators, coaches, students). Normal practice is no longer going to be accepted by university administrators. This is the vision for change.

References

A boom in black coaches. *Ebony.* (1986, April) pp. 59-62.

Acosta, R.V., & Carpenter, L.J. (1990a). *Perceived causes of the declining representation of women leaders in intercollegiate sport—1988 update.* (ERIC Document Reproduction Service, No. ED 314 381).

Acosta, R.V., & Carpenter, L.J. (1990b, February). *Women in intercollegiate sport: A longitudinal study— thirteen year update 1977-1990.* Paper presented at the Symposium for Girls and Women in Sports, Slippery Rock University, Slippery Rock, PA.

Allen, W.R. (1988). Black students in U.S. higher education: Toward improved access, adjustment, and achievement. *The Urban Review, 20,* 165-188.

American Institute for Research, (1989). *Report No. 3: The experiences of black intercollegiate athletes at NCAA Division I institutions.* Palo Alto, CA.

And then there were none. *The Chronicle of Higher Education*, (1992, January 29). p. A36.

Banks, O. (1979). How black coaches view entering the job market at major colleges. *Journal of Physical Education and Recreation, 50*, 62.

Berghorn, F.J., Yetman, N., & Hanna, W.C. (1988). Racial participation and integration in men's and women's intercollegiate basketball: Continuity and change, 1958-1985. *Sociology of Sport Journal, 5*(20), 107-124.

Best, C. (1987). Experience and career length in professional football: The effect of positional segregation. *Sociology of Sport Journal, 4*, 410-420.

Big 10's home black grid coach accepts record. *Jet* (1981, December 3) p. 48.

Birrell, S. (1989). Racial relations theories and sport: Suggestions for a more critical analysis. *Sociology of Sport Journal, 6*, 212-227.

Black access, white flight: where are they taking sports in the USA? *USA Today* (1991, December 19), p. 9C.

Black coaches accept big college basketball jobs. *Jet* (1983, April 25) p. 46.

Black coaches seek change in Atlantic Coast Conference. *Black Issues in Higher Education*. (1987, July) *1*, p. 14.

Black head coaches: taking change in major campuses. *Ebony* (1982, May) pp. 57-62.

Blalock, H.M. (1962). Occupational discrimination: Some theoretical propositions. *Social Problems, 9*, 240-247.

Blalock, H.M. (1967). *Toward a theory of minority group relations*. New York, John Wiley and Sons.

Boeck, G. & Shuster, R. (1991, March 19). College 'old boy network' hard to crack. *USA Today*, p. 11A.

Braddock, J.H., (1980). Race, sports and social mobility: A critical review. *Sociological Symposium, 30*, 17-38.

Brooks, D., Althouse, R., & Brown, R. (1990). Black coaching mobility: An investigation of the stem and branch structural model. Unpublished paper presented at the North Central Sociology Meeting, Louisville, Kentucky. March 22-23.

Brooks, D., Althouse, R., King, V., & Brown, R. (1989). Opportunities for coaching achievement and the black experience: Have we put marginality into the system? *Proceedings of the 32nd Annual ICHPER*

Conference. pp. 246-254.

Buhrmann, H.G. (1971). Scholarship and athletics in junior high school. *International Review of Sport Sociology, 7,* 119- 128.

Carter, D., & Wilson, R. (1989). Eighth annual status report: minorities in higher education. Washington, DC: American Council on Education.

Christiano, K.J. (1986). Salary discrimination in major league baseball: The effect of race. *Sociology of Sport Journal, 3,* 144-153.

Christiano, K.J. (1988). Salaries and race in professional baseball: discrimination 10 years later. *Sociology of Sport Journal, 5,* 136-149.

Chu, D.B., & Segrave, J.O. (1981). Leadership and ethnic stratification in basketball. *Journal of Sport and Social Issues, 5*(1), 15-32.

Coakley, J.J. (1986). *Sport in society: Issues and controversies* (3rd ed.). St. Louis: Times Mirror/Mosby.

Coleman, J. (1961). *The adolescent society.* New York: Free Press.

Collins, R. (1975). *Conflict sociology: Toward an explanatory science.* New York: Academic Press.

Curtis, J.E., & Loy, J.W. (1978a). Positional segregation in professional baseball: Replication, trend data and critical observation. *International Review of Sport Sociology, 4,* 5-21.

Curtis, J.E., & Loy, J.W. (1978b). Race/ethnicity and relative centrality of playing positions in team sports. *Exercise and Sport Science Review, 6,* 285-313.

Dent, D. (1987). Black coaches remain scarce in college ranks. *Black Enterprise, 18*(5), 34.

Edwards, H. (1969). *The revolt of the black athlete.* New York: Free Press.

Edwards, H. (1973). *Sociology of sport.* Illinois: Daisy Press.

Edwards, H. (1979a, March-April). The Olympic project for human rights: An assessment ten years later. *Black Scholar, 10* (6-7), 2-8.

Edwards, H. (1979b, September). Sport within the veil: The triumphs, tragedies, and challenges of Afro-American involvement. *Annals, AAPSS, 445,* 116-127.

Edwards, H. (1982a). On the issue of race in contemporary American sports. *Western Journal of Black Studies, 6*(3), 138-144.

Edwards, H. (1982b). Race in contemporary American sports. *Phi Kappa Phi Journal, 62*(1), 19-22.

Edwards, H. (1987). Race in contemporary America. In A.Yiannakis, T.McIntyre, M.Melnick, and D.Hart (Eds), *Sports in sport sociology: Contemporary themes,* (3rd edition) (pp.158-166).Dubuque, IA:

Kendall/Hunt Publishing Company.

Eitzen, D.S., & David, C.S. (1975). The segregation of blacks by playing position in football: Accident or design? *Social Science Quarterly, 55*, 948-59.

Eitzen, D.S., & Furst, D. (1989). Racial bias in women's collegiate volleyball. *Journal of Sport and Social Issues, 13*(1), 46-51.

Eitzen, D.S., & Sage, G.H. (1989). *Sociology of North American sport* (4th ed.). Dubuque, IA: Wm. C. Brown.

Eitzen, D.S., & Sanford, D. (1975). The segregation of blacks by playing positions in football: Accident or design? *Social Science Quarterly, 55*, p. 948-959.

Eitzen, D.S., & Tessendorf, I. (1978). Racial segregation by position in sports: The special case of basketball. *Review of Sport & Leisure, 3*(1), 109-128.

Eitzen, D.S., & Yetman, N.R. (1977). Immune from racism. *Civil Rights Digest, 9*, 3-13.

Eliopolous, E., Brown, R., & Rebach, R.L. (1991, January 17). Black coaches on the rise. *The National Sports Daily*.

Fabianic, D. (1984). Minority managers in professional baseball. *Sociology of Sport Journal, 1*(2), 163-171.

Farrell, C. (1987a, September 23). NCAA effort to spur black coach hirings gets mixed reviews. *The Chronicle of Higher Education*, pp. 39-40.

Farrell, C.S. (1987b, May 6). Scarcity of blacks in top jobs in college sports prompts founding of group to monitor hiring. *The Chronicle of Higher Education*, pp. 40-42.

Freischlag, J., & Jacob, R. (1988). Developmental factors among college men basketball coaches. *Journal of Applied Research in Coaching and Athletics, 3*(2), 87-93.

Green, T.S., Oglesby, C., Alexander, A., & Franke, N. (1981) *Black women in sport*. Reston, VA: AAHPERD.

Grenfell, C., & Freischlag, J. (1989, April). *Developmental pathways of men's and women's college basketball coaches*. Paper presented at the AAHPERD Convention. Boston, MA.

Grusky, O. (1963). The effects of formal structure on managerial recruitment: A study of baseball organization. *Sociometry, 26*, 345-353.

Hanks, M.P., & Eckland, B.K. (1976). Athletics and social participation in the educational attainment process. *Sociology of Education, 49*, 271-294.

Ivey, L. (1988, Winter). An interview with Rudy Washington. *BCA Journal*, 1, 4-5.

Johnson, W.O. (1991, August 5). A matter of black and white. *Sports Illustrated*, 44-58.

Jones, G.A., Leonard, W.M., Schmitt, R.L., Smith, D.R. & Tolone, W.L. (1987). Racial discrimination in college football. *Social Science Quarterly, 68*, 1, 7-83.

Keegan, T., & Towle, M. (1991, January 17). Black coaches on the rise. *The National Sports Daily.*

Krasnow, S. (1988). Survey: Major colleges shun black coaches. *Sport, 79*(6), 11.

Lapchick, R.C. (1989, Spring). Future of the black student athlete: Ethical issues of the 1990's. *Educational Record, 70*, 32-35.

Latimer, S., & Mathes, S. (1985). Black college football coaches social, educational, athletic and career pattern characteristics. *Journal of Sport Behavior, 8*(3), 149-162.

Lederman, D. (1988, April). Black coaches movement gains momentum: First annual meeting attracts 300. *The Chronicle of Higher Education, 43-44.*

Leonard, W. (1977, June). Stacking and performance differentials of whites, blacks, and latins in professional baseball. *Review of Sport and Literature, 2,* 77-106.

Leonard, W. (1986). The sports experience of black college athletes: Exploitation in the academy. *International Review for the Sociology of Sport, 21*(1), 35-49.

Leonard, W. (1987). Stacking in college basketball: A neglected analysis. *Sociology of Sport Journal, 4,* 403-409.

Leonard, W. (1989). Salaries and race/ethnicity in major league baseball: The pitching component. *Sociology of Sport Journal, 6*(2), 152-162.

Leonard, W., & Reyman, T. (1988). The odds of attaining professional athlete status: Refining the computations. *Sociology of Sport Journal, 5,* 162-169.

Leonard, W. & Schmidt, S. (1975). *Observations on the changing social organization of collegiate and professional basketball.* Midwest Sociological Society's Annual Meeting. Chicago, Illinois, April 10, 1975.

Loy, J.W. (1969). The study of sport and social mobility. In Gerald S. Kenyon (Ed.), *Aspect of Contemporary Sport Sociology* (pp. 101-

119). Chicago, Ill.: Athletic Institute.

Loy, J.W., & McElvogue, J. (1970). Racial segregation in American sport. *International Review of Sport Sociology, 5*, 5-24.

Loy, J.W. & Sage, G. H. (1978). Athletic personnel in the academic market place: A study of the interorganizational mobility patterns of college coaches. *Sociology of Work and Occupations, 5*(4), 446-469.

Massengale, J.D. (1974). Coaching as an occupational subculture. *Phi Delta Kappan, 56*(2), 140-142.

Massengale, J.D., & Farrington, S.K. (1977). The influence of playing position centrality on the careers of college football coaches. *Review of Sport and Leisure, 2*, 107-115.

McPherson, B.D. (1975). The segregation by playing position hypothesis in sport: An alternative explanation. *Social Science Quarterly, 55*, 960-966.

Medoff, M.M. (1977). Position segregation and professional baseball. *International Review of Sport Sociology, 12*(1), 49- 54.

Medoff, M.M. (1986). Positive segregation and the economic hypothesis. *Sociology of Sport Journal, 3*, 297-304.

Miller, D., & Form, W. (1964). *Industrial Sociology.* New York: Harper & Row.

Miller Brewing Company (1983). *Miller Lite report on American attitudes towards sports.* Milwaukee: Author.

Mississippi hires Gibson as 1st black head coach. *Jet* (1985, July 29), p. 46.

Mogull, R.G. (1975). Salary discrimination in major league baseball. *Review of black political economy, 5*, 269-279.

Money and fame: who reaps the rewards and benefits? *USA Today* (1991, December 18), p. 4C.

NCAA's first black head football coach is ready to tackle the pressure. *Jet* (1979, March 22), p. 48

NCAA. (1988). Summary to the survey of NCAA member institutions and conferences on minority representation. *Report to the NCAA Council Subcommittee to Review Minority Opportunities in Intercollegiate Athletics.* Mission, KS.

Nettles, M.T. (1988). *Toward black undergraduate student equality in American higher education.* Westport, CT: Greenwood Press.

Oberlander, S. (1989, April 10). University-paid membership in all-white club ignite controversy after Tennessee hires black head coach. *The Chronicle of Higher Education,* p. A33.

Oliver, M.L. (1980). Race, class and the family's orientation to mobility through sport. *Sociological Symposium 30* (Spring), 62-86.

Otto, L., & Alwin, D. (1977). Athletics, aspirations and attainments. *Sociology of Education, 42*, 102-114.

Picou, J.S. (1978). Race, athletics, achievement and educational aspirations. *The Sociological Quarterly, 19*(3),429-438.

Rehberg, R.A., & Schafer, W.S. (1968). Participation in interscholastic athletics and college expectations. *American Journal of Sociology, 63*, 732-740.

Rooney, J.R. (1974). *A geography of American sport from Cabin Creek to Anaheim.* Reading, MA: Addison Wesley Publishing Company.

Rosenberg, E. (1980). Sports as work: Characteristics and career patterns. *Sociological Symposium 30* (Spring), 39-61.

Rosenblatt, A. (1967). Negroes in baseball: The failing of success. *Transaction, 4*, 51-53.

Sage, G. (1980). Sociology of physical educator/coaches: Personal attributes controversy. *Research Quarterly for Exercise and Sport, 51*(1), 110-121.

Sage, G.H., & Loy, J.W. (1978). Geographical mobility patterns of college coaches. *Urban Life, 7*(2), 253-280.

Schneider, J.J., & Eitzen, S.D. (1979). Racial discrimination in American sport: continuity or change? *Journal of Sport Behavior, 2*, 136-142.

Schafer, W.E., & Armer, J.M. (1968, November). Athletics are not for inferior students. *Transaction, 5*, 21-26, 61-62.

Snyder, E.E., & Spreitzer, E.A. (1989). *Social Aspects of Sport* (3rd ed.). Englewood Cliffs, NJ: Prentice-Hall.

Spady, W.G. (1970). Lament for the letterman: The effects of peer status and extracurricular activities in goals and achievements. *American Journal of Sociology, 75*, 680-702.

Stacking: a widespread practice that determines who get to play where. *USA Today*, (1991, March 17), p.6C.

Stevenson, C.L. (1975). Socialization effects of participation in sports: A critical review of the research. *Research Quarterly, 46*, 287-301.

Turner, R.H. (1960). Sponsored and contest mobility in the school system. *American Sociology Review, 25*, 855-867.

University of Arkansas names black basketball coach. *Jet* (1985, April 29), p. 46.

USA Today poll shows blacks and whites often accept the same stereotype about athletes. *USA Today,* (1991, December 16), p. 1.

Watson, B.C. (1979, October). Through the academic gateway. *Change, 11*(7), 24-28.

Weiberg, S. (1991, December 17). Stereotypical notions often come into play when finding athletes. *USA Today,* p. 6C.

Williams, R.L. & Youssef, Z.I. (1975). Division of labor in college football along racial lines. *International Journal of Sport Psychology, 6*(1), 3-13.

Wulf, S. (1987). Opportunity knocks (NCAA to work for black coaches). *Sports Illustrated,* 5.

Yetman, N.R. (1987). Positional segregation and the economic hypothesis: A critique. *Sociology of Sport Journal, 4,* 274-277.

Yetman, N.R., Berghorn, F.J., & Thomas, F.R. (1982). Racial participation and integration in intercollegiate basketball, 1958-1980. *Journal of Sport Behavior, 5,* 44-56.

Essay 5

Black Student-Athletes: Reaping the Benefits or Recovering from the Exploitation

Robert M. Sellers

Abstract: The present essay examines quality of life that black student-athletes experience after their retirement from athletics. The author argues that student-athletes' life experiences on the college campus play an important role in influencing their subsequent life experiences. Specifically, former black student athletes will show more positive psychological adjustment to the extent that their university experiences offered them true educational opportunities rather than exploitation of their athletic ability and to the extent that athletes themselves took advantage of educational opportunities.

Data suggest that black student-athletes come to college with poorer academic preparation and from poorer socioeconomic backgrounds and, once enrolled, perform poorly academically. Because research literature is inclusive, this essay presents a framework by which to evaluate the quality of the educational experiences of black student-athletes. A critique of the movement within intercollegiate athletics is presented as a backdrop for a set of proposed reforms to the current system. These reforms focus on proactive measures that the NCAA, individual institutions, and black student-athletes and their families can take to enhance the educational experiences of black student-athletes.

Introduction

One of the most hotly debated arguments surrounding the black athlete focuses on the role of sports in the black community. Specifically, have sports helped or hindered the black community? Those who argue that sports have been a benefit to the black community point to the relatively colorblind nature of athletic competition. Sport is viewed as one of the few meritocracies in this country. On a football field, skin color is not as important as speed, strength, and skill level. They point to the fact that despite constituting only 13% of the population and around 4% of student body at the predominantly white Division I universities, black athletes make up 37% of the football players, 33% of the women's basketball players, and 56% of the men's basketball players (Center for the Study of Athletics, 1989). The proponents of the "sports-provide opportunities-to-the-black-community" perspective also focus their arguments on the social mobility that sports have provided those who are athletically gifted and financially smart enough to exploit the sport system. Because of the *relatively* few racist barriers in sports, barriers that are prevalent in most of the other legal avenues of social mobility in this country, they argue sports provide blacks with one of the few legal opportunities to change their station in life. Sports provide educational and career opportunities, which are often beyond the reach of some of their more academically gifted, but less athletically endowed black classmates, to black athletes from under-privileged backgrounds.

The opposing side contends that sports have exploited black athletes. This argument focuses not on the successful black athletes, but instead on those athletes who do not reap the benefits of sports participation. Opponents emphasize the extremely long odds that face any high school athlete with career aspirations of playing professional sports. For example, a black high school football player has a 1 in 43 chance of playing for a Division I college football team. His chances of playing in the National Football League (NFL) are 6,318 to 1. A black male high school basketball player has about a 1 in 130 chance of playing for a Division I basketball team and the odds are 10,345 to 1 against his playing in the National Basketball Association (NBA) (Lapchick, 1991). The supporters of the exploitation argument also point out that only 1 of 4 black Division I athletes has graduated from his or her university five years after arrival (National Collegiate Athletic Association, 1991).

Those who support the "sports-exploit-the-black-community" perspective argue that participation in sports does not enhance most black athletes' opportunity for upward social mobility. On the contrary, they argue that the lure of sports blinds too many black athletes from other, more stable, avenues up the social stratum such as academic excellence. The sports establishment benefits from the black athletes' skills and labor by providing the illusion of an opportunity at fame, fortune, and education. However, in the end, the majority of the black athletes are exploited without any measurable compensation for their service. Noted sport sociologist Harry Edwards (1979) eloquently sums up this argument:

This channeling process tragically leads millions of blacks to pursue a goal that is foredoomed to elude all but an insignificant few.... The impact of what would otherwise be personal career tragedies reverberates throughout black society both because of the tremendous proportion of black youth channeled into sport and the fact that serious sport involvement often dictates neglect of other important spheres of development. Further the skills cultivated through sport are utterly worthless beyond the sport realm.... (p. 119)

Whereas those who view sports as a positive force for the black community point to the potential benefits that can be reaped from participating in sports such as obtaining a college education and/or playing professional sports, their opposition argues that far too few black athletes receive a college education and even fewer obtain the opportunity to play professional sports.

This debate over the value of sports to the overall welfare of the black community hinges on the question of what happens to black athletes once their athletic careers end. Unfortunately, there is very little empirical work to document what actually happens to black athletes after their college careers are finished. Much of the evidence regarding the influence athletics has on the quality of life of former black college athletes is anecdotal. For example, there are the stories like Kevin Ross's (Lapchick, 1991, p. 259). Kevin Ross was a basketball player at Creighton University. Ross spent four years at Creighton as a member of the basketball team and ostensibly a member of student body. However, after his athletic eligibility was exhausted and he was unable to succeed with an NBA team, he found himself a functional illiterate with over 70 credit hours of college course work. He made national headlines by enrolling in Marva Collins' Westside Preparatory School in Chicago beginning as a fifth grader. At present,

Kevin Ross is suing Creighton University.

However, there are other stories similar to the one experienced by Thomas LaVeist (LaVeist, T., Personal Communication, 1992, March). Thomas LaVeist grew up in a rough section of Brooklyn. Although very intelligent, LaVeist never truly applied himself academically during his high school days. He was a student with "A" ability, but he performed at "C" level. He was fortunate enough to receive a football scholarship from the University of Maryland-Eastern Shore. While at UMES, LaVeist became a more diligent student. He went on to receive a Ph.D. in medical sociology. Today, Dr. Thomas LaVeist is a very successful professor at The Johns Hopkins University School of Public Health as well as the president of The Alexandria Consortium, a prominent consulting firm. Dr. LaVeist credits a much of his success to the educational opportunity he received. Because of his poor high school academic record and his family's financial situation, he would never have been able to go to college without an athletic scholarship.

Unfortunately, we do not know which ending is most typical of the athletic experience of the black athlete. Does participation in college athletics provide black student-athletes with the opportunity for an education, or does it exploit their physical skills without providing fair compensation? This is the central question of the present essay. In general, the quality of life for black student-athletes will be better if they have received a college education than if they participate in college athletics without receiving a fair opportunity for an education. In order to address this question properly, the present essay will also examine a number of other relevant questions. Are the life experiences of black student-athletes unique? What does the research literature say about the influence of athletic participation on the quality of life of former black student-athletes? What should black student-athletes reasonably expect to receive as compensation for their athletic services? How will the current reform movement within intercollegiate athletics affect the quality of postathletic life for black student-athletes? What can be done to improve the quality of black student-athletes' postathletic lives?

First, I will provide a brief description of the black student-athlete at NCAA Division I schools. Next, I will briefly review the relevant research that has focused on athletic retirement as well as on race differences in career aspiration. Then, I will present a framework by which to evaluate whether a college student-athlete is provided equitable compensation for participation in intercollegiate athletics, followed by a discussion of the current reform movement within the NCAA and its impact on the postathletic career of the black student-athlete. Finally, I will present some recommendations that I feel will provide the black athlete with a better opportunity to maximize his collegiate experience.

Before I begin to address these issues, it is important that I provide an overview of my perspective on the black athlete. Any analysis of the life experience of the black athlete must view the black student-athlete as both a unique entity as well as a composite of other related groups of students. At first glance this perspective may seem paradoxical. However, any meaningful investigation of the black student-athlete must be aware of both the similarities and differences in the life experiences of black student-athletes as compared to those of all student-athletes and all black college students. The life experiences of these analogous groups should be used as a point of reference, not as an evaluative yardstick. Black student-athletes' experiences can only be evaluated from their own world-view. Black student-athletes also do not exist in a vacuum. They are a function of their environment. Thus, one should also be aware of the societal context and its influence on black student-athletes' life experiences before, during, and after their college athletic careers are over.

The major premise of the present essay is that the quality of black student-athletes' postathletic lives is significantly influenced by the extent to which their college experience was one of opportunity or exploitation. Because of the lack of systematic evidence on the processes involved in the postathletic adjustment of black student-athletes, the present essay will avoid the temptation to develop a model based on idiosyncratic anecdotes. Instead, the focus will be on ways to enhance the educational experiences of black student-athletes during their stay in college with the assumption that these experiences will have a positive influence on the quality of postathletic life.

Black Student-Athletes: Experiences and World View

Black student-athletes represent unique entities on our college campuses. They often come from backgrounds that are very different from those of the rest of the student body. Moreover, black student-athletes are different from the two student constituencies with whom they share the most in common, white student-athletes and black nonathletic students (Selle.s, Kuperminc, & Waddell, 1991). Whereas the median black enrollment of black students at Division I universities is approximately 4%, blacks constitute approximately 12% of the student-athlete population. Interestingly, the proportion of black student-athletes roughly corresponds with the proportion of blacks in the overall population (13%). The problem is not that blacks are overrepresented in college athletics; the problem is that black students are underrepresented in college.

In one of the few studies to focus specifically on the unique college experiences of black student-athletes, Sellers and his colleagues (1991) compared black student-athletes to white student-athletes and other black college students on four important areas: Demographic and Academic Background, College Life Experiences, Mental Health, and Social Support. The data came from a national, representative survey of black and white student-athletes in revenue-producing sports (football, and men's and women's basketball) at 42 NCAA Division I schools. The study also surveyed a random sample of nonathletic black students from these same institutions. The study found interesting differences between black student-athletes and both comparison groups across all four domains.

One important finding was that black student-athletes enter college with educational and sociocultural backgrounds very different from those of both white student-athletes and other black students. They come from families that have significantly lower incomes and that are headed by less educated parents. Once enrolled, black student-athletes perform worse than their counterparts (Ervin, Saunders, Gillis, & Hogrebe, 1985; Kiger & Lorentzen, 1986; Purdy, Eitzen, & Hufnagel, 1982; Sellers, 1992; Shapiro, 1984). With regard to academic performance, the average black student-athlete hovers perilously close to the NCAA minimum requirements for initial eligibility (average SAT score of 753; score of 700 necessary for eligibility). This trend continues after entering college (average GPA of 2.14; GPA of 2.00 necessary for eligibility).

Broadly stated, the college life of black student-athletes more closely resembles that of white student-athletes than of other black students (Sellers et al., 1991). Black and white student-athletes do not differ in the importance they ascribe to earning a degree, their satisfaction with their relationship with coaches, and their overall satisfaction with life. For the most part, black and white student-athletes also perceive similar levels of difficulty with achieving personal growth as a result of athletics. However, black student-athletes feel that it is easier to become more assertive as a result of being an athlete. Black student-athletes seem to be aware of the increased status that is accorded them as a result of being an athlete. This elevated status often results in their having greater and more familiar access to influential alumni and university officials. At the same time, their relationships with other black students (who may have the least access to important individuals within the university) make black student-athletes more conscious than white student-athletes of their opportunities to be assertive. Black student-athletes are more likely to report experiencing racial isolation than are white student-athletes. This finding is consistent with the reported increase in overt racism on campuses and the racial make-up of most universities. However, black student-athletes reported feeling less different as a result of being athletes than did their white counterparts. Although these last two findings seem contradictory, they are actually complementary. Because they are more likely to experience racial isolation, black student-athletes may be attributing their feelings of being different more to the fact that they are black and less to the fact that they are athletes. For black student-athletes, being black makes them different from the mainstream. But being a student-athlete provides them with some privileges that are not experienced by the average white student.

Sellers (1991) also found important differences in the college experiences for black student-athletes and other black students. Black student-athletes seem to feel that their college experience is more worthwhile and more satisfying than do other black students. This may be as much an indicator of the social difficulties that many black students experience at predominantly white colleges as it is a measure of the quality of the black student-athlete's college experiences (Allen, 1988). Although both groups are highly motivated to obtain a degree, black student-athletes perceive greater personal growth from being an athlete than black students perceive from being students (Sellers et al., 1991). Black student-athletes also reported feeling less racial isolation than do other black students. The study attributed this finding to the possibility that black student-athletes' enhanced status as athletes provides them with opportunities to socialize with people who are inaccessible to other black students. Thus, it may be easier for black student-athletes to interact with white students from very different backgrounds because of their status as athletes. White students are more likely to make an effort to get to know the black student-athlete than they would be for a nonathletic black student.

Black student-athletes also differ from white student-athletes and other black students with regard to their mental health. As the result of historical experiences with powerful others and cultural influences, in general, blacks are more likely to perceive an external locus of control than whites (Gurin, Gurin, & Morrison, 1978). Black student-athletes are also more likely to attribute their locus of control to external factors such as luck and powerful others than are other black students (Sellers et al., 1991). The study attributed this finding to the fact that college athletes' lives actually are more externally controlled than are the lives of most college students. The study also found that black student-athletes reported more depressive symptoms than did white student-athletes. (However, the scores for both groups were not high enough to signal clinical depression.)

With regard to social support, the study found that black student-athletes are less likely than white student-athletes to report that they have someone to talk to about their problems. Black and white student-athletes also differ in the groups of people with whom they are most likely to discuss their problems. Black student-athletes are less likely to discuss their problems with peers (teammates, other students, and other friends) and more likely to talk with an academic advisor. The study concluded that the relative social distance that black student-athletes report from their teammates and other students on campus may be a function of sociocultural background differences. The greater utilization of, and contact with, the academic advisor for emotional support may be a function of black student-athletes' poorer academic performances, which may in turn lead to greater contact with academic advisors. While black student-athletes and other black students are more similar in their perception of overall emotional support, the structure of that support does differ. Black student-athletes are less likely than other black students to talk to peers (other students and friends) and are more likely than other black students to receive support from loved ones who are not on campus (parents and siblings).

Black student-athletes' reliance on off-campus support interacts with their socioeconomic background to place them at greater risk. Black student-athletes come from poorer families, and their support systems are more likely to be located away from campus. Thus, it is more difficult for them to personally access their support systems. This problem is exacerbated by the fact that NCAA rules forbid athletes from working during the school year. Yet the NCAA does not permit universities to provide athletes with any money beyond tuition, room, and board. Another potential problem for black student-athletes is that although their support networks may be very effective in providing emotional support, they may have more difficulty obtaining instrumental support. Instrumental support refers to the type of support such as information that helps the individual to solve the problem. In the case of problems associated with being a college student, oftentimes instrumental support can be provided only by a person who has had some college experience. It would be difficult for someone without any college experience to advise a student interested in medical school on whether to major in premed or biology. Because the average black student-athlete has parents who have never attended college and is more likely to seek support from parents, she or he is often limited in the type of support that these networks are able to provide (Sellers et al., 1991). The NCAA must look at developing legislation that will provide a means by which black student-athletes may access their support systems more frequently. For example, the NCAA could subsidize an annual visit home. On the other hand, universities must also be aware of the potential of inadequate educational experiences from some black student-athletes' support networks. The universities should make every effort to provide black student-athletes with access to persons who have the experiences necessary to provide instrumental support.

Tracking the Problem

As stated earlier, there is a dearth of empirical studies that have specifically documented what happens to black student-athletes once their athletic careers are completed. However, there are two areas of studies that may aid in providing a glimpse of what former black student-athletes may be experiencing. First, there is a growing literature that has investigated the retirement process of student-athletes in general. This literature examines the psychological consequences associated with the end of an athlete's sport career. The second area of study has focused on the relationship between athletic participation and career attainment. This area of research typically examines differences between athletes and nonathletes on such direct measures of career attainment as postathletic career occupation as well as such indirect measures as career aspirations and academic performance. The main emphasis in this area of research is on the impact that being a student-athlete has on the person's social status later in life.

Athletic Retirement and Psychological Adjustment

The research literature has approached retirement from sport from the perspective that sport retirement leads to a significant adjustment within the life of the student-athlete (Danish, 1983; Harris & Eitzen, 1978; Lerch, 1982). The quality of the athlete's adjustment is influenced by whether the athlete was forced to retire or voluntarily retired from his or her sport. In general, athletes whose athletic careers ended abruptly because of such things as career-ending injuries report less satisfaction than those who were able to complete their athletic careers without an unexpected disruption (Kleiber, Greendorfer, Blinde, & Samdahl, 1987). Harris and Eitzen (1978) suggest that those individuals who feel that their athletic careers end as a result of their own failure are at a greater risk of having problems adjusting to life after athletics. They argue that such an experience can damage the individual's athletic self-esteem. This damage may be especially extensive and pervasive if the individual's athletic self-esteem is central to his or her overall self-concept. Thus, "the consequences of failure for an athlete who intends to be an athletic success and has no alternative can be quite serious." (Harris & Eitzen, 1978, p. 185)

Other research suggests that for many former student-athletes the adjustment to life after an athletic career is not particularly difficult. Greendorfer and Blinde (1985) surveyed 1,123 former male and female athletes from the Big Ten conference on their experiences during their athletic career, their postathletic career sport participation, and their adjustment to sport retirement. The majority of their sample did not report experiencing any long-lasting emotional hardship as a result of the completion of their sports career. The study paints a picture in which most student-athletes adjust to life after their athletic career by slowly de-emphasizing the importance of athletics in their lives while continuing to participate in athletic activities. This pattern does not seem to differ for either men or women. Coakley (1983) has even suggested that retirement from sport may actually be a rebirth. It may allow an athlete the opportunity to pursue other activities and roles that had to be sacrificed or de-emphasized as a consequence of the demands associated with being a college athlete. Retirement from an athletic career may also signal the end of an unpleasant association with a coach or a teammate. It is not uncommon for college athletes to talk about how much their college athletic experience differs from their high school experience. Often they perceive this change as being for the worse.

Unfortunately, the research literature on the psychological consequences of athletic retirement has several conceptual shortcomings that severely limit our understanding of postathletic life for black athletes. First, the research literature has conceptualized postathletic retirement as a monolithic event with all athletes having similar reasons for their participation in athletics. It is assumed that all athletes participate in intercollegiate athletics because of their love for the sport. Such an assumption overlooks those student-athletes who view participation in college athletics as an experience that is tolerated in exchange for an opportunity for an education. Another limitation of the research literature is that it has ignored possible influences of race and socioeconomic status on adjustment. A number of authors have argued that there are race and socioeconomic status differences in the orientation to sport so that athletics are more central for blacks from poorer backgrounds than for middle-class whites (Cashmore, 1982; Eitzen & Tessendorf, 1978; Snyder & Spreitzer; 1978). Such cultural and structural differences in sport orientation suggest that there should be similar cultural and structural differences in postathletic career adjustment. However, to date there is little evidence either to support or refute this hypothesis.

Along with the conceptual shortcomings, the research literature on the psychological consequences also suffers from methodological limitations. Most of the research has utilized retrospective techniques to assess changes in individuals' perceptions of their athletic experience and adjustment. In other words, the former athletes are asked questions in the present about what their perceptions of their experiences were at a previous point in time when they were athletes. Such techniques are vulnerable to distortions and deficits in the subject's memory, as well as to the possibility of the athletes' providing responses that make them appear more favorable. Another limitation of many of these studies is their failure to use representative samples of student-athletes, which makes generalizing the findings beyond the samples in the studies very tenuous. Finally, the lack of clarity and uniformity in the definition of such concepts as athletic retirement, psychological adjustment, and life satisfaction has resulted in the use of imprecise measures of these concepts. In order for this research literature to progress in a meaningful manner, researchers must develop more sophisticated models of retirement. These models should be sensitive to differences in athletic experience and orientation that are the result of such demographic factors as the athlete's race, gender, and socioeconomic status.

Athletic Participation and Career Attainment

Another area of relevant research is the literature on the influence of athletic participation on career attainment. Over the past 20 years, a number of studies have attempted to determine whether participating in athletics enhances or detracts from the athlete's subsequent career status. Do athletics build skills and provide opportunities that translate into success outside of the playing field? Or do the role demands of being an athlete exact a toll on preparation and performance in other domains outside athletics? The research in this area has taken two approaches in investigating this link. These approaches consist of studies that have tried to (a) examine a direct association between athletic participation and career attainment and (b) examine an indirect association between athletic participation and career attainment through intermediate processes such as educational and career aspirations and academic performance.

The literature that has analyzed the direct relationship between athletic participation and subsequent career status has been somewhat inconclusive. In his extensive review of the literature regarding race, sport, and social mobility, Braddock (1980) delineates two opposing hypotheses within the literature. The *sport-enhances-mobility* hypothesis argues that traditionally sport has served as a vehicle to social mobility for minority groups. The *sport-impedes-mobility* hypothesis argues that the deceitful allure of an athletic career with its truncated career options has blinded minority groups from other more viable career paths. Braddock noted that both hypotheses assume that lower class minority youths would place greater importance on sport than would white middle-class youths. Interestingly, Braddock (1980) presented little empirical evidence to support the notion that blacks place more importance on athletics than do whites. In fact, he cited evidence that suggests that younger white males may actually place a greater value on sport (Hurtsfield, 1978). However, with regard to the present essay, the most relevant finding of his review was that of the 16 studies that investigated the direct relationship between sport participation and occupational attainment, only 1 study found that nonathletes obtained higher status occupation, and 3 studies found that athletes obtained higher status occupations. The other 12 studies found no statistically significant difference between the two groups. It should be noted, however, that 7 of the 12 studies found a statistically nonsignificant relationship for athletes obtaining higher career status.

Braddock's (1980) review of the research, focusing on the influence of athletic participation on the intermediate process of social mobility, suggests that there may be moderate support for the notion that athletics have a positive influence on educational and occupational aspirations. Of the 25 studies that examined educational and occupational attainment, 19 (6 statistically significant) yielded differences that favored athletic participation. This is in contrast to only 2 studies that yielded statistically nonsignificant differences in support of nonathletes. For example, Picou (1978) examined the achievement behaviors and social mobility attitudes of 691 male athletes and 838 male nonathletes from a representative sample of Louisiana high school seniors. Picou found that participation in athletics was associated with higher educational aspirations. He also found significant race differences in his results. For black students, there was a direct association between athletic participation and educational aspirations. On the other hand, for white student-athletes, Picou found the association was mediated by a college-oriented peer group. White student-athletes were more likely to interact with a college oriented peer group, which in turn was associated with higher educational aspirations.

Growing evidence that suggests that participation in intercollegiate athletics, in at least some sports, is associated with poorer academic performance. Purdy et al. (1982) examined the academic potential and performance of more than two thousand student-athletes from the Western Athletic Conference across a ten-year period. They found that student-athletes came to college with significantly lower academic credentials and performed more poorly as students while there. In contrast, Shapiro (1984) studied the graduation rates at Michigan State University (MSU) from 1950 to 1980 and found that MSU athletes graduated at a rate similar or superior to that of MSU nonathletes. However, recent evidence released by the NCAA strongly suggests that academically, athletes are not performing as well as nonathletes.

In 1986, the Center for the Study of Athletics at the American Institutes for Research (AIR) was commissioned by the Presidents' Commission of the NCAA to survey student-athletes at 42 Division I universities. In their initial report, the Center for the Study of Athletics (1988) found that student-athletes had lower college GPAs than a sample of students who participated in 20 or more hours of extracurricular activities. Black student-athletes had lower GPAs than both white student-athletes and other black nonathletes (Center for the Study of Athletics, 1989; Sellers, et al., 1991). Recently, the NCAA reported results from a five-year study of the graduation rates of Division I student-athletes (National Collegiate Athletic Association, 1991). The analysis of the graduation rates for the first cohort of student-athletes revealed that only 46% of the student-athletes in the sample had graduated five years after first enrolling in college. Within that group, white student athletes graduated at about twice the rate (52.3%) of black student-athletes (26.6%).

As one can see, the findings in the research literature focusing on the links between athletic participation and career attainment are rather complex. It seems that athletic participation in high school may be positively associated with indicators of upward social mobility (e.g., Picou, 1978). On the other hand, participation in intercollegiate athletics is associated with poorer academic performance (e.g., Purdy et al., 1982). There also appear to be race differences in the relationship between athletic participation and career attainment. Unfortunately, limitations in the studies make any firm conclusions about this literature precarious. Prospective longitudinal designs are needed before any firm conclusions regarding the causal relationship between athletic participation and career attainment can be made. Subsequent research is also needed that uses large representative samples of both athletes and nonathletes from as similar backgrounds as possible and that follows them throughout their high school, college, and postcollege years. Such research is quite expensive and time consuming. However, it is the kind of research that is necessary to enhance our understanding of these phenomena.

Framing Educational Opportunity: When is the Check Cashed?

One objective of this essay is to evaluate whether black student-athletes receive fair compensation for their participation in sport. If black student-athletes are receiving fair compensation, then athletics constitute a valuable opportunity. On the other hand, if they are not receiving fair compensation then black student-athletes are being exploited. The assumption here is that the exploitation of black student-athletes results in their experiencing negative psychological, social, and financial adjustments to life after sports. In order to evaluate accurately the fairness of the exchange between black student-athletes and their university, a set of expectations to be met by both parties must be developed. With regard to their obligation to the university, black student-athletes must participate in athletics fully with a commitment to excel to the best of their abilities. In return for black student-athletes' commitment to athletic excellence, the university is obligated to provide them with a reasonable opportunity to receive a college education.

One should note that I argue for the opportunity for a college education, not for a college education itself. The most that a university can provide a student is the opportunity for an education. Ultimately, it is the individual's responsibility to take advantage of the opportunity. Nonetheless, it is the university's obligation to provide any support service that will enhance the black student-athletes' chances of receiving a college education. These services include appropriate academic support programs and career counseling. (I will discuss this point in greater detail later in the essay.) The university must also insure that the student-athlete will have the time necessary to pursue an education. During the season, student-athletes in the revenue-producing sports spend more time participating in sport-related activities than they do preparing and attending class (Center for the Study of Athletics, 1988). This is analogous to giving athletes a generous check for their athletic services but prohibiting them from going to the bank to cash it. Although the athletes have something of great value in their possession, it is worthless to them because they are unable to convert it to usable currency.

It should also be noted that I argue for the opportunity for a college education and not a college degree. The two are not synonymous. A degree is a necessary, but insufficient, element of a college education. Not all individuals who receive degrees from accredited universities receive college educations. There are three elements to a college education that are important to black student-athletes: (a) the refinement of personal competence, (b) the upward social mobility, and (c) the earning of a degree. All three elements of a college education are important to all student-athletes; however, the last two elements are especially significant for black student-athletes.

College life consists of numerous experiences that help students to develop personal competence. Most of these experiences occur outside of the classroom. Student-athletes may have a head start over other college students with regard to personal competence. Danish (1983) argues that participating in athletics leads to experiences that may enhance personal competence. Personal competence consists of both interpersonal skills and intrapersonal skills (Danish, Galambos, & Laqquatra, 1983). Interpersonal skills can be simply defined as the individual's ability to relate well with others. Such skills are important in the obtaining of social support and the projection of a positive image of oneself to others. Interpersonal skills allow one to win friends and influence people. The novel experience of entering college forces freshmen to develop new social networks without the aid or hindrance of their previous social networks and reputations. On the other hand, intrapersonal skills refer to those skills associated with the development and successful completion of tasks important to the overall success and well-being of the individual. Intrapersonal skills associated with personal competence include goal setting, knowledge acquisition, risk taking, self-confidence, and self-discipline. Such collegiate activities as writing a research paper, being active in a student organization, and planning for one's career help to develop intrapersonal competence skills.

Also, the lack of structure in college forces students to be responsible for their own actions, which in turn hones their intrapersonal skills.

A college education should also provide an opportunity for upward social mobility. Black student-athletes come to college from poorer socioeconomic backgrounds than those of both other white student-athletes and other black college students at their schools (Sellers et al., 1991). Average black student-athletes are also likely to be the first generation within their families to receive a college education. A college education can lead to upward social mobility for black student-athletes in two ways. First, the skills and the credentials associated with having attended college provide black student-athletes with greater access to higher status career opportunities. The second way in which it may enhance upward mobility for the black student-athlete involves exposure. Black student-athletes on a college campus are often exposed to numerous career options that they never knew existed. For example, a student-athlete with an aptitude for drawing who has her mind set on becoming an architect may become exposed to a number of careers such as drafting or graphic design that she may find more appealing. College is also a setting in which black student-athletes can form social relationships that may lead to career advancement in the future. The business world is replete with examples of successful partnerships forged from college friendships.

The final element of a college education that is important to black student-athletes is obtaining a college degree. More than anything else, a college degree is, and has always been, a credential of achievement rather than a certification of competence. Traditionally, a college degree was a ticket to "the good life." Ironically, opportunities for obtaining college degrees were usually reserved for those persons whose family were already living the good life. Those few individuals from less educated families who were somehow able to go to college and earn a degree greatly enhanced their social and financial status. In the past, a college degree was a great advantage in earning a good living, but it was not a requirement for earning one. Today, with the technological advances in the work force, a college degree no longer means the same thing as it did 15 years ago. It is no longer an advantage in today's labor market. It is a necessity. There are fewer viable opportunities for noncollege- educated persons to earn an income sufficient enough to support a family. Although the skills that black student-athletes learn in college may or may not transfer to the performance of their jobs, the college degree is often required for them to get hired in the first place.

Black student-athletes who have fulfilled their athletic commitment to the university have the right to expect the university to provide them with the opportunity to develop personal competence, improve their social status, and earn a degree. In order for a university to live up to its end of the commitment, it must provide an environment that enhances black student-athletes' chances for success. Paramount to that success is the balance between institutional support and personal freedom and responsibility. Later in this essay, I discuss some recommendations for building such an environment. However, we will examine next the direction taken by the current reform movement within intercollegiate athletics.

The Current Reform Movement Within Intercollegiate Athletics
Over the past 10 years, influenced in part by a number of embarrassing and tragic incidents, a reform movement has swept through intercollegiate athletics. These incidents include point-shaving scandals at Tulane and Boston College, the NCAA's suspension of the football program at Southern Methodist University, the drug-related death of Len Bias and the ensuing investigation of the University of Maryland basketball program, and the academic indiscretions of such schools as the University of Iowa and Temple University during the trial of sports agents Nordby and Walsh, as well as the stunning evidence of violations associated with the University of Oklahoma football program. In 1988, the University of Oklahoma football team was placed on three years probation for "major violations" including offering money and cars to recruits. Since their probation a number of other incidents have occurred including: three players being charged with raping a women in the athletic dorm; one player shooting another player during an argument; and still another player being convicted of distributing cocaine (Telander & Sullivan, 1989). Incidents such as these have left big-time college athletics with a major image problem. The negative publicity has forced university presidents to get involved with the management of their athletic programs. Until recently, university presidents were content to delegate their responsibility for intercollegiate athletics to their athletic directors. At many institutions, it was as if the athletic department had become a separate entity from the rest of the university. Indeed, some athletic departments became corporations in hopes of increasing their money-making potential. With the athletic programs' increasingly negative publicity tarnishing the reputation of the entire university, the presidents were forced to get involved. Thus, the NCAA's Presidents Commission

was formed in the early 1980s. The organization's expressed goal has been to reform the current structure of intercollegiate athletics. The reform movement as led by the Presidents Commission has focused on a number of areas within the governance of intercollegiate athletics from institutional control to cost containment. However, the movement's most visible reforms have come from its efforts to restore academic integrity to intercollegiate athletics.

Recent NCAA conventions have been testaments to the Presidents Commission's commitment to reform. In 1989, the NCAA passed legislation (Proposition 42) that eliminated the partial qualifier from Proposition 48. Proposition 48 stated that potential student-athletes had to obtain a high school GPA of 2.0 in a set of 12 core curriculum courses as well as at least a 700 combined score on the SAT to be eligible to participate in athletics during their first year. Potential student-athletes who met only one of the requirements were considered partial qualifiers and were ruled ineligible to compete during their first year. However, the partial qualifier was allowed to receive an athletic scholarship. As originally stated, Proposition 42 would not allow partial qualifiers to receive any financial assistance in their first year. (Proposition 42 was revised in 1990 to allow the partial qualifier to receive need- based financial aid). In 1991, the NCAA also passed legislation that would limit to 20 hours a week the amount of time an athlete can participate in activities related to their sport. In 1992, the NCAA passed legislation that will further raise the initial eligibility requirements of Proposition 42 by implementing a sliding scale for the high school GPA and SAT requirements. Now, a potential student-athlete with a 2.0 high school GPA in a set of 15 core curriculum courses will have to earn a score of 900 on his SAT in order to be eligible to receive an athletic scholarship. Also, a potential student-athlete with a 700 SAT score must have a 2.5 high school GPA in order to be eligible.

Black student-athletes have been affected more by the present reform movement than has any other group. Black student-athletes score significantly lower than their white counterparts on the SAT and ACT (Center for the Study of Athletics, 1989). In a study conducted by the NCAA in 1984, two years before Proposition 48 went into effect, it was reported that 54% of black male athletes and 48% of black female athletes who attended and subsequently graduated from the surveyed institutions would have been disqualified from freshman eligibility by the standardized test requirement (NCAA, 1984). Meanwhile, only 9% of the white male and female athletes would have suffered the same fate. Similarly,

Walter, Smith, Hoey, and Wilhelm (1987) reported that 60% of the black football players at the University of Michigan from 1974-83 would not have been eligible under Propositions 48 and 42. Further, they found that 87% of those black football players who would have been excluded under Propositions 48 and 42 actually graduated.

On the surface the goal of restoring academic integrity in intercollegiate athletics is a noble one. Unfortunately, the reform movement has adopted a strategy that assumes that the problem regarding student-athletes' relatively poor academic performance resides in student-athletes' poor academic preparation prior to arriving to college. The movement's current strategy also assumes that the reasons for the poor academic preparation is that many student-athletes are not sufficiently motivated to achieve academically. The student-athletes value athletics more than they do academics. Thus, by raising the initial eligibility requirements of student-athletes, the reform movement argues that it is sending a message to potential student-athletes that they must do a better job academically if they want to play college athletics. Supporters of the current reform movement have also argued that these increases in initial eligibility standards will send a message to the secondary school systems throughout the country that they must also do a better job of educating high school athletes. Surprisingly, little research has investigated the role of motivation in the academic performance of student-athletes. What little evidence that does exist suggests that an overwhelming majority of student-athletes value a college education (Center for the Study of Athletics, 1988; 1989) and that at least for black student-athletes academic motivation is not a predictor of subsequent academic performance (Sellers, 1992).

The current direction of the movement is based on erroneous premises and does nothing to address the real problems that are influencing the relatively poor academic performance of student-athletes. The student-athletes' lack of motivation is not the problem. The current movement takes an unnecessarily exclusionary approach that will lead to deleterious consequences for black student-athletes. The poor academic preparation of many black student-athletes can be traced to the current state of the public education systems in our inner cities. For example, the Chicago public school system, which is 68% black, has an overall dropout rate of 40%. Meanwhile its neighbor to the north, Evanston, has a dropout rate of approximately 3% (Harrison, 1991). The national high school dropout rate is approximately 12%. Clearly, there is a great deal of variance between the educational experiences of students in our inner cities and those students who live just a few miles away in the suburbs. The current reform movement does not begin to address this societal problem, which is adversely affecting the life chances of far too many potential black college students and student-athletes. The present legislation on initial eligibility requirements does nothing to alleviate these discrepancies in educational preparation. The present legislation does not provide the school system in Gary, Indiana, with funds to help offset the fact that it spends 38% less per student than does the public school system in Evanston (Harrison, 1991). Yet, the present NCAA legislation views the educational opportunities of students from the Gary and Chicago public school systems as being equal to the educational opportunities of students coming from the Evanston public school system.

Black student-athletes are not only coming from poorer socioeconomic backgrounds, but they may also be coming to college from poorer school districts. They may represent a number of other black students trapped in deplorable educational systems for whom a college education is not a workable option. Given the frightening state of affairs associated with our inner-city schools, these black students are not likely to meet the criteria for college admission if those criteria are based on the academic performance of students who are coming from superior educational environments. One might suspect that universities with a surplus of applicants for admission would show an interest in only those individuals from poorer educational backgrounds who have skills that are unique and valuable, individuals such as the athlete. Nonathletic students from the same high school who have performed better academically than their athletic classmates may not have as many educational opportunities because they do not possess skills that the universities value. The poor reputation of their high schools undermines the black nonathletic students' chances of being admitted to college. Thus, the problem of the relatively poor performance of black student-athletes is not one of focusing too much on athletics. In fact, their athletic achievement may actually have provided them with an educational opportunity that would not have otherwise existed if they were not athletes. In actuality, the black student-athlete is the only connection between the postsecondary school system and the problems of the inner-city educational system. The reform movement would be better served to adopt more inclusive policies regarding initial eligibility and focus more on enhancing the black student-athletes' educational experiences once they are on campus.

Recommendations and Solutions

Before recommending possible interventions that will enhance the quality of postathletic life for black student-athletes, it is important to keep in mind the major premise of the present essay. The quality of black student-athletes' lives after sports is directly influenced by the quality of their experiences in college, which in turn, is a function of the quality of the education that they received. If an athlete receives a quality education then she or he is more apt to have a productive and positive postathletic experience. On the other hand, if an athlete does not receive a college education then she or he is at greater risk for a poorer quality of life. One should remember that a college education consists of the opportunity to develop personal competency, to move up the socioeconomic ladder, and to receive a degree. Clearly, there are exceptions to this premise. Perhaps the most obvious exceptions are those athletes who leave college without a degree to play professional athletics and are fortunate enough to use that experience to gain some of the same benefits associated with a college education. However, this is a rather rare occurrence. Very few athletes succeed professionally. Too many of those who do, do not learn the personal competence skills necessary to lead productive lives outside sports. In general, black student-athletes who receive an opportunity for a college education are going to be better prepared for life after athletics than are those black student-athletes who did not receive that opportunity. Thus, the following recommendations focus on interventions directed at black student-athletes' educational experiences during their tenure in college.

The problems facing black student-athletes in their efforts to get a college education are quite complex and need solutions that are sensitive to these complexities. For some black student-athletes, many of their academic problems stem from inferior academic preparation in the elementary and secondary school systems. This problem is not unique to the black student-athlete. It is one that affects most of the students who are educated in these dilapidated systems. The black student-athlete just happens to have skills that are coveted by universities. Another problem facing many black student-athletes is the cruel irony that besides having poorer academic preparation, they also have to participate in an activity (athletics) that is comparable to working a full-time job. Add to this the fact that they are coming from very different backgrounds and experiences, and it is easy to understand why many black student-athletes report feeling as if they are strangers in a strange land. There are various influences that affect black student-athletes' educational opportunities. These influences exist at a number of levels including the societal level, the institutional level, the departmental level, and the individual level. A presentation of recommendations to address societal influences is beyond the scope of the present essay. It is sufficient to say that the decay of our public school systems adversely affects the educational opportunities of many black student-athletes. Instead, the following are recommendations that are designed to improve the quality of black student-athletes' postathletic lives by enhancing their educational opportunity while they are in college. These recommendations are addressed to the following constituencies: researchers in sport sociology and psychology, the NCAA, individual institutions, and the black student-athlete and her or his family. Most of these recommendations would be beneficial to all student-athletes, but are especially proposed with black student-athletes in mind.

Recommendations for Researchers in
Sport Sociology and Sport Psychology

As stated earlier, there has been very little empirical documentation of what happens to most black student-athletes after their playing days are over. Researchers in sport sociology and sport psychology must begin to build a systematic body of literature that addresses this issue. This literature must be sensitive to the unique life experiences of black student-athletes when investigating possible factors that predict successful adjustment. Researchers that use control groups of nonathletes to examine the effects of athletic participation on the career achievement of black student-athletes must be sure that their control group is an appropriate one. Because many black student-athletes are coming from very different backgrounds from even other black college students, it is more appropriate to use a control group of the student-athletes' high school peers. Future studies must also employ longitudinal designs in order to provide a better understanding of the different processes black student-athletes undergo during their adjustment to life after athletics. How traumatic is the ending of an athletic career for black student-athletes? Is the adjustment to life after athletics a gradual one? What variables mediate the success of this adjustment? These are all-important questions that can best be studied within a longitudinal design.

Finally, researchers must also understand that black student-athletes are a heterogeneous group. Black student-athletes vary with regard to gender and socioeconomic differences. Analyses of these differences should not simply be parcelled out, but fully investigated. They should be studied as contributors of important information. Thus, the postathletic career adjustment of black student-athletes is a topic worthy of study, in itself, without other comparison groups to provide texture.

Recommendations for the NCAA

It is obvious to even the casual observer that intercollegiate athletics are in need of reform. However, it is imperative that reformers such as the Presidents Commission of the NCAA focus less on solutions that are designed to regain the public's confidence in intercollegiate athletics and focus more on developing a system that will actually promote the educational mission of the colleges themselves. The NCAA should place greater emphasis on developing strategies that will provide student-athletes with the greatest opportunity to receive college educations while they are on campus. Less emphasis should be placed on legislation that focuses on student-athletes' academic preparation prior to college. The NCAA has no influence over the quality of the elementary and secondary school systems. The organization would be better served to focus its energies on enhancing the quality of the educational experience being provided by colleges, institutions over which the NCAA has some jurisdiction. The following recommendations are made in concert with this perspective.

First, the NCAA should adopt legislation that requires competent academic support systems for all student-athletes (Sellers et al., 1991). The NCAA should regulate these support programs. Although academic support programs for student-athletes are fairly widespread, many of them provide very little educational benefit to the student-athlete. Many of them are supervised by underqualified individuals such as assistant coaches and graduate students. Dick Schultz, the Executive Director of the NCAA, has advocated the implementation of an accreditation process for athletic departments whereby they would have to meet a set of criteria before the NCAA would recognize the athletic department. Within such an accreditation process, the NCAA should include a thorough evaluation of the academic support programs for the student-athletes. Second, the NCAA must enforce its newly passed legislation restricting the amount of time to 20 hours per week that student-athletes may spend involved with activities related to their sport. This increase in free time will provide the student-athletes with a greater opportunity to interact with other students as well as time to complete their course work.

Thirdly, the NCAA should make all student-athletes ineligible to participate as freshmen. Currently, at some schools freshman football players play in three games before ever attending their first class. Most freshmen would benefit from a year to adjust to college life without the added pressure of athletic competition. Freshman ineligibility would greatly enhance the academic potential of those black student-athletes who are coming from academically impaired backgrounds by allowing them to take courses that teach basic study skills. Athletic programs should grant five-year scholarships that allow student-athletes to compete intercollegiately during the last four years. At many institutions, most nonathletic students take five years or more to graduate anyway. During their freshman year, student-athletes should be allowed to participate in athletic related activities for only 15 hours per week. Fifteen hours per week is 5 hours less than the new NCAA time limit for all student-athletes. The 5-hour difference per week in athletic participation roughly corresponds to the amount of time team sports spend watching film of an upcoming opponent.

Finally, the NCAA must take a more inclusive stance regarding admissions of student-athletes. I argue that such an approach would not undermine the academic integrity of our institutions of higher education. In fact, educating those student-athletes who come from disadvantaged backgrounds enhances rather than erodes academic integrity. It is the mission of most public universities to provide community service, and an important part of that mission is to provide access to educational opportunities for those who have been historically denied access. Public institutions are also responsible for educating citizens to help them become productive members of society. If America is to continue to compete effectively in the next century it is clear that it is going to have to do a much better job of preparing its human resources. However, the most important argument for educating those student-athletes is that it is the mission of all institutions of higher education to pursue understanding and knowledge. Individuals from diverse backgrounds provide a valuable resource to that pursuit. Their unique life experiences provide important new perspectives on the theoretical and applied problems that face academia today. Thus, the emphasis in reform should not be to eliminate those individuals who "do not belong" in college, but instead to provide those same individuals with the best opportunity to succeed.

Anyone who has seen a playbook from any college football team would have to admit that it must take a great deal of intelligence and motivation to master it. Unlike in the classroom, where scoring 90% earns the student-athlete a spot on the Dean's List, on the football field such a score earns him only a seat on the bench. A coach will not allow a player to take the field if he knows that the player is going to miss an assignment 1 out of every 10 plays. Yet, the same athletes whose SAT scores suggest that they are not qualified to be in college are able to master a playbook that is every bit as complex as any history textbook. For example, the date in which the Declaration of Independence was signed does not change from class period to class period, let alone during a single class period. However, players must think and adjust their assignments on the field almost instantly. On the playing field, the correct answer (reaction) to a set of test stimuli (plays) changes as a function of a number of game situation variables such as down and distance, the assignments of one's teammates, the time of the game, and the tendencies of the other team. If the NCAA recognizes that these student-athletes from disadvantaged backgrounds do have the ability to be as successful academically as they are athletically and provides legislation that enhances the quality of student-athletes' educational opportunity, then they cannot help but have a better life chance after their athletic careers.

Recommendation to Individual Institutions

One structure that already exists in many institutions and that has enormous potential to nurture the overall development of black student-athletes is the academic support programs. Most of the academic support programs for student-athletes are housed in athletic departments. In previous work, my colleagues and I have argued that these programs must focus on the long-term development of the student-athlete (Sellers et al., 1991). A program that focuses on the long-term development of the student-athlete would emphasize future competence in areas both inside and outside the classroom. Unfortunately, many support programs are forced to focus on the short-term goal of maintaining student-athletes' athletic eligibility instead of their potential academic development. This results in the student-athletes' pursuing a curriculum that may be to their advantage in the short term, but undermines their pursuit of long-term goals. Another characteristic of short term thinking is that the support staff (often tutors) is spending all of its efforts in getting student-athletes through some course instead of teaching them better writing skills.

On the other hand, an academic support program focusing on long-term development would emphasize academic skill-building activities. These academic skills consist of such activities as writing, note taking, time management, and reading comprehension. Upon entrance to that institution, each student-athlete would be assessed for strengths and weaknesses, and a support program would be designed tailored specifically for the student-athlete's needs. This means that many student-athletes, black and white, would have programs that would have some remedial courses during their first year or two which might force them to adopt a five- or maybe even a six-year educational track. A student-athlete who takes six years to graduate, but does so with a college education, is preferable to one who graduates in four or five years without a true education. This is especially important for black student-athletes when only 1 out of 10 black students has received a bachelor's degree within six years of their high school graduation (Chronicle of Higher Education, 1991). Institutions must be willing to redshirt student-athletes who have particularly deficient academic preparation and spend the time, money, and effort to strengthen them academically. This recommendation is for a commitment to the academic development of black student-athletes that is no different from the current commitment athletic programs display toward the athletic development of black student-athletes. Most athletic programs assess student-athletes' physical strengths and design individualized fitness regimens tailored for the student-athletes' needs. The same practice should be done for student-athletes' academic needs.

A program with a long-term focus would also emphasize a holistic approach to the student-athletes' development. Such a support program would facilitate black student-athletes' efforts to further develop personal competencies as well as improve their chances for a successful career after athletics. With regard to the development of personal competence, the support program must allow student-athletes to feel a sense of power and responsibility over their education. Student-athletes should be encouraged to make decisions for themselves and allowed to experience the consequences of those decisions. Such an approach teaches self-discipline, responsibility, and decision-making skills. It also promotes an overall sense of self-efficacy. Unfortunately, too many institutions do not allow student-athletes the opportunity of developing the intra- and interpersonal skills that one must rely upon when one makes decisions. Institutions make decisions for the student-athletes that may be in their best interest in the short term, but deprive them of a valuable aspect of learning. However, this does not mean that support programs should not assist student-athletes with many of these decisions. They should provide any resources that will help the student-athletes make the right decisions. The support program must walk the often fine line between supporting and controlling.

Academic support programs can do much to help black student-athletes enhance their vocational potential by providing career planning and placement programs throughout the student-athletes' tenure at the school. Evidence suggests that student-athletes may not be particularly sophisticated in their career aspirations (Blann, 1985). A study using a nationally representative sample of Division I student-athletes found that despite their placing a greater importance on financial importance than did nonathletes, the jobs the student-athletes hoped to have at age 40 were significantly lower in socioeconomic status than were those chosen by nonathletes (Center for the Study of Athletics, 1988). Career counseling early in student-athletes' tenure at college has been shown to positively influence both the student-athletes' career choices and their overall academic performance (Nelson, 1982). The greater exposure to different career paths increases the chances of the student-athletes' finding a career that matches both their aptitudes and their aspirations. Such a match can only increase the student's intrinsic motivation and performance.

Another area in which institutions can make an important impact in enhancing the educational opportunities of black student-athletes is in the hiring of more black coaches and administrators within the athletic department (Sellers et al., 1991). Black coaches and athletic administrators (particularly former black student-athletes) are more likely to understand the unique experiences of the black student-athlete. Lapchick (1991) has noted that white coaches' treatment of black student-athletes is sometimes influenced by their own stereotypical notions regarding black athletes. Thus, black coaches and administrators are more qualified to design programs that will enhance black student-athletes' life chances. Black coaches and athletic administrators also provide important role models for both black and white student-athletes. This is especially important to black student-athletes because of their dependence on support systems located off campus.

In 1990, at predominantly white Division I schools there were only 47 black head coaches out of 1,165 head coaching positions in football, men's and women's basketball, track, and baseball (Lapchick, 1991). This equals to roughly 4 percent of the coaching positions. Blacks make up approximately one percent of the athletic directors, assistant and associate athletic directors, business and ticket managers, and sports information directors at these schools. Currently, there are no black head football coaches at any of the predominantly white Division I schools. The few assistant coaches who are at these institutions are relegated to recruiter status, in which their primary function is to recruit black student-athletes to the schools. Besides being a role that does not often lead to head coaching responsibilities, the role of recruiter also keeps black coaches on the road for significant periods of time. The road-warrior existence of the recruiter makes it more difficult sustain a supportive relationship with the black student-athletes who are on campus. Universities should not only hire more blacks in their athletic departments but should also place blacks in a greater variety of positions.

Recommendations for the Black Student-Athlete and Family

Black student-athletes and their families can also play a significant role in increasing the chances of the student-athletes' receiving a quality college education. First, student-athletes and their families must understand that they are ultimately responsible for their education. They are the ones who will suffer the consequences of not receiving a college education. Black student-athletes and their families should adopt this understanding before choosing a college. They should make the quality of the educational opportunity offered a major criterion for evaluating which college the student-athlete will be attending. Black student-athletes and their families should be proactive in the recruiting process. They should evaluate every aspect of the school from academics to athletics to social climate. An important part of any evaluation should be an examination and under-standing of the graduation rates of previous student-athletes. (Recent NCAA legislation requires each school to provide information on its graduation rates of student-athletes over the past 10 years to student-athletes whom it is recruiting.) Black student-athletes and their families should also obtain as much information about the educational experiences and career status of as many student-athletes from similar backgrounds as possible. The student-athletes and their families should also investigate the academic support programs that are offered for student-athletes. Are the support programs adequate for the student-athlete's specific needs?

Once in college, student-athletes must be willing to take the extra steps necessary to receive a college education. These extra steps may mean that the student-athlete must go out of the way to interact with other students who are not student-athletes. This is especially important for black student-athletes. Allen (1988) found that for black students, interacting with other black students was positively associated with academic achieve-ment. Interaction with other black students provides black students with both the emotional and instrumental support necessary to navigate a sometimes hostile environment. Black student-athletes should try to become involved with campus activities such as clubs, fraternities and sororities, and volunteer organizations. Besides providing a much-needed perspective on college life outside the athletic realm, involvement with nonathletes also provides an opportunity to build a wider social network, which may lead to unforeseen benefits later in life. These unforeseen benefits include future business relationships, medical relationships, and legal relationships.

Conclusions

The quality of black student-athletes' lives after their playing days are over is likely to be related to the quality of their college education. Those black student-athletes who are able to obtain a college education are likely to enjoy greater economic, social, and psychological benefits than are those who end their college athletic careers without receiving equitable compensation. Coming from very different backgrounds than their fellow student-athletes and fellow black college students, black student-athletes may have unique postathletic career experience. Unfortunately, the research literature has virtually ignored this experience, and the present reform movement in college athletics threatens to extinguish it. More enlightened efforts by the NCAA and individual institutions can enhance the chances of black student-athletes' spending their postathletic days reaping the benefits of a college education instead of recovering from exploitation. Since black student-athletes and their families are the ones who will have to endure the consequences of an exploitative athletic career, they are the ones who must ultimately shoulder the responsibility for obtaining a meaningful college education in a system that is not as responsive to their needs as it should be.

References

Allen, W.R. (1988). Black students in U. S. higher education: Toward improved access, adjustment and achievement. *The Urban Review, 20*(3), 165-188.

Blann, F.W. (1985). Intercollegiate athletic competition and student's educational and career plans. *Journal of College Student Personnel, 26*(2), 115-118.

Braddock, J.H. (1980). Race, sports, and social mobility: A critical review. *Sociology Symposium, 2*, 18-37.

Cashmore, E. (1982). *Black sportsmen.* Boston: Routledge & Regan

Paul.

Center for the Study of Athletics (1988). *Report No. 1: Summary results from the 1987-88 national study of intercollegiate athletes*. Palo Alto: American Institutes for Research.

Center for the Study of Athletics (1989). *Report No. 3: The life experiences of black intercollegiate athletes at NCAA Division I universities*. Palo Alto: American Institutes for Research.

Chronicle of Higher Education (1991). *1991 Almanac, 38*(1), p.11.

Coakley, J.J. (1983). Leaving competitive sport: Retirement or rebirth? *Quest, 35,* 1-11.

Danish, S.J. (1983). Musings about personal competence: The contributions of sport, health, and fitness. *American Journal of Community Psychology, 11*(3), 221-240.

Danish, S.J., Galambos, N.L., & Laqquatra, I. (1983). Life development intervention: Skill training for personal competence. In R. D. Felner, L. A. Jason, J. Moritsugu, & S. S. Farber (Eds.), *Preventive psychology: Theory research and practice*, (pp. 49-61). Elmsford, NY: Pergamon Press.

Edwards, H. (1979). Sport within the veil: The triumphs, tragedies, and challenges of Afro-American involvement. *Annals, AAPSS, 445,* 116-127.

Eitzen, S.D., & Tessendorf, I. (1978). Racial segregation by position in sports: The special case of basketball. *Review of Sport and Leisure, 3,* 109-128.

Ervin, L., Saunders, S.A., Gillis, H.L., & Hogrebe, M.C. (1985). Academic performance of student athletes in revenue-producing sports. *Journal of College Student Personnel, 26* (2), 119-124.

Greendorfer, S.L., & Blinde, E.M. (1985). "Retirement" from intercollegiate sport: Theoretical and empirical considerations. *Sociology of Sport Journal, 2,* 101-110.

Gurin, P., Gurin, G., & Morrison, B.M. (1978). Personal and deological aspects of internal and external locus of control. *Social Psychology, 41,* 275-296.

Harris, D.S., & Eitzen, D.S. (1978). The consequences of failure in sport. *Urban Life, 7* (2), 177-188.

Harrison, C.H. (1991). *Peterson's public schools USA: A comparative guide to school districts* (2nd ed). Peterson's Guide Inc.

Hurtsfield, J. (1978). Internal colonialism: White, black, Chicano self-conceptions. *Ethnic and Racial Studies, 1* (1), 60-79.

Kiger, G., & Lorentzen, D. (1986). The relative effect of gender, race, and sport on university academic performance. *Sociology of Sport Journal, 3*, 160-167.

Kleiber, D., Greendorfer, S., Blinde, E., & Samdahl, D. (1987). Quality of exit from university sports and life satisfaction in early adulthood. *Sociology of Sport Journal, 4*, 28-36.

Lapchick, R. (1991). *Five minutes to midnight: Race and sport in the 1990's*. Lanham, MD: Madison Books.

Lerch, S. (1982). *Athletic retirement as social death: an overview*. Paper presented at third annual meeting of NASSS, Toronto, November.

National Collegiate Athletic Association (1984). *Study of freshman eligibility standards: Executive summary*. Reston, VA: Social Sciences Division, Advanced Technology, Inc.

National Collegiate Athletic Association (1991). *NCAA academic performance study report 91-01: A description of college graduation rates for 1984 and 1985 freshmen student-athletes*. Overland Park, MO: NCAA Publications.

Nelson, E. S. (1982). The effects of career counseling on freshman college athletes. *Journal of Sport Psychology, 4*, 32-40.

Picou, J. S. (1978). Race, athletic achievement, and educational aspirations. *The Sociological Quarterly, 19*, 429-438.

Purdy, D., Eitzen, D.S., & Hufnagel, R. (1982). Are athletes also students?: The educational attainment of college athletes. *Social Problems, 29* (4), 439-448.

Sellers, R.M. (1992). Racial differences in the predictors of academic achievement of Division I student-athletes. *Sociology of Sport Journal, 9*, 48-59.

Sellers, R.M., Kuperminc, G.P., & Waddell, A.S. (1991). Life experiences of black student-athletes in revenue producing sports: A descriptive empirical analysis. *Academic Athletic Journal*, Fall, 21-38.

Shapiro, B.J. (1984). Intercollegiate athletic participation and academic achievement: A case study of Michigan State University student-athletes, 1950-1980. *Sociology of Sport Journal, 1*, 46-51.

Snyder, E.E., & Spreitzer, E.A. (1978). *Social aspects of sports*, Englewood Cliffs, NJ: Prentice-Hall.

Telander, R. & Sullivan, R. (1989, February 27). You reap what you sow. Sports Illustrated, 70, 20-26

Walter, T., Smith, D.E.P., Hoey, G., & Wilhelm, R. (1987). Predicting the academic success of college athletes. *Research Quarterly for Exercise and Sport, 58*(2), 273-279.

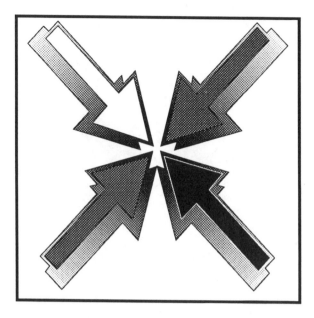

Section Three:
Gender and Race
Intersections in
College Athletics

Section Three

Gender and Race Intersections in College Athletics

The opportunity for women to gain parity in college sport barely exists; even worse, much of the work dealing with African-American women reaffirms stereotypes and myths of sports role or ability that do not contribute toward the social mobility of black women. Title IX was supposed to have stimulated a dramatic increase for participating in high school and college sport, but the treatment of female athletes reveals powerful racial and sexual barriers. Antiracist work and feminist analysis may offer some recommendations for implementing affirmative action programs and building alliances to assault the prevailing gender stereotypes and treatment of sportswomen of color.

The initial essay on "The African-American Female in Collegiate Sport: Sexism and Racism," by Doris Corbett (sport sociologist) and William Johnson (college coach), focuses on gender stereotypes, the impact of NCAA policies and discrimination, and the treatment of the African-American female athletes at historically black colleges and universities. The authors cite various studies of the sexual and racial barriers that have resulted in underrepresentation of African-American women in college sport. Some suggestions to change these societal and collegiate conditions are highlighted such as developing more nurturing institutions, changing media exposure of the African-American female athletes, improving HBCU athletic programs, and building support networks to surmount these barriers.

An optimistic outlook is provided in Tina Sloan Green's (college coach) essay on "The Future of African-American Female Athletes."

Female participation in basketball, track and field, and baseball is likely to continue. New facilities as well as those inherited due to white flight from cities provide the spark for an array of inner city recreational projects sponsored by professional and amateur associations as well as by the reformed YWCA, girls' clubs, scouts and the NCAA-NYSP organizations. Although the African-American female athlete must deal with problems such as long hours of practice, travel, and demands for academic achievement, Sloan Green offers optimistic advice to sports participants to help them to strengthen themselves. A plea is made to conduct more research to highlight the experiences and demands facing African-American female athletes.

In undertaking a comprehensive analysis of current scholarship on race relations, Alison Dewar (sport sociologist) focuses her work on challenging oppression in racist structures and sport practices. Regarding sport as a system of power and privilege allows us to see that oppression is built into its social structures and is legitimated by cultural beliefs and social codes. Dewar looks at how the dominant views of race relations obscure blacks' experiences and strategies for success. Dewar thus joins Corbett and Johnson to challenge NCAA member institutions to conduct antiracist work that includes implementing affirmative action plans, conducting workshops, and building new coalitions and alliances. The success of these programs depends on commitment to act from those at all levels of the sport hierarchy, including administrators, coaches, parents, players, and students.

Essay 6

The African-American Female in Collegiate Sport: Sexism and Racism

Doris Corbett and William Johnson

Abstract: The authors explore the relationship between racism and sexism in collegiate sport. This relationship continues to be a complex issue that causes Americans, especially African-Americans, to be particularly sensitive. This chapter addresses the cultural milieu of the African-American woman from a "her"storical and sociological perspective. Also discussed is the impact of Title IX at historically black institutions of higher learning on African-American sportswomen, implications of Proposition 48 for the black woman in sport, racial and sexual barriers as well as the attitude of the media toward women of color in sport. One feature of the chapter is a focus on outstanding African-American sportswomen who have excelled in a variety of sports. Recommendations and solutions are offered to improve the plight of the African-American woman in sport.

Introduction

The subject of racism and sexism in collegiate sport has been a complex issue that causes Americans to be particularly sensitive. The fact that there have been too few African-American sportswomen who serve as role models is a reflection of the problems in this area. Even as we swiftly approach the twenty-first century, American society is vaguely aware of the sporting experience of the African-American sportswoman. This chapter will address the cultural milieu of the African-American sportswoman from a historical and sociological perspective. The impact of Title IX on women of color in the historically black institutions of higher learning will be evaluated. The racial and sexual barriers women of color face will be discussed, as will be the attitude of the media toward the African-American sportswoman.

A Historical and Sociological Perspective of the African-American Female

The concern regarding women in sport has brought with it a focus on African-American women in particular. A new scholarship about women of color has been strengthened by the growing acceptance of African-American and women's studies as distinct areas of inquiry.

In order to better understand the psychological and sociological nature of the African-American woman in sport, the cultural milieu of the African-American woman in society must first be reviewed.

Society has viewed and treated African-American women differently from white women in the United States. African-American women have suffered many hardships and have not been treated as status symbols of their spouses or placed in a protected position in society.

Although the women's liberation movement has focused on a number of theories regarding female inequality, very few models have examined the constraints of both racism and sexism. It is a historical fact that African-American women were excluded and denied mainstream participation in the political-economic development of the larger society until the civil rights movement of the sixties. Prior to that time, the law denied African-American people normal adult prerogatives. Widely sanctioned acts such as rape, sexual exploitation of African-American women, low wages, menial jobs, and substandard educational programs all functioned as stringent barriers to participation in the political and economic process.

Like the African-American woman, the white woman is also victimized. However, the stereotypic traits differ and are quite often the opposite. For example, almost without exception African-American women are portrayed as aggressive whereas white women are pictured as passive or nonassertive. Other stereotypic African-American/White opposites include (a) independent-dependent, (b) loud-coy, (c) dominating-submissive, and (d) castrating-seductive (Gump, 1975).

The history of the African-American woman has shaped concepts of her identity as well as her ideals, attitudes, behavior, role, and responsibilities. The African-American female is believed to be instilled with skills essential to her maintenance and conducive to her survival. Lewis (1975), Bonner (1974), and Giddings (1974) have suggested that young African-American women have not been socialized to conform to stereotypic behavior patterns. Instead, society has allowed the African-American female to be assertive, nonconforming, and self-reliant (Staples, 1970).

In the American culture, the African-American skin is defined as inferior, and rigid caste barriers are erected in order to maintain the low social status of the African-American people. The result is that people of color assume identities in an environment steeped in the symbolism of African-American inferiority. They have been exposed to few successful African-American role models or instances in which people of color exert control over their existence. It is therefore not very surprising that under these conditions, it can be concluded that the negative self-images of many African-Americans can be expected (Katz, 1969; Pettigrew, 1964).

African-American women have used, and continue to use, a variety of techniques in self-development. Skin-bleaching creams and process hairstyles more clearly reflect the attempts by African-American women to enhance their appearance. These efforts appear to be in the direction of self-augmentation rather than self-depreciation. It is suggested that a reassessment of a number of the behaviors of African-Americans that have previously been interpreted as self-negating, self-depreciating, and maladaptive (i.e. straightening of hair and the bleaching of skin) might more accurately be viewed as self-actualizing, self-enhancing, and adaptive. It is possible for African-American women to exist in a difficult and oppressive environment without developing self-attitudes of hatred and rejection. The African-American community has played a unique and valuable role as a buffer to the negative influences of the larger society.

A closer look at some of the perceptions and stereotypes that society has held about the sportswoman of color will help us better understand the African-American woman in society and in sport.

The African-American Woman in Society and Sport

There are "herstorical" differences between African-American women and white women that tend to create a different social milieu that surrounds each race. Although the United States is ethnically diverse, the North American standard of female beauty has tended to be defined by

European history and European literature created primarily by men. The standard for assessing feminine beauty until recently has been described as white complexion, golden hair, and fragile build; the ideal woman is light, soft, small, and delicate. White women have been portrayed as the ideal housewife and the symbol of love and motherhood. The antithesis of this standard is dark complexion, kinky hair, and sturdy build. The black woman was considered to be a tough person and a hard-working matriarch (King, 1973).

Cultural and ethnic conceptions of masculinity and femininity, the degree of sex-typing according to class, and the dominant-submissive relationship between the sexes tend to vary within and among all the various ethnic groups. As individuals and families adopt the mores and folkways of the United States, each generation will tend to blur ethnic differences as their members are absorbed into the urbanized, industrialized culture. First-generation Americans and first-generation migrants from rural areas are usually more patriarchal and traditional in their conceptions of masculinity and femininity. This pattern varies according to the cultural heritage, the unique herstorical experiences of the group, and the current availability of educational and economic opportunities to various ethnic groups (Yorburg, 1974).

For the African-American woman, there was the presumption by society as a whole that because she represented an inferior status in society (not limited to, but featured as a tough, hard-working domestic or working-class individual), the roughness and toughness of the sporting world would only be a natural and an acceptable activity at which she would be competent.

In an era when minorities have been vocal about a wide range of social issues, African-American women have been relatively silent with respect to their status in athletics.

The black woman's role in sports in the so-called Golden Era of sports in the 1930's and 1940's was nearly non-existent. The shackle of segregation handicapped the black female in sport, but a few did excel in several sports including basketball, tennis, track and golf. (Pinkey, 1975, p. 58)

Women in general have protested the lack of attention, respectability, and professional opportunities available to them in sport that the male athlete has traditionally enjoyed. The African-American male has aggressively sought leadership roles and careers in athletics beyond his active years of competition. The African-American female has not been proportionately represented in athletics at all levels, such as interschool competition, coaching, officiating, administration, policy making, and league work (Houzer, 1971).

Houzer (1971) reported that African-American women appeared to be moving toward a position of less interest and involvement in sport and athletics. Her findings reflected a decline in interest and sport involvement by African-American women due to socially based factors. Similarly, Alexander (1979), in a study of the status of minority women in the Association for Intercollegiate Athletics for Women (AIAW), suggested that various factors account for the underrepresentation of minority women in athletics: (a) lack of money for lessons and equipment, (b) availability and rental of facilities; (c) lack of racial role models; (d) time commitments for child care, study responsibilities, and wage earning responsibilities; and (e) available opportunities in geographic areas of minority population concentration.

In spite of segregation and racism, many African-American women had the opportunity to participate in sports through clubs organized especially for that purpose, such as the Alpha, Physical Culture Club, Smart Set, and St. Christopher (Young, 1963). African-American women have been participating in sports and athletics for many years. During the years of black-white segregation, however, they were forced to compete only against other black women in tournaments that to the country as a whole did not count. One of the most widely held myths about the African-American woman in sport is the belief that African-American women favor track and field in light of their successes in these events.

According to Houzer (1971), there is no substantial evidence that African-American women favor participation in track and field. A 1969 study sampled 265 female students enrolled in five predominantly black colleges in South Carolina. From data collected, it was found that the subjects were generally negative in their attitudes toward track and field. Softball, volleyball, basketball, modern dance, and bowling were the five most preferred physical education classes. The subjects also indicated significant interest in tennis, badminton, swimming, gymnastics, square dance, soccer, and archery. Metheny (1972) argues that participation in track and field was related more to limited opportunities than to individual preferences.

With an increase in interest and support in general for women in sport, particularly post-Title IX, more and more women are not only being physically active but they are also more inclined to participate competitively in sport. Although the African-American culture has traditionally embraced the black male sportsman, Marie Hart (1980), after discussing the plight of the woman in sport, commented: "In startling contrast is the black woman athlete. In the black community, it seems a woman can be strong and competent in sport and still not deny her womanliness. She can even win respect and status. Wilma Rudolph is an example" (p.207). Hart (1974) suggests that within the black culture, sport involvement provides women of color status and prestige.

Coakley (1982) has supported the notion that the African-American community places few constraints on the black sportswoman. If this is true, then it might be suggested that gender role expectations for African-American women are less constraining in the black culture than are similar expectations for white women in the dominant culture. For example, black women more often have traditionally been represented in basketball, softball, and track and field. For the white sportswoman public acceptance of participation in these sports has not been encouraged (Del Rey, 1977; Snyder & Kivlin, 1975; Snyder & Spreitzer, 1975). White women are most represented in the individual sports of tennis, swimming, and gymnastics. These sports remain the most acceptable sports for white women (Metheny, 1965). Metheny (1965) found that sports that require application of force to a heavy object, body contact, or hard running and throwing are generally discouraged for the white female.

Oglesby (1981) in her writings, "myths and realities of black women in sport," differs with Coakley and Hart. Oglesby submits that the socioeconomic, political, and psychological environment in the United States has not been supportive of the advancement of the black woman in sport. Oglesby argues that black women have been a casualty to the double affliction of racism and sexism. The fact that black women have systematically been neglected in the research literature simply supports this point of view. Further, Oglesby (1981) reports that most of the investigations on minorities and women have examined the sporting experiences of the black male and the white woman without exploring the sport experience of the black woman.

In our view, the limited number of studies that have been conducted are tainted in their findings because they do not examine the sporting experience of black women in its context. Not only do the few studies that exist neglect the sporting activities of the African-American woman, but they also fail to depict how African-Americans perceive women of color participating in sport. Much of the literature documents the achievements of a select group of African-American women in primarily one or two sports. For example, the struggles and accomplishments of Wilma Rudolph in track and Althea Gibson in tennis have been reflected as the norm for women of color in sport. Their stories are used to reaffirm the myth that sport is a means of upward social mobility, and therefore, the existence of racism and discrimination in sport and society becomes disguised. Their experiences reflect their fight to compete with whites and to gain recognition from whites. By focusing on the few available highly acknowledged examples of female African-American athletes such as Althea Gibson and Wilma Rudolph, the authors believe that the stereotypes and myths regarding the African-American sportswomen are reaffirmed. Although many African-American women competed and contributed to sport before and after Althea Gibson and Wilma Rudolph, these two women are considered the most significant athletic forces among African-American women in sport history. The reality that the participation of African-American women has been restricted to just a few sports is an issue that has caused considerable discussion. The following African-American sportswomen, however, represent a selection of noteable women of color who have excelled in basketball, fencing, golf, handball, lacrosse, rowing, field hockey, ice skating, tennis, figure skating, track and field, and volleyball (Boutilier & SanGiovanni, 1983; Corbett, 1987; and Green, Oglesby, Alexander, & Franke, 1981).

Outstanding African-American Women in Sport

Athlete	Sport	Comment
Lucia Harris	Basketball	Three-time All-American player averaging 31 points per game; 1977 Broderick Cup winner.
Cheryl Miller	Basketball	Former star, University of Southern California women's basketball team; won 1982 national championship.
Marian E. Washington	Basketball	United States Women's National Team - 1969, 1970, 1971; and AAU All-American Team - 1972 and 1974.
Carla Dunlap	Body Building	Accomplished and nationally acclaimed body builder.

Outstanding African-American Women in Sport (cont'd)

Athlete	Sport	Comment
Cherly Daniel	Bowling	Champion bowler.
Nikki Franke	Fencing	1975 National Fencing Champion; 1975 Pan American Team (Second Place); member of the 1976 Olympic Team.
Ruth White	Fencing	In 1969 first African-American and youngest to ever win the National Fencing title; Won five major fencing titles.
Tina Sloan Green	Field Hockey	U.S. Women's Lacrosse team in 1969 and 1970; member U.S. Field Hockey Squad in 1969 and the U.S. Women's National Lacrosse Team in 1968 and 1972.
Renee Powell	Golf	The second African-American female to tour the professional golf circuits since Althea Gibson, has been with the LPGA since 1967.
Diane Durham	Gymnastics	Outstanding nationally recognized gymnast.
Tai Babilonia	Ice Skating	First African-American woman to make the U.S. Ice Skating team and compete in world class competition.
Debbie Thomas	Ice Skating	Olympian and former world champion.
Anita DeFrantz	Rowing	Member of the 1976 Olympic Rowing team and is currently a member of the International Olympic Committee (IOC).
Camille Benjamin	Tennis	Outstanding professional tennis player.
Renee Blount	Tennis	Outstanding professional tennis player.

Outstanding African-American Women in Sport (cont'd)

Athlete	Sport	Comment
Zina Garrison	Tennis	Highest ranking African-American professional female tennis player.
Althea Gibson	Tennis	Champion-Wimbledon and Forest Hill.
Cheryl Jones	Tennis	Outstanding professional tennis player.
Lori McNeil	Tennis	One of the highest ranking professional players; often plays as Zina Garrison's doubles partner.
Kim Sands	Tennis	Outstanding professional tennis player.
Evelyn Ashford	Track	Broke Wilma Rudolph's twenty year old record in the 100 meters; top sprinter in the world.
Valerie Brisco-Hooks	Track	Has set Olympic and American records in all her finals; in the 1984 Los Angeles Olympics she won three gold medals for the 200 meter, the 400 meter, and 1600 sprint relay; in 1988 she won a silver medal in Seoul as a member of the 2nd place 1600 meter relay team..
Florence Griffith-Joyner	Track	Has brought fashion, flair, and high finance to women's track; at Seoul Summer Olympics in 1988, she won three gold medals in the 100 and 200 meter races and the 400 meter relay, and a silver medal in the 1600 meter relay; she has surpassed Wilma Rudolph's record.

Outstanding African-American Women in Sport (cont'd)

Athlete	Sport	Comment
Nell C. Jackson	Track	American record 200 meter; Member US Olympic Track and Field Team, 1948; Member U.S. Pan American Track & Field team 1951, and AAU champion in 200 meter 1949, 1950, 1951 in 400 meter relay.
Jackie Joyner-Kersey	Track	Holds the world record in the seven-event heptathlon and winner of two Olympic Gold Medals.
Madeline Manning Mims	Track	Member of 4 Olympic Teams- 1968, 1972, 1976 and 1980; Gold Medalist in 800 meter event in 1968 Olympics; five time 800 meter National Champion.
Wilma Rudolph	Track	Won three Olympic Gold Medals.
Wyomia Tyus	Track	Gold medal in the 1964 Olympics for the 100 meter, and a silver medal for the 400 meter relay; 1968 Olympics won a gold medal for the 100 meter, and another gold medal for the 400 meter relay.
Willye White	Track	Considered the grand old lady of track; silver medal in the long jump; silver medal on the 400 meter relay team; and won four medals in the 1959, 1963 and 1967 Pan-American Games; 17 national indoor and outdoor track titles.
Lucinda Williams-Adams	Track	The third runner on the 1960 Olympic relay team with

Outstanding African-American Women in Sport (cont'd)

Athlete	Sport	Comment
		Wilma Rudolph. They called her "Lady Dancer." At the Pan-American Games in 1959 with 33 countries competing, she won the 100 and 200 meter races.
Flo Hyman	Volleyball	First team All American to the United States Volleyball Association (USVBA); Amateur Athletic Union (AAU) most valuable player.
Verneda Thomas	Volleyball	Member of Olympic Volleyball team in 1964.

Very little is written about the sporting experience of African-American women within the black culture (Henderson, 1968; Gibson, 1958; Twin, 1979 ;Young, 1963). Although Althea Gibson is the most outstanding African-American female tennis player in the history of the sport, she did not perceive herself as a Negro Champion even though society perceives her as a model for Negroes. Gibson (1958) commented that she perceived herself as a tennis player and that she, "never set herself up as a champion of the Negro race" (p. 35). Oftentimes white America holds a different interpretation of the role and function of sport in the black community and, as a consequence, ideological generalizations, stereotypes, discrepancies, and contradictions are promoted in the research and popular literature.

The little research about the African-American sportswoman that has been done is descriptive. The existing studies assume that the sex role and gender expectations for the black woman have functioned to diminish her participation in sport. Gergen (1971) points out that the female has continued to engage in sport in spite of the stigma associated with her participation. Gergen (1971) explains this behavior by stating that the female in sport is able to shed the stereotypical female role because it is not a frame of reference for her, and consequently, she is not cognizant of a role conflict.

In order for an individual to experience discord, the person must be aware of the conflict. Oglesby (1978) contends that sport provides neither masculinity nor femininity training but is instead androgynous training. Therefore, through sport, the qualities that cause human beings to be fully functioning individuals are potentially communicable-reenforceable.

An androgynous person has been conceptualized as having both masculine and feminine qualities. The presumption is that the androgynous individual has in his or her repertoire a much broader and more effective behavior option, than does the highly sex-typed individual (Kelly & Worell, 1977). The highly sex-typed individuals (Kagan, 1964; Kohlberg, 1966) are motivated to keep their behavior consistent with how they perceive themselves. The perception is then internalized according to the sex-appropriate role. This type of behavior narrows the self-concept and does not allow the individual to engage freely in both "masculine" and "feminine" behaviors. Corbett (1981), in a study of the relationships between androgyny, self-concept, and social status among minority female athletes and nonathletes found that social status and sex-role orientation were important and significant variables that affected the type of sport African-American women select. Specifically, Corbett (1981) found that the black, female, androgynous athlete showed greater role adaptability and flexibility than did the black, female nonathletes who were sex-typed feminine, masculine, or undifferentiated. It is the authors' view that the white, female, androgynous athletes also display greater role flexibility and adaptability.

When examining the social status of black women, Corbett (1981) reported that the black, female, androgynous athletes were significantly lower in social status than the black female nonathletes who were sex-typed feminine, masculine, or androgynous.

The African-American woman's unique cultural heritage and experiences have contained great hardship. However, the contemporary African-American woman has become socialized or enculturated to accept the normative values of the larger society; in so doing, middle-class African-American sportswomen experience sex-role conflict and restrictions similar to those experienced by white female sportswomen (Corbett, 1981). For the disadvantaged black woman, the African-American community provides a sense of personal security, identity, and belonging, and a different criteria for self-evaluation (Watson, 1974).

However, 20 years after the passage of Title IX, the federal regulation prohibiting discrimination on the basis of sex in college education has gone a long way to enhance sporting opportunities for women in general but particularly the African-American woman in the historically black institutions of higher learning. Title IX has played an important role in the creation and development of program opportunities for the black sportswoman.

The Impact of Title IX at Historically
Black Institutions of Higher Learning

Title IX assures everyone (regardless of sex) an equal chance to learn skills, choose an area of study, partake of an opportunity for advancement in status, participate in sport, receive a scholarship, or otherwise benefit from the contributions of any institution supported by federal aid (United States Commission on Civil Rights, 1980). The regulations apply in three main areas: admission of students, treatment of students, and employment in the institution. Treatment of students is related to access to and participation in course offerings and extracurricular activities including student organizations and athletics. It is the area of intercollegiate athletics that provoked bitter discussion and controversy. Compliance is determined by the elimination of discrimination in athletic programs. Title IX does not require equal aggregate expenditure for male and female athletics. Some of the provisions of Title IX regarding sports programs are summarized as follows (United States Commission on Civil Rights, 1980):

1. All physical education classes in elementary, secondary and post-secondary schools must be offered to both sexes.

2. There shall be no discrimination in competitive athletics. It allows, but does not require separate teams for members of each sex; the "nature" of the particular sport should be taken into account. Contact sports need not be open to both sexes; however, institutions are required to open intramural and club teams to members of both sexes.

3. Males and females must receive equal opportunity in: selection of sport, levels of competition, provision of equipment and supplies, scheduling of games and practices, coaching, academic tutoring, practice and competitive facilities, publicity and athletic scholarships. (pp. 9-10)

Despite the fact that negative attitudes toward women in sport persist, major changes in the level and patterns of participation for women have improved. Since the implementation of Title IX in 1975, the opportunity for female athletes to participate in intercollegiate sport has increased substantially. For example, in 1977, one year before the Title IX compliance date, the number of sports offered women was 5.61 per school. In 1980 the number had grown to 6.48, in 1986 to 7.15, and in 1988 to 7.31. The number for 1990 has dropped slightly to 7.24 (Acosta & Carpenter, 1990).

The enforcement of Title IX has suffered setbacks in recent years. The 1984 U.S. Supreme Court Grove City decision effectively denied the application of Title IX to nonfederally funded programs such as college departments of physical education and athletics. In March of 1988, however, Congress enacted over a presidential veto, the Civil Rights Restoration Act, which effectively renewed jurisdiction of Title IX over college departments of physical education and athletics. The four years without Title IX was a time in which athletic scholarships for women were reduced and other negative changes were made in some women's intercollegiate athletic programs (Acosta & Carpenter, 1990).

African-American sportswomen and their athletic programs have also experienced the evils of sexism in the historically black institutions of higher learning. Male athletic directors at historically black colleges and universities have been reluctant to share revenue with the female athletes (Alston, 1980). The enforcement of Title IX has posed some hardships for most institutions. Eliminating sexism like eliminating racism is not an easy goal.

Historically, black male athletic programs have functioned as second-class citizens striving to develop into NCAA Division I programs. The majority of the athletic programs in the black institutions of higher learning have not been able to produce revenue at a level that would qualify them to be major players in the big league. Athletic administrators in these institutions have witnessed the success of the athletic programs in the major white institutions and have observed their white colleagues as they enjoy the financial rewards that come with bowl games and media coverage as well as other lucrative benefits. Many of the males responsible for the implementation of athletic programs have taken the position that selected male sport programs, especially football and basketball, should not have to suffer in order to support the female programs (Alston, 1980). In reality, however, this concern is not a legitimate one. Very few athletic programs generate sufficient revenue to support themselves. This is true not only for the women's athletic programs but also for the minor male sport programs in the historically black institutions. The majority of the money spent for intercollegiate athletics for both male and female programs is still derived from student fees.

Not until recently have many of the athletic programs in historically black institutions sought to achieve Division I status. Because a commitment to achieve Division I status is a costly one, some of the black institutions experienced difficulty in adhering to the Title IX mandate, while building or rebuilding their programs with limited funds. Consequently, the decree to provide resources fairly has not received a warm reception in the black institutions of higher learning (Simmons, 1979). The idealist, however, might argue that a minority institution's athletic program would be more receptive to providing equitable opportunities to women for moral and ethical reasons.

As a former coach, a member of the historic Board of Directors of the AIAW and a past president of the National Association of Girls and Women in Sport (NAGWS), and as a result of numerous dialogues with fellow colleagues in the Historical Black Colleges and Universities (HBCU) and as an active observer of the status of women's athletics in the predominantly black institutions of higher learning, this writer is keenly aware that black institutions have attempted to take as long as they can to do as little as possible to comply with Title IX. A few black institutions have moved ahead to comply with the letter of the law and, in some instances, the spirit of the law. However, in the area of scholarship, often no systematic approach to the financial awards process has ever been used. For the most part, the commitment to equitable opportunity in the area of scholarships is no more than a paper commitment. Improvements have been found in travel and per diem as well as in dining and training facilities. The worst news, however, is in coaching. Fewer women are coaches, hold leadership position, or have an opportunity to make important decisions regarding their athletic programs. Female coaches have to work longer hours with less pay and with a shorter contract term than do their male coach counterparts (Alston, 1980).

Although the African-American sportswoman is tired of a second-class status, she has long become accustomed to discrimination due to race and gender and, therefore, holds little expectation that equity in sport will exist for her. There is no doubt that the problems encountered at the historically black institution are any different from the problems that exist at predominantly white institutions of similar size. Regardless, the historically black institutions must seek to train, identify, and employ minority female coaches who are sensitive to the problems and are willing to stand tall to address the inequities in order to enhance the welfare of the next generation of sportswomen of color.

Although Title IX has improved the status and program opportunities for women, racial and sexual barriers must be addressed.

Racial and Sexual Barriers in Women's Collegiate Sport

Racial and sexual barriers surrounding the involvement of the African-American woman in athletics include:

1) **Limited financial support.** The lack of funds diminishes the opportunity for the minority female to receive quality training and have excess to the best equipment for use.

2) **Lack of background to coach competitive teams.** The success of African-American women in the sports of basketball, and track and field has real implications for the physical education teacher who is socialized to emphasize these activities as they prepare for their professional career. Myths and stereotypes continue to exclude the African-American woman who wishes to develop coaching and teaching skills in the individual sports of golf, tennis, gymnastics, and swimming. The success of African-American women in track and field and basketball has led many individuals to believe that these activities are the only ones in which blacks are better prepared to teach, train/coach, and officiate.

3) **Lack of administrative support where competitive programs and interest exist.** The major problems surrounding involvement of African-American women in sport include limited financial support for athletes and athletic programs; along with lack of encouragement and support to attend and participate in workshop and training programs; and with the increase in the numbers of African-American women entering collegiate sport programs with undeveloped skills, greater coaching attention is necessary.

4) **Lack of positive opinion leaders as role models who are African-American sportswomen.** It is difficult for a minority to select to enter an organization that is 90% white male.

5) **The tendency of white coaches to associate the black female athletes with only certain sports (i.e., basketball and track and field).** The high participation in track and field by black women is probably more related to limited opportunities than to individual preferences. The commonly accepted belief that women of color are naturally gifted athletes in some sports and totally inept in others create

a barrier for them to be accepted in other sports. The result is a limitation in the variety of sports offered to them. Opportunities must be provided to African-American women who can derive benefits from athletic programs other than basketball and track and field.

6) **Discrimination in team selection, particularly in the sports of volleyball and basketball**. Racial stacking is evident for the African-American female in sport. In volleyball, African-Americans are underrepresented at the setter position and they are overrepresented as hitters, a position requiring jumping, agility, and reaction--all physical characteristics. Whites are found in positions high in interaction, coordinative tasks, leadership, and outcome control. African-Americans, in contrast, are found in peripheral positions where these traits are low and physical skills are paramount. Stacking is stronger in volleyball than in basketball (Eitzen & Furst, 1989; Furst & Heaps, 1987; Kanter, 1977; Simmel, 1950; Yetman et al., 1982).

7) **Discrimination in hiring**. Women of color are less likely to be recruited as coaches, athletic directors or officials. Therefore, too few African-American women are actively involved in preparing for careers in coaching, officiating, or athletic administration.

8) **Limited skill development opportunities**. African-American women athletes are underrepresented in such sports as tennis, gymnastics, and swimming. Minority women are nearly absent in these sports because they do not have access to both the human and financial resources to develop these skills. Special training, facilities, and equipment are essential in the development and maintenance of skills for these activities.

9) **Coaches' hours**. Female coaches have to work longer hours with a more difficult goal to attain, have fewer financial rewards, and a shorter term of contracts than male coaches. Coaches are required to take too many hours away from their family. All too often the female coach and particularly the African-American female coach is without coaching assistants who would enable coaches to have more time to spend with their families. Long coaching hours and the lack of coaching assistants also deter many capable minority women from pursuing a coaching career.

10) **Officials**. African-American female athletes lack motivation to be an official because traditionally this is considered male territory.

11) **Intimidation from male coaches and fans**. Support systems must be developed and maintained that will provide the African-American

woman with the confidence that she can do the job. There is an unspoken message conveyed by the majority society that she is not qualified, will never be qualified, and will never be as competent as a male coach.

12) **Unwillingness to travel.** The demands to travel are greater for the African-American coach, who must often function without assistants and therefore must also serve as a coach, scout, recruiter, trainer, and counselor.

Understandably, the solutions to eliminating these barriers are not simple. Institutions must first develop a nurturing and supportive environment where concerns can be acknowledged and admit that racism and sexism are legitimate issues and that there are problems to be solved. Professionals who express concern about both racism and sexism should be supported, not discouraged. Denying that the barriers exist only hampers progressive behavior by everyone. Administrators must closely examine their own programs and define avenues by which:

1. A much greater number of African-American women will hold positions of authority as athletic directors, coaches, athletic trainers, and officials. Role models in these positions are essential to the successful recruitment and retention of African-American women in these roles.
2. Adequate financial resources are in place to develop, support, and maintain quality athletic programs.
3. Female coaching salaries will be comparable to the male coaches' salary in the same sports.
4. African-American women will be encouraged to participate in a variety of sports without being singularly directed into the sports of basketball, and track and field.
5. Institutions can expand and provide locker rooms and other facilities including training facilities to accommodate increased female participation. In many instances in the historically black institutions, the male athletes and coaches have not been willing to share these facilities.

Rule 48: Implications for the African-American Sportswoman

Another barrier to participation in sport has been the institution of Proposition 48. At least this is a position of many African-American college presidents, athletic directors, coaches, and some civil rights leaders. These leaders strongly believe that Proposition 48 reduces participation opportunities for African-American athletes (Warfield, 1984). Rule 48 stipulates that with the start of the academic year, freshman athletes who want to participate in sports in any of the 277 Division I colleges and universities must have obtained a minimum score of 700 (of a possible 1,600) on the Scholastic Aptitude Test (SAT) or a score of 15 (of a possible 36) on the American College Test (ACT), and must have achieved a "C" average in 11 designated high school courses, including English, mathematics, social sciences, and physical sciences (Chu, Seagrave & Becker, 1985). The storm surrounding Proposition 48 has been over those provisions specifying minimum test scores as a condition for sports participation. The fundamental arguments against Proposition 48 are that (a) the minimum SAT score requirement was arbitrary and (b) that the SAT and ACT are racist diagnostic tests that display a cultural bias that favors whites only. It is argued that the 700 SAT and 15 ACT score requirement is punitive for the African-American student- athletes because statistics show that 55% of African-American students generally score lower than 700 on the SAT and 69% score lower than 15 on the ACT (Chu et al., 1985).

Certainly one could also argue that Proposition 48 forces the interscholastic athlete to take seriously the whole notion of being a student first and then an athlete. The controversy continues, and although there is some empirical evidence to show the impact Proposition 48 has had on the African-American athlete, there are no data to date to show its effect on the African-American sportswoman. It is the authors' view that African-American women have not been as negatively affected by Proposition 48 as has the black male athlete. Generally speaking, the female athlete is more successful academically. Barriers can be overcome, and the media can effect a significant difference.

Media Attitude Toward the
African-American Sportswoman

The media serves more to reenforce previously existing attitudes and behaviors than to introduce new ones. This view casts the media as a preserver of the status quo rather than an agent of social change (Rintala & Birrell, 1984). It has been well documented that African-Americans have made tremendous strides in American sport, but little research has examined the extent of media coverage awarded the African-American sportswoman.

The media coverage that women of color receive in the leading magazines reflects our public awareness and says a great deal about our level of acceptability for the sportswomen of color. What the leading magazines report serves as a medium to illustrate our cultural values and stretches our definition of excellence beyond just public recognition of one's success. The media portrayal of the African-American sportswoman serves as a mirror of society, and it is our truth teller.

If we reflect on our expectations before the 1984 Olympic Games began in Los Angeles, the majority of sport fans and athletes felt that the Games would serve as the impetus to lift the black gold medalist into the world of commercial endorsements, unlimited exposure, and infinite respect. However, 48 gold medals and four years later, most of the African-American Olympic heroes and heroines are still waiting to be celebrated. There has been a general lack of recognition and respect for the latest group of African-American Olympians and other highly talented and outstanding sportswomen of color.

Since the Olympic Games have ended, it appears that an outpouring of affection and adoration, media exposure and commercial endorsements have been directed at the United States all-white swimming and gymnastic teams, whereas African-American gold medalists who excelled in track and field have remained essentially on the sidelines. A graphic example of this situation can be found when comparing the post-Olympic lives of Mary Lou Retton, a white gymnast who won only one gold medal in 1984, and Valerie Brisco-Hooks, who won an amazing three gold medals in track in the 1984 Olympic games. Retton quickly signed endorsement contracts with McDonald's and Vidal Sassoon. She appeared on the Wheaties cereal boxes and the cover of numerous magazines. Brisco-Hooks is still waiting to get a major endorsement and is still relatively unknown ("Slap," 1985). Williams, Lawrence and Rowe (1985) explain this phenomenon by stating that women's increased participation is severely impeded by social inequities in society. One must remember that a considerable number of whites perceive African-Americans as natural athletes; and they, therefore, expect black people to excel in sports. Consequently, when women of color perform well, as they did in the 1984 and 1988 Olympic Games, there is often a feeling among the majority (primarily white America) that the sport achievement of blacks, regardless of how exceptional, does not deserve special acclaim in the form of special recognition and awards. Edwards (1969) explains that:

> Many black athletes have felt at one time or another that they were discriminated against. Aside from the money, prestige is the greatest incentive to professional sports participation. In amateur athletics, it is the main incentive, along with love of the game.

Prestige is typically accrued and measured by the frequency and general tone of publicity that an athlete receives in the various reporting media. Black athletes as a whole feel many sports reporters have not always given credit where credit is due. (p. 109)

Because the mass media are recognized as one of the most powerful institutions in our society, they serves as an important vehicle for communicating social values and identifying role models. The extent to which women of color in sport are invisible in the media suggests a symbolic annihilation of them. The African-American sportswoman's perspective in sport is lost to the public for examination.

Corbett (1987) investigated the portrayal of African-American sportswomen in 14 leading magazines (*Cosmopolitan, Glamour, Good Housekeeping, Ladies Home Journal, Ms, Redbook, Women Sport and Fitness, Woman's Day, Working Woman, Black Family, Crisis, Ebony, Essence,* and *Jet*) for a two-year period (1985 and 1986) immediately following the 1984 Olympic Games. Twenty African-American sportswomen were identified in the review of 286 issues. Her findings clearly indicated that sportswomen of color were underrepresented in the popular literature reviewed. The pattern of coverage revealed that the African-American sportswoman is essentially invisible, that she is more likely to participate in very specific individual sports, and that the sports she most often represents are the least costly sports. Athletes participating in basketball and track and field received more attention. The white female Olympian received considerable attention in the media and was represented in a variety of sports.

Although the media have the power to act as an agent of social change and can affect on society's attitude toward the African-American sportswoman, they have not done so in a positive and progressive way. It is revealing to note that Corbett (1987) in her two-year study of the portrayal of sportswomen of color, reported that *Ms* Magazine featured only one black sportswoman (Lynette Woodard - basketball) in the two-year period investigated. During this same period, three white women (Diana Nyad – swimmer, Greta Waitz–runner, and Beverly Francis–body builder) were featured. Similarly, *Essence* magazine in May 1985 did a celebration of black women without any mention of an African-American sportswoman. *Ebony* magazine in its November 1985 issue depicted black women in history who have made outstanding contributions to society. However, no mention or recognition was given to the African-American sportswoman. Valerie Brisco-Hooks said it best in an interview in 1985 when she commented, "I'm still waiting for some good things to happen" ("*Slap*," 1985, p. 29).

Summary

The experiences of the African-American female in society, and particularly in sports, have been different from those of the white female. For her, the African-American community has played an instrumental role in protecting the self-esteem of women of color by functioning as a buffer to the negative influences of the larger society. The African-American community provides a sense of personal security, identity and belonging, and a different criteria for self-assessment. The stage has been set for a workable solution to improve the status and overall conditions of athletic programs in the historically black institutions. Title IX has made a difference. Although all is not well, significant changes have occurred post-Title IX. African-American sportswomen must become more vocal about the issues of racism and sexism if change is to evolve. There are supportive and caring networks of professionals who want to make a difference and are willing to provide a supportive sport environment. Society needs to know about the African-American sportswoman's achievements and how her experiences compare to those of women of other cultures. The public must know that there are many African-American sportswomen other than Althea Gibson and Wilma Rudolph who have made significant contributions. The attitude of the media towards the African-American sportswoman forces us to recognize that the issue comes down to a balance between social responsibility and economic rationality. The dominant philosophy in journalism remains largely that the media should cover the events and issues that have the widest public interest. Unfortunately, in North America, this philosophy rarely embraces the African-American sportswoman. The struggle continues, and the recent successful litigation by Brooklyn College of New York points the way for other Title IX complaints to be levied. Brooklyn College received financial damages because of the inequities in the women's and men's athletic program. Administrators must now think harder and longer about whether they are willing to spend more dollars on women's athletic programs or take the risk of a lawsuit (Herwig, 1992).

References

Acosta, R.V., & Carpenter, L.J. (1990). *Women intercollegiate sport a longitudinal study —Thirteen year update 1977-1990.* New York:

Brooklyn College.

Alexander, A. (1979). *Status of minority women in the Association on Intercollegiate Athletics for Women.* Unpublished master's thesis, Temple University, Philadelphia.

Alston, D.J., (1980, January). *Title IX and the minority women in sport at historically black institutions.* Paper presented at the National Minority Woman in Sport Conference, Washington, DC.

Bonner, F. B. (1974). Black women and white women: a comparative analysis of perceptions of sex roles for self, ideal-self and the ideal-male. *The Journal of Afro-American Issues, 2,* 12-19.

Boutilier, M.A., & SanGiovanni, L. (1983). *The sporting woman.*Illinois: Human Kinetics Publishers.

Chu, D., Seagrave, J.O., & Becker, B.J. (1985). *Sport and higher education.* Champaign, IL: Human Kinetics Publishers.

Coakley, J.J. (1982). *Sport in society: Issues and controversies.* St. Louis, MO: C.V. Mosby.

Corbett, D. (1981). *The relationship between androgyny, self-concept, and social status among minority female athletes and non-athletes.* Unpublished doctoral dissertation. University of Maryland.

Corbett, D. (1987). The magazine media portrayal of sportswomen of color. *ICHPER/CAHPER World Conference Towards the 21st Century Conference Proceedings* (pp. 190-195). Vancouver, British Columbia, Canada: University of British Columbia.

Del Rey, P. (1977). In support of apologetic for women in sport. *International Journal of Sport Psychology, 8,* 218-223.

Edwards, H. (1969). *The revolt of the black athlete.* New York: Free Press.

Eitzen, D.S., & Furst, D. (1989). Racial bias in women's collegiate volleyball. *Journal of Sport and Social Issues, 13*(1), 46-51.

Furst, D.M., & Heaps, J.E. (1987). *Stacking in women's intercollegiate basketball.* Paper presented at the annual meeting of the North American Society for the Sociology of Sport, Edmonton, Alberta, Canada.

Gergen, K.J. (1971). *The concept of self.* New York: Holt, Rinehart & Winston.

Gibson, A. (1958). *I always wanted to be somebody.* Philadelphia: Harper and Row.

Giddings, P. (1984). *When and where I enter: The impact of black women on race and sex in America,* (pp. 327, 354, & 356). New York:

William Morrow & Company.

Green, T.S., Oglesby, C.A., Alexander, A., & Franke, N. (1981). *Black women in sport.* Reston, VA: American Alliance for Health, Physical Education, Recreation and Dance.

Gump, J.P. (1975). Comparative analysis of black women and white women sex role attitudes. *Journal of Consulting and Clinical Psychology, 43,* 858-863.

Hart, M. M. (1974). Stigma or prestige: the all-American choice. In G.. McGlynn (Ed.), *Issues in physical education and sports* (pp. 214-220). Palo Alto, California: National Press Books.

Hart, M.M. (1980). Sport: women sit in the back of the bus. In D.F. Sabo Jr. and R. Runfola (Eds.), *Jock: Sports and male identity* (pp. 205-211). Englewood Cliffs, New Jersey: Prentice-Hall.

Henderson, E.B. (1968). International library of negro life and history. *The black athlete: Emergence and arrival (*pp. 241-274*).* Washington, DC: Publishers Company.

Herwig, C. (1992). Reactions to Title IX ruling. *USA Today,* February 28.

Houzer, S. P. (1971). *The importance of selected physical education activities to women students in predominately black South Carolina colleges.* Unpublished master's thesis, Springfield College, Massachusetts.

Kagan, J. (1964). Acquisition and significance of sex-typing and sex role identity. In M.L. Hoffman and L.W. Hoffman (Eds.), *Review of Child Development Research* (pp. 53-61). New York: Russell Sage Foundation.

Kanter, R.M. (1977). Some effects of group life: Skewed sex ratios and responses to token women. *American Journal of Sociology, 82,* 965-1006.

Katz, I. (1969). A critique of personality approaches to negro performance with research suggestions. *Journal of Social Issues, 25, 13-27*

Kelly, H.A., & Worell, J. (1977). New formulations of sex roles and androgyny: a critical review. *Journal of Consulting and Clinical Psychology, 45*(6), 1101-1115.

King, M.C. (1973). The politics of sexual stereotypes. *The Black Scholar,* March-April, pp.17-24.

Kohlberg, L.A. (1966). A cognitive developmental analysis of children's sex role concept and attitudes. In E.C. Maccoby (Ed.), *The Development of sex differences* (pp. 186, 188, 189, 210). Stanford, California:

Stanford University Press.

Lewis, D. (1975). The black family: socialization and sex roles. *Phylon, Fall, 36,* 221-237.

Metheny, E. (1965). *Connotations of movement in sport and dance.* Dubuque, IA: William C. Brown.

Metheny, E. (1972). Symbolic forms of movement: The feminine image in sports. In M.H. Hart (Ed.), *Sports in the socio-cultural process* (pp. 277-290). Dubuque, IA: William C. Brown.

Oglesby, C.A. (1978). The masculinity femininity game: Called on account of . . . In C.A. Oglesby, *Women and sport: From myth to reality* (p. 82). Philadelphia: Lea & Febiger.

Oglesby, C.A. (1981). Myths and realities of black women in sport. In T.S. Green, C.A. Oglesby, A. Alexander and N. Franke (Eds.), *Black Women in Sport,* (pp. 1-2). Reston, Virginia: AAHPERD Publications.

Pettigrew, T.F. (1964). *A profile of the Negro American.* Princeton, NJ: Van Nostrand.

Pinkey, R. (1975, June-July). Taking a sporting chance. *Encore,* (pp. 58-63).

Rintala, J., & Birrell, S.(1984). Fair treatment for the active female: A content analysis of young athlete magazine. *Sociology of Sport Journal, 1*(3), 231-250.

Simmel, G. (1950). *The sociology of George Simmel.* (Kurt H. Wolff, Trans.). Glencoe, IL: Free Press.

Simmons, G.L., (1979). *The impact of implementing Title IX in a predominantly black public university.* Washington, DC: U.S. Department of Health, Education & Welfare National Institute of Education.

Slap in the face (1985, Summer). *Ebony Magazine, 6,* 29.

Snyder, E.E., & Kivlin, J.E. (1975). Women athletes and aspects of psychological well-being. *Research Quarterly, 46,* 191-199.

Snyder, E.E., & Spreitzer, J.E. (1975). The female athlete: Analysis of objective and subjective conflict. In D.M. Landers (Ed.), *Psychology of sports and motor behavior* (p. 165). University Park: Pennsylvania State University.

Staples, R. (1970). The myth of the black matriarchy. *The Black Scholar, 1,* 8.

Twin, S.L. (1979). *Out of the bleachers: Writings on women and sport.* New York: McGraw-Hill Book Company.

United States Commission on Civil Rights, (1980). *More hurdles to clear.* Washington, DC: Clearinghouse Publication #63.

Warfield, J.L. (1984). NCAA Rule 49, black leaders and collegiate student-athletes' bill of rights: A critique. *Center for African and Afro-American Studies and Research.* Austin, TX: University of Texas-Austin, Vester Center.

Watson, V. (1974). Self-concept formation and the Afro-American woman. *Journal of Afro-American Issues, 11,* 225-233.

Williams, C., Lawrence, G., & Rowe, D. (1985). Women and sport: A lost ideal. *Women's Studies International Forum, 8*(6), 639-645.

Yetman, N.R., Berghorn, F.J., & Thomas, F.R. (1982). Racial participation and integration in intercollegiate basketball, 1958-1980. *Journal of Sport Behavior, 5,* 44-56.

Yorburg, B. (1974). *Sexual identity, sex roles and social change.* New York: John Wiley & Sons.

Young, A.S. (1963). *Negro firsts in sports.* Chicago: Johnson Publishing Company.

Essay 7

The Future of African-American Female Athletes

Tina Sloan Green

Abstract: The author provides a historical and social overview of African-American women's participation in college athletics. Despite the lack of existing data, the author is optimistic about the future of African-American female participation in sport. Organizations such as PGM Golf, YWCA's, Girls Clubs, and the National Youth Sport Program will continue to enhance participation opportunities for females.

The essay targets the future of the elite African-American female athlete. Particular attention is given to her capitalization on the American commercial market and greater prominence gained through media exposure. As we approach the next century, it is predicted the number of African-American females participating in college and professional sports in foreign countries will increase. However, barriers such as racism, sexism, and politics will continue in the twenty-first century.

Recommendations to eradicate sexism and racism include having African-American females apply for sport-related jobs, creating jobs in the African-American community, establishing sport camps and clinics, and serving as sport interns.

Introduction

What is the future of African-American women in sports and athletics? The predictions that follow are based on my discussions and interactions with contemporary African-American female athletes, administrators, and coaches. All agree that economics will be one of the primary factors affecting the future of these African-American women. Although limited research has been conducted on the contributions and participation levels of African-American sportswomen, the literature available indicates that there has been limited but increased involvement during the twentieth century.

In categorizing some current research on the representation of African-American women in sport, Beatrice Smith (1986) reports that 281 African-American females made major contributions to sports between 1900-1979 in 35 different areas. Focusing on the mid-1970s, Alpha Alexander's (1978) data indicated there were 17,000 women athletes in the Association of Intercollegiate Association for Women (AIAW) during the 1976-1977 academic year, of which 1,000 were African-American (5.8%). Approximately one decade later, Acosta and Carpenter (1990) found between 1986-1987 African-American women accounted for 10.3% of intercollegiate athletic participants. A study reported by the Center for the Study of Athletics (1989) for the National Collegiate Athletic Association revealed that 33% of women's basketball players on NCAA Division I teams were African-American, whereas African-Americans constituted only 8% of all other sports combined.

Evidence of an apparent lack of participation of African-American female athletes in scholastic sport programs has also been documented. According to the Women's Sport Foundation report (1989) on minorities in sport, the National Federation of State High Schools Association found that about 5.25 million youths participated in varsity sports in 1987-1988. Yet black females represented only 4.4% of the total sample of varsity athletes in 1980-1982.

One factor that may allow more African-Americans to participate in sport may be an increase in their economic status. Historically, African-American women have not had time to participate in games or sports (Corbett, 1981). It was necessary to work for whatever salary was available while nonworking hours were spent mothering and tending to household chores. Today, among the African-American middle and upper classes, more time and money may be available to pursue sport activities including enrollment of young children in sports programs. Regardless of some modest affluence, in the remaining years of this century, however, the majority of African-Americans will continue to experience economic oppression and a very large number will remain poor.

Among African-American women who are struggling to provide the basic necessities of life while making financial ends meet for their families and themselves, sport will remain a frivolous commodity --one that they will have neither the time nor the energy to pursue. In my estimate, public schools must provide realistic and inexpensive lifetime sport and fitness training for African-American females from childhood through high school. Perhaps if African-American women develop positive attitudes and habits concerning physical activity when they are young, these practices will continue into their adult lives.

Recreational Sport and the African-American Female

According to Warwick (1991), the scope of recreation programs in urban areas has improved and should continue improving in the future. If this is so, African-American children growing up in low-income environments may have more access to recreational sports than has been the case in the past. A variety of reasons may help us to understand changes in participation levels.

First of all, Title IX legislation and feminist groups have pressured agencies and sports organizations to provide more recreational sports activities for females. We may see more and more African-American girls involved in league basketball, track and field, and softball. Secondly, many facilities--tennis courts, pools, outdoor fields--in urban areas now are available for use by African-Americans.

Finally, changes in residential patterns and neighborhood composition may also affect the availability of recreational resources: As whites fled the city, they left behind facilities that may be used by African-Americans moving into these communities. The availability of facilities in African-American neighborhoods, in turn, places pressure on local recreation leaders to provide instruction and supervision in swimming, tennis, field hockey, and other sport activities. This "replacement" phenomenon was best exemplified in some Philadelphia residential areas during the late '70s as African-Americans moved into Germantown, Mt. Airy, and other residential areas of west and north Philadelphia. In areas like these more African-American children than ever before are swimming on a daily basis, participating in summer tennis camps, and playing basketball year-round.

Indications are that local fiscal and budgetary crises confronting cities will force some regional and national sport-governing bodies, nonprofit associations as well as youth organizations and clubs, to assume more responsibility for providing resources for youth sports. Government funds and Olympic development funds may be more commonly available for sport programs that are offered as alternatives for drugs and key on maintaining the fitness of our youth. Current projects undertaken by the United States Tennis Association, the Amateur Athletic Union, Track Athletic Congress, United States Field Hockey Association, United States Golf Association and others may enhance sport opportunities for the inner-city African-American population (Williams, 1990). Some observers suspect that tennis, golf, and other such sports may forge new economic markets by revealing that the African-American population is a viable economic market for equipment, foot gear, and athletic talent.

In the professional arena, the white-dominated sport organization and associations raise million of dollars using grassroots involvement as a giving incentive. Although domination has grown less blatant, economic influence continues to exclude blacks from economic participation, certainly from economic power. One suspects that it is in the best interest of sports organizations to control the funding for minority programs and to continue striving to monopolize the administration of sports while also controlling how African-Americans may be allowed to succeed. Tempering such oppressiveness, if these organizations do not build programs for minorities, they will be subject to lawsuits alleging discrimination. Likewise, providing minority programs also avoids the threat of African-Americans' developing their own programs, producing talented athletes, and bypassing the national organizing body.

For young inner-city women, the YWCA, Girls' Clubs, and the Girl Scouts have recognized that girls have an array of social and recreational interests and many have strong interests in sport (Alexander, 1991). These organizations will continue to encourage sports activities in their programs. Indeed, one suspects that since many clubs are located in the city and their former white clientele has moved to the suburbs, the clubs' leadership will be forced to gear their programs toward the African-American, Hispanic, and other minority populations that now occupy the neighborhoods.

The YWCA initiated grassroot programs for girls in field hockey, basketball, tennis, volleyball, and gymnastics, as well as swimming and fitness. It has a long-standing commitment to provide leadership positions for minority women and to eliminate racism and sexism in sport programs. These efforts should also aid in promoting sports participation among minorities.

Another nationwide association of groups that is geared to fight minority oppression through the provision of opportunities for personal growth and social development by focusing on an array of recreational activities is the NCAA's National Youth Sports Program (NYSP). The NYSP programs are now held during the summer at 139 universities, and continue to have an impact on increasing participation of young African-American girls and women involved in sports and sport-related fields. Largely the offspring of activist public conscience of the civil rights movement, the NYSP was created in the summer of 1968 and is presently administered by the NCAA Office of Community Services (OCS), Family Support Administration, United States Department of Health and Human Services (DHHS), and selected colleges and universities. In 1990 the NYSP serviced 57,545 disadvantaged youths between the ages of 10-16 in 119 different cities. Since the NYSP has strong affiliations with historically black colleges and urban universities, the majority of the participants are African-Americans.

Elite Sport and the African-American Female

It is likely that improved sport programs and facilities in urban areas result in an increased recreational participation among young African-American women and men. At the same time, what may be needed to raise the skill level of African-American female athletes to that of the elite athlete is a significant improvement in the quality of programs (facilities, instruction, support services). Unless the programs in the African-American neighborhoods can compete in quality with the established white programs, it is doubtful that significant numbers of African-American female champions will emerge during the next decade.

The possibility to compete successfully for more athletic scholarships will encourage some exceptional African-American female athletes in urban areas to pursue their sports seriously. Title IX has forced universities all over the country to offer scholarships for women. Just as African-American men have used scholarships as a means to acquire an education and a profession, so too will African-American females. Chances have increased for African-American female athletes to attend ''top name'' colleges that were previously out of their economic and social ranges.

The exploitation of student-athletes is documented, and in their quest for a championship team, colleges must not exploit the African-American female athlete as they have the African-American male athlete (Wiley, 1990). For example, to maintain a competitive program, coaches are apt to place heavy, sometimes extraordinary, demands on their African-American scholarship athletes. Even though African-American women may come to college for academic achievement, sport forces them to devote long hours to practicing, traveling, and competing, with very little time left for their academic studies. A demanding schedule, in turn, may encourage some African-American female athletes to take easy courses held at convenient times. Faculty members may also contribute to the exploitative system by "giving grades" to female athletes who rarely attend class. Some also complain about being forced to compete when they are injured, about being prohibited from going home for scheduled holiday weekends, and about being restricted in their social development. In the end, the athlete is left too often with an inferior education and usually no degree.

The new NCAA legislation, which restricts practice and competition time for athletes, will help eliminate some of the exploitation and reduce the injustices. Tutoring and academic support services, structures that should be included in every program--certainly in every Division I athletic program--may also help offset the effects of exploiting athletes. Focusing on equalizing the outcomes to ensure minority education, financial aid and academic advising must not only be available for the student-athlete during her four years of eligibility but must also prove successful to support her after eligibility expires to ensure her educational goals. When a university offers a minority student an athletic scholarship and accepts her into the institution, it is imperative that the institution also provide all the support the student needs for academic survival (Clark, 1988; Matthews, 1988).

The African-American female athlete is no more prepared to define educational goals than is any other student, and she may find it very difficult to refine and adapt goals to be assured success. African-American female athletes must make sure that they earn a degree as well as a varsity sport letter, because after four years of collegiate participation, the opportunity to enter the professional sport arena will be very slim. It is unlikely that professional basketball or professional track and field for females will flourish in the United States in the next decade, and the global market for sports is probably even more confined for women than for elite male athletes.

Sexism has had and will continue to have serious penalties for women in professional sport. Sponsors and spectators spend millions of dollars in support of men's basketball and track teams, but sponsors and spectators do not support female athletes and teams. This is not simply a lack of parity; it is sheer exclusion, with the exception of a few white-dominated, media-driven games like golf and tennis, which receive scant attention and control from the NCAA. Although there have been several attempts to establish professional female basketball leagues in the United States, these efforts were unsuccessful because, I believe, there was a lack of public interest, low salaries, and lack of sponsorship. A few elite African-American women athletes who are willing to travel will find greater financial opportunities in basketball, or in track and field in the European and Japanese markets.

One suspects that African-American female athletes who deal with economic hardships in new, largely corporate and media-driven sports tours and matches like golf and tennis will need to rely on new sources of backing. Currently, promising white tennis and golf pros begin to train very young, at ages six through eight. Parents usually are well-to-do business professionals, with access to sponsoring networks (money) and to expertise for training their daughters. In a 1988 report by the United States Tennis Association, Ron Woods, Director of the Player Development Program said, "We found that the average national junior player comes from a family that was making $80,000" (cited in Markowitz, 1991, p. 7). In addition, it is not uncommon for top juniors to move to warm climates in order to practice year round.

In tennis, only Zina Garrison (a top 20 player) and Lori McNeal and Stacy Martin (doubles) are highly ranked professional players. People like Arthur Ashe, Althea Gibson, Bill Cosby, and John H. Johnson of Johnson Publishing Company have helped with financial obligations of these current African-American female tennis players. Undoubtedly, improving the play, thus increasing the number, of African-American females playing tennis and golf, will rely on, and awaits, increased corporate sponsorship.

The absence and poor quality of facilities for training and tournament play of African-Americans is one barrier that can begin to be corrected with money. Not long ago, the Chairman of the Black Tennis and Sports Foundation announced the formation of a minority support program to assist promising minority and disadvantaged junior tennis players. With such organizational assistance, promising upcoming juniors like Chanda Rubin, Traci Green, Jodie Anglin, Joy Mitchell, and Venus Williams could possibly break into top professional tennis ranks.

There are strong indications that initiatives are also being implemented to attract and support young African-American females in golf. For example, since 1971, the PGM Golf Clinic, Inc., a golf program for African-American youth in Philadelphia, has been responsible for introducing golf skills to African-American girls and boys on playgrounds, school yards, in church basements, and on public golf courses. The United States Golf Association has recently established a minority program to attract and retain minority junior golfers. Working with this program, Rose Elder has been very influential in raising funds for promising young African-American golfers. The chances are still slim that the African-American female tennis or golf pro will suddenly emerge from the collegiate scene in the next decade without extensive training, strong parental support, and broad media exposure beyond the collegiate experience.

Role of the Media
Greater prominence through media exposure is an advantage that the new upcoming generation of collegiate African-American women athletes can and will enjoy. Although media exposure will surely generate a more ubiquitous, and probably vicariously known African-American female role model, chances are good that a collection of elite women will stand as candidates for this role model. African-American youth hold to the old sayings "seeing is believing" and "a picture is worth a thousand words." Minority role models (including African-American males and females) in sport will make children and parents believers. If youngsters have the opportunity to watch highly skilled African-American athletes on television, their motivation to pursue the sport as participants may increase.

In order for the elite African-American female athlete to capitalize on the United States commercial market, the sport as well as the athlete must appeal to the white upper- middle classes. We can compare this to fashion, where many trends originate in lower class subcultures but usually do not become popular until they are sanctioned by the socially elite. Sport practitioners must work together to get the white economically elite to value and identify with the "Flo-Jo"s and Zina Garrisons.

Top-level women's team sports like basketball, field hockey, lacrosse, and soccer have been and will continue to be predominantly participation sports rather than spectator sports, and have almost no chance to capture very much media exposure. Florence Griffith Joyner (Flo-Jo) has been one of a few African-American talents able to take advantage of commercial markets. Her unique running attire appealed not only to female track stars but also to female joggers, walkers, and fitness buffs. She also became a sex symbol for men. In general, not many women have lucrative, endorsement contracts, but most women who do, possess Eurocentric features and manners: Jennifer Capriati, Monica Seles and Chris Evert (all tennis players) represent types of female images appreciated by the upper-middle-class white establishment.

It has been my experience that racism and sexism are critical forces that will prevent the African-American female "star" athlete from achieving commercial success. Either she will have to be talented and also portray an appealing middle-class image, or she will need to possess exceptional talent. Like successful entertainers who create a flamboyant and creative image package, she may have to develop something (hair, clothing, or personality) that makes her stand out from the crowd.

The media should be more accessible to women, and more vulnerable to concerted efforts among African-Americans. African-American political factions, especially women's groups, must put pressure on the media and sponsors for greater coverage. Sponsors must be convinced that there is an untapped economic market in African-American communities for sport gear. The African-American media must also play a greater role in promoting African-American female athletes. African-American female athletes may find more financial success in foreign markets like Europe or Japan where their Afrocentric differences have gained recognition.

According to June Rogers, professor of black studies at California State University at Fresno, "Afrocentricism is an important new educational emphasis on the African and African-American experience and contributions to human culture"(Wiley, 1991, p. 1). Afrocentricism gives credibility, respect, and value to the African-American heritage, which oftentimes in the past has been ignored or misrepresented by the dominant, American, Eurocentric ideology (Wiley, 1991). Dark skin, curly hair, large facial features, and body shape prevent many African-American females from fitting the profile of the All-American white girl, a fair-skinned, blue-eyed blonde with petite hips and waist. Cultural differences in speech, body language, and customs prevent many African-American females from being accepted by the dominant white culture. For purposes of social and economic mobility, African-Americans sometimes find it necessary to modify their behavior and appearance so that they can resemble the dominant model.

From a personal perspective, I toured with the United States Women's Lacrosse team to Australia and Japan in 1969, and for the first time in my playing career I felt like a star. Much to the surprise of my white teammates, in these countries I was given very special treatment and media publicity. The Australians and the Japanese had many questions about the African-American experience in white America. Eurocentricism does not encourage the African-American athlete to feel good about her differences, but Afrocentricism encourages the African-American athlete to value her diversity.

Even though the African-American female athlete will have greater career opportunities in foreign countries in the year 2000, she will face other obstacles that will affect the longevity of her playing career. Isolation from family and friends will be a very significant problem. It will be very difficult to establish and retain a romantic relationship. Likewise, it will be very costly to call home to say "Hi" or "Happy Birthday," or to attend family funerals, weddings, or parties. Other obstacles to overcome include demanding travel schedules; limited availability of black hair care or cosmetics; and the absence of favorite foods, music, and cultural events. In order to make positive adjustments, it is imperative that the gifted African-American athlete experience travel to foreign countries early in her career. It is also important that she have enough corporate sponsorship so that she can travel not only with a coach but also with family members and/or a significant other.

School Sport and the African-American Female
The role of school sport and athletics has changed dramatically over the decades. The extent to which the gifted African-American female athlete will be able to advance in her sport in a school setting will depend on her educational background, the positive advice and support that she receives from family and coaches/teachers, and her own self-discipline, work ethic, and motivation. Sport should be used by educators as a vehicle for fostering academic achievement. Some literature tends to support this concept. For example, a study by the Women's Sport Foundation (1989) concluded that athletic participation enhanced involvement in school and community activities. It was interesting to note that minority athletes actually performed better academically than did nonathletes. In addition,

sport involvement lowered the dropout rate among some minorities in suburban and rural schools.

These findings justify the inclusion of a variety of sports in schools to capture the interest and talents of a variety of students. In order for the student to participate in high school sports, however, there should be minimum academic requirements such as (a) regular class attendance, (b) an acceptable GPA, and (c) good citizenship. It is my belief that if the student does not meet these requirements, she should not be allowed to participate in sports.

Students should know that coaches care about and monitor their progress. Once students know that they need to fulfill certain requirements for participation and that the rules will be enforced, they are more likely to assume responsibility for their actions and adjust their behavior in order to play. Coaches should inform parents if they think the student-athlete has potential for college athletics, but is not achieving academically. Maybe the home and school together can find an answer for the student's lack of success.

Student-athletes who think they want to go on to college should see their counselors and/or coaches in the eighth or ninth grade to plan their course selections. The academic school policy for athletic participation should be well publicized and enforced. In addition, each student-athlete and coach should be made aware of NCAA Proposal 48, which defines GPA standards, core curriculum minimums, and minimum standardized test scores. High schools must invest in tutoring programs, and student-athletes must be encouraged to take advantage of them. Each school district should offer a college board preparatory course or make available to students information on extension courses that deal with how to take the SAT and ACT. Students should be encouraged to take the exam in 10th grade, just for practice. The outstanding academic achievement of student-athletes should be publicized in the school and local papers, and coaches and staff should send letters of commendation to such students. Student-athletes should sit down with their coaches and parents and establish career goals at the start of the 9th and 10th grade. Too often students reach the 12th grade only to discover that they have not taken the right courses for entrance to college. Students should be encouraged to dream, to strive for excellence, to take risks, and to love themselves.

Coaches of schoolgirl athletes will influence the lives of many African-American female athletes. They should not lower their expectations for the minority athlete, whether it be in academics or athletics. If their high school coaches had not encouraged academic achievement, many of today's professional people would never have earned a college degree. A good coach will assist her student-athletes and their parents with the selection of colleges (M. Jackson, personal communication, 1991). The coach should help the athlete realistically evaluate her ability and advise the athlete of the probability of her playing on a Division I, II, or III collegiate level. The coach should talk with these students and send them where they are most likely to survive academically and socially. Coaches should assist athletes with completing college forms and meeting deadlines, and encourage them to visit the school of their choice. Although the coach will be in a position to influence the college selection for some athletes, the African-American student-athlete along with her parents should also take responsibility for evaluating all the given information and choosing the college that best fits her needs.

The high school student-athlete should also know the difference between BEOG (need-based grant) and an athletic performance grant. She should write the NCAA for a booklet about the recruitment rules. She should visit the colleges of her choice and interview the coaches. She should ask the coach about coaching philosophy, coaching style, practice and travel schedule, and the role that the student will have on the team. The coach's answers should be honest and reflect a concern for the athlete as a student and a person. The student athlete should find out how many minority athletes are presently enrolled in the university and how many have graduated from the college. She should talk with those minority female athletes on campus about the campus atmosphere and make sure the university offers her career choice. The urban high school African-American student-athlete must realize that even though she has good grades, good study skills, and has completed all the college application procedures in a timely fashion, the possibility of a scholarship aid will be quite limited.

Unless academic performance drastically improves in the urban schools, the reduction of the number of NCAA athletic performance grants and the enforcement of NCAA rules that increase academic standards will negatively affect the numbers of African-American female athletes completing degrees at Division I universities. Those exceptional athletes with strong academic credentials will be highly recruited and financed by Division I colleges. Basketball and track and field will continue to have a high African-American participation rate on many campuses (Acosta & Carpenter, 1990). However, those African-American student-athletes who are educationally disadvantaged will be denied entrance to, and financial support from, Division I institutions. Some will choose not to attend college, thus ending their athletic career. Others will attend junior college hoping to transfer to a major institution at a later date.

Attending a junior college is an excellent alternative for those who do not qualify academically or financially for a four-year institution. Many community colleges are less expensive than four-year institutions and are more sensitive to serving the needs of educationally disadvantaged students. According to Jill R. Triplett (1991), "One fourth of the students enrolled in Junior Colleges are minorities" (p. 38).

For a variety of reasons, however, community college students have a low transfer rate, and Blacks and Hispanics have a lower transfer rate than both whites and Asians. Because the community colleges are possible sources for increasing the pool of minority professionals, there is presently a concerted effort to encourage community college students to transfer to four-year institutions. Four-year institutions are developing transfer agreements with community colleges and establishing better community college recruitment programs. Programs that target minority community college students will address two critical issues facing the nation: increasing the total number of black students earning baccalaureate degrees and providing a large pool of prospective teachers (Triplett, 1991).

Many community colleges are trying to establish a campus-like environment that will encourage students to stay on campus after classes. Intercollegiate athletic programs are being created and improved to enhance campus life. This will have positive implications for the student-athlete who does not initially qualify academically for a four-year institution. The community college will provide the student the opportunity to maintain her athletic skills, improve her academic skills, and transfer in good standing. Because of the expected increase in academic standards in the next decade, I see community colleges playing a greater role in providing opportunities for African-American female athletes to attend a four-year institution.

Historically black colleges will also continue to play a major role in providing educational opportunities for educationally disadvantaged female student-athletes. With the proper nurturing, some of these student-athletes will thrive academically and receive their degree. However, because of the inequality of competition, lack of media exposure, and lack of political connections, many of these athletes will not receive top recognition in their sports. After they receive their degree, will there be opportunities for these African-American female athletes in sport-related fields?

Sport Careers and the African-American Female

With the projected increase of sports participants and evident affirmative action guidelines, it would seem natural that one would predict an increase in the numbers of African-American females in sport-related fields such as administration, coaching, commentating, officiating, athletic training, and sports information. However, in the past 18 years, the number of female coaches and athletic administrators has drastically decreased. Furthermore, black women as athletic directors and coaches in sports are rapidly becoming invisible (Acosta & Carpenter, 1990). I believe that there will continue to be great barriers to increasing the numbers of African-American females in high authority sport occupations.

Abney and Richey (1991) surveyed and interviewed black female administrators and coaches at both black and white institutions and recorded the social and institutional barriers that affect their mobility. The black women at both white and black institutions listed low salaries as a great obstacle in their career development. It is well established in this country that black women are paid less than white men, black men, and white women. Abney's study also revealed that black women lacked support groups. There was an expressed need for role models and mentors. Being a woman was listed as another barrier that was cited by these women. In addition, they constantly had to deal with challenges to their competence and with peer disrespect. Many, especially those employed at white institutions, expressed a feeling of isolation and loneliness because of the lack of cultural and social activities. Being black presented another barrier for black women at white institutions where they were expected to be the black expert on all black issues. Employer discrimination in the promotion practices was another cited barrier. And lastly low expectations by administrators and others was mentioned. In other words, black women were given titles without significant or challenging responsibility.

It was believed that these barriers could be reduced if black women could continue to compete for jobs and maintain a strong self-concept in spite of the obstacles. They were encouraged to create or find mentoring programs. It was suggested that black women constantly improve their administrative skills and actively seek administrative leadership roles in sports organizations. They should also try to replace themselves by mentoring promising African-American females who have an interest in sports (Abney & Richey, 1991).

As a former All-American collegiate athlete in field hockey and lacrosse, and current head coach and professor of physical education in an urban university, and as a result of conversations with other players and colleagues, my experiences indicate that racism, sexism, and politics continue to influence hiring practices. The African-American male has dominated the sports of basketball and football, but how many black head coaches, athletic directors, sports promoters and commentators have been seen in the past 20 years? As coaching female athletes becomes more financially and socially lucrative, the white male, the white female, the African-American male, and other minorities will compete with the African-American female for the same job. Lack of sufficient experience will be the cited reason for not hiring African-American females (Edwards, 1983). Those few African-American females who are hired will be either super-qualified or young graduates who can enter the work force at minimal salaries.

The current trend, which will continue over the next decade without significant affirmative action efforts, is a decrease in the numbers of female athletic directors and coaches. Mergers of departments will force reorganization and in many cases create male leadership. I believe that those few African-American females who are currently athletic directors or associate athletic directors will be replaced by men or by white women. The trends indicate that the "old white girls" have been replaced by the "old white boys" and in a few cases by the "old black boys" in administration and coaching (Acosta & Carpenter, 1990). In 1972, 90% were headed by a female. In 1990, only 16% of women's programs were headed by a female. The NCAA has made an attempt to reverse the trend by proposing that each school that receives NCAA basketball revenue have at least one senior female administrator for women's sports.

Sport in the Year 2000 and the
African-American Female: Future Strategies

My experiences have lead me to believe that racism, sexism, and politics will still exist in the next century. Even though we erase or change discriminatory laws and practices, racist and sexist attitudes and feelings will be hard to change. Minorities must continue to insist on representation in the administrative committee structure and professional staff of each sport organization. We need sensitive minorities on each committee to scrutinize the process, to protect the welfare of our African-American athletes, and to support inclusive rather than exclusive legislation. We also need to encourage the hiring of minority role models on every level of sport.

Young African-American athletes must be prepared for the racist, sexist, and political roadblocks that they will face. They have to realize that to be successful they cannot be just average but must be high achievers, superstars. There must be strong support systems for the African-American female athlete at every level. Even after working hard and achieving, there will be times when she will be frustrated and disgusted. In times like these, she will need reassurance from her support group or mentor. The few African-American pioneers who succeed as coaches, commentators, or athletic administrators will become important role models for others.

It is important that African-American women continue to apply for sport-related jobs. After applying for several jobs and being rejected time and time again, it is only natural to lose some self-confidence and to adopt a negative attitude. However, it is important not to become lost in self-blame but to look at the employment system and the process. A large-scale study of high-achieving students in historically black colleges showed that these students were able to perceive appropriate levels of system blame (Epps & Gurin, 1975).

It will also be necessary for African-American women to create jobs in the African-American communities so that they can obtain the experience necessary to compete in the national market. It appears that young African-American women are prevented from getting jobs. But how does one obtain experience if one is not hired?

Sports camps and clinics have traditionally been excellent training grounds for aspiring young coaches, officials, and clinicians. It is very difficult for the young African-American woman to find work at well-established camps and clinics. African-American females are encouraged to establish camps and clinics in and for the African-American community. They can then gain coaching, officiating, and administrative experience.

Volunteering to be an intern in established programs in community Y's, recreation centers, or schools is another way of gaining valuable work experience. The United States Olympic Committee (USOC) and the National Collegiate Athletic Association (NCAA, 1988)) have excellent internship opportunities for athletes pursuing experience in sports administration. The NCAA also provides graduate scholarships to promising minority and female applicants who wish to complete a master's or doctoral degrees in sports administration. Some African-American females have taken advantage of these programs, and I suspect others may take advantage of these opportunities in the future.

Finally, since sport reflects society, it is highly unlikely that the African-American female athlete in this country will receive the recognition and status of the male athlete. It will continue to be a struggle to eliminate sexist attitudes about the role of sport in the lives of girls and women. Based on my experience as a college coach and former athlete, once girls participate regularly in a sport it is likely that their spectator interest will also increase. Young African-American girls must see and identify with their mothers, sisters, and friends who enjoy competing in sport, in order to reinforce their own participation as being normal, acceptable behavior. The possibility of obtaining an athletic scholarship has helped to positively influence mothers' and fathers' opinions about women in sport. As a result, many more parents are encouraging their daughters to participate in sports in hope of their earning a college degree.

In spite of racism, sexism, and inadequate financial support, we will still find those African-American women who will succeed and break barriers in sport. Why? Because of their internal fortitude, desire, and courage to overcome the obstacles placed before them. The real future of the African-American woman in sport rests in the strength of the African-American girl. Will she be able to endure the struggle? Will the struggle be worthwhile? There will be some women willing to fight and to sacrifice for a goal or a dream. In the next 20 years those who attempt to achieve excellence in sport will have the exhortation and the knowledge of those who have endured and succeeded.

I say to the young African-American girl, believe in yourself, and dare to be great. You can if you think you can. Be proud of being African-American, be proud of being a woman, be proud of being an athlete. Draw strength from reading about the struggles of past successful African-American women in sport. It is hoped that your name will be added to the list of outstanding African-American females in sport.

I appeal to the whites, African-Americans, and other people of color to work together to support and encourage African-American female participation in sport and athletics. By valuing diversity and making every effort to eliminate sexism and racism in sport, together we will improve the quality of life for all Americans.

References

Abney, R., & Richey, D. (1991). Barriers encountered by black female administrators and coaches. *Journal of Physical Education, Recreation, and Dance, 62,* 18-21.

Acosta, R.V., & Carpenter, L.J. (1990). *Women in intercollegiate sport: A longitudinal study thirteen-year update, 1977-1990.* New York: Brooklyn College.

Alexander, A. (1978). *Status of minority women in the association of intercollegiate athletics for women.* Unpublished master's thesis, Temple University, Philadelphia.

Alexander, A. (1991). New programs in girl-serving agencies. *Women's Sports Foundation Annual Conference Proceedings.* New York: Women's Sport Foundation, pp. 101-107.

Center for the Study of Athletics (1989). Report No 3: *The life experiences of black intercollegiate athletes at NCAA Division I universities.* Palo Alto: American Institutes for Research.

Clark, G. (1988, February 15). Campus environment critical to minority retention. *Black Issues in Higher Education, 4*(26) p. 12.

Corbett, D. (1981). *Learned social identity of the black female athlete and non-athlete.* Paper presented at the North American Society for Sociology of Sport, Ft. Worth, TX, p. 13.

Edwards, H. (1983, August). Educating black athletes. *Atlantic Monthly,* pp. 31-38.

Epps, E.E., & Gurin, P. (1975). *Black consciousness identity and achievement: A study of students in historically black colleges.* New York: Wiley Publishers.

Markowitz, D. (1991, February 12). Charges of racism now a tennis problem. *New York Times.*

Matthews, J. (1988, June 1). Mentor programs brings students, faculty together. *Black Issues in Higher Education, 5*(7), pp. 11-16.

National Collegiate Athletic Association (1988). Summary to the survey of NCAA member institutions and conferences on minority representation. KS: Author.

Sloan, T., Oglesby, C., Alexander, A., & Franke, N. (1981). *Black women in sport.* Reston, Virginia: AAHPERD.

Smith, B.A. (1986). *Contributions of black women to sport in America: A reference catalog.* Unpublished master's thesis. Philadelphia: Temple University.

Triplett, J.R. (1991, August 29). The nation's community colleges are an untapped resource for new minority teachers. *Black Issues in Higher Education,* 8(14), p. 88.

Warwick, R. (1991, October). African-American recreation participation trends 1980-88. 1991 Leisure Research Symposium, Baltimore, MD, p. 4.

Wiley, E. (1990, May 10). Forum addresses solution to education plight of black athletes. *Black Issues in Higher Education,* 7(5), p. 18-20.

Wiley, E., III (1991, October 24). Afrocentricism: Many things to many people. *Black Issues in Higher Education,* 8(18), pp. 1, 20.

Williams, R. (1990, November). Is tennis doing the right thing for blacks. *Tennis,* p. 46.

Women's Sport Foundation (1989). *Minorities in sport.* New York: Author, pp. 4-5.

Essay 8

Intergroup Race Relations: Success or Failure?

Alison Dewar

Abstract: In this essay I argue for the development of antiracist policies and practices in sport. I present an analysis and critique of existing work on race in the sociology of sport and argue for inclusive feminist analyses of racism in sport. The essay concludes with strategies for challenging racism in sport and argues for the development of both policies and practices that work towards a recognition and celebration of difference.

Introduction

Prejudice does hurt, however, just as the absence of it can nourish and shelter. Discrimination can repel and vilify, ostracize and alienate. Any white person who doesn't believe it should spend a week telling everyone she meets that one of her parents or grandparents was black. (Williams, 1991, p. 61)

... if we are to understand gender and racial relations in sport, particularly as they relate to women of color, we cannot remain in our old theoretical homes, for we have seen how that approach has limited us. Instead we need to increase our awareness of issues in the lives of women of color as they themselves articulate these issues. (Birrell, 1990, p. 195)

I begin with these statements from Patricia Williams and Susan Birrell because they help to set the scene for this essay. Both of these quotations, taken from very different works on racism in the law and racism in sport, remind me of the importance of challenging oppression and of doing so in ways that make explicit the fact that race relations are always developed, articulated, and understood within systems of power and privilege that define and structure these relations.

This essay addresses oppressive practices in sport and focuses on the importance of challenging and changing the racist structures and practices that exist within intercollegiate sport. This is not an easy task or one that can be achieved in a short essay. In order to make my arguments I will limit my analysis to race relations in women's sport. I do this for two reasons. First, as a white, radical feminist I am concerned that much of our work in the sociology of sport is and continues to be Eurocentric. We have tended to develop analyses in which sexism is defined as a primary form of oppression, which has meant that we have tended to make invisible other forms of oppression, particularly racism, that exist in sport.[1] Secondly, as a white, middle-class, lesbian feminist my attempts to understand and locate myself within the systems of power, privilege, and oppression that exist in the world have meant that I have turned to the work of feminists and womanists for help. Although this feminist, womanist work is not about sport or sporting practices as we commonly think of them, it is important because it is directed towards challenging oppression and developing ways of knowing and being in the world that work against all forms of oppression in all women's lives.

The purpose of this essay is to examine the nature of intergroup race relations in collegiate athletics. I argue that in order to understand the dynamics of this process it is important to examine the ways in which racism, sexism, heterosexism, and classism shape these relations. In this essay I argue for theories and actual practices that are designed to work against oppression. I also argue for the development of theories and practices that provide ways of relating in which alliances are possible between groups of individuals who are differently located in the various systems of power and privilege that help to define relations among groups.

The essay begins with a discussion and definition of intergroup race relations. In this discussion dominant ways of viewing race relations in sport are examined. Alternatives to the dominant view are presented. These alternatives are developed from the work of feminists, womanists, and feminist sport sociologists who have been attempting to develop antiracist theories and practices in their work and their lives. This discussion will examine what it means to do antiracist work. It will also explore what it means to create practices whereby alliances can develop between different groups in ways that promote relationships built on trust, sharing, and learning, and that foster commitments to continued growth and development in an environment that challenges racist and sexist oppression.

The essay concludes with an exploration of the ways in which this analysis can be implemented and applied to group relations in college sport. The paper will develop suggestions for both theoretical work in sport sociology as well as provide examples of practices that might be implemented in athletic programs.

Intergroup Race Relations: Integration, Assimilation, or Alliances? Dominant Views of Intergroup Race Relations in Sport

The title of this subheading may be misleading. Given the paucity of work in the sociology of sport on race relations, what I am naming as "dominant" is what I see as an emergent trend in existing work. This becomes even more difficult to discuss in relation to work on women's sport as there is so little of such work that it is impossible to identify a dominant view or emergent trend. What is possible, however, is to name and critique what I see as possible directions that work might take and to locate these directions within dominant ideological discourses on race and racism.

One place to begin to identify emergent trends in the work on race relations in sport is with Susan Birrell's (1989) review and critique. Birrell argues that despite the existence of critical analyses of sporting practices in our culture: "We have yet to launch any sort of sophisticated analysis of racial relations in sport. To date our focus on race has been, in reality, a focus on Black male athletes" (Birrell, 1989, p. 213).

This focus is problematic for Birrell for a number of reasons. First, it presents a simplistic, reductive view of race in which race and diversity are equated with a narrow interpretation of African-American male experiences in sport. This reductionist view is simplistic because what is absent from these analyses is a recognition of the diversity that exists within the lives and experiences of both African-Americans and other racial and ethnic groups.

Secondly, this research also obscures the complex ways in which racism is connected with other forms of oppression. When isolated and reduced to a variable for analysis such research promotes simplistic analyses of very complex relations. For example, identifying and describing patterns of involvement of African-American men and women in intercollegiate sport (which is usually translated to mean basketball, football, baseball or track) provide important data that help us to quantify the results of the oppression that exists in the structures and practices that constitute intercollegiate sport. However, what these data do not allow for is an analysis of the ways in which these patterns reflect relationships between different oppressive formations. To be more specific, when we have data that show that in 1985, 76% of women's college basketball teams and 95% of men's college basketball teams had African-American players (Berghorn, Yetman, & Hanna, 1988), what we have is a numerical representation of the presence of African-American players in a specific sport in a specific year. What is missing and obscured are the experiences of the players these data represented. Who are they? Why were they recruited? How do their experiences as athletes and students reflect racist, classist, sexist, heterosexist power relations? What kinds of strategies do they use to survive in these oppressive educational and sporting systems? What prices do they pay when they make choices to become involved with, stay involved with or withdraw from sport? How are these choices embedded within the systems of power and privilege that exist in sport, education and society? In what ways are individuals expected to accommodate, and to become incorporated within, existing systems of power and privilege? How are these systems resisted, challenged, and changed?

When questions like the ones outlined above are obscured, our focus becomes centered on only *describing* the racial composition of the individuals involved in collegiate sport. This kind of analysis makes it tempting to see race relations in terms of the presence or absence of different categories of individuals at different levels of sport. This is not enough. Challenging the overrepresentation of European-Americans in sport is only one step towards challenging, working against, and eliminating racism.[2] The fact that the majority of our work on race in sport describes and documents patterns of participation suggests that for many equalizing access to sport is seen as the way to achieve racial equality in sport. This view is one that defines the problem of race relations in sport largely in terms of opportunity and access. Equality is seen in terms of the opportunities available to different categories of individuals within sport, and problems are identified in terms of the nature of the distribution and allocation of opportunities and rewards within existing sporting systems. Distribution patterns are evaluated in this work in terms of their "representativeness." This means that equality is defined in relation to the degree to which racial distributions in sport match racial distributions in society. Research comparing the participation rates, playing positions, graduation rates, salaries, and post playing career opportunities (in areas such as coaching and administration) in sport of African-American and European-American athletes is then used to identify and describe the nature of any inequities that exist in sport.

This distributive research[3] is predicated on a number of assumptions about the nature of race relations in sport. First, it assumes that equality of opportunity will lead to an integrated sport system. Integration appears to be a primary goal of this work, and a goal that is assumed to be both possible and desirable. The achievement of equality is deemed possible through the identification and removal of existing barriers. One way to achieve this has been through legislative reform. Legislation such as Title IX, which prohibits discrimination on the basis of sex, and affirmative action legislation, which is an attempt to remedy the inequities that exist in the work force through the selective recruitment and hiring of categories of individuals who have typically been excluded from the work place, are examples of remedies or solutions being sought. Even if these solutions were possible (which is highly questionable given the successful challenges that have been made against both kinds of legislation) what do these solutions imply for intergroup race relations? At face value they seem to imply that changes occur at the level of the individual, while sporting structures themselves remain the same. Thus, when women of color are recruited into sport they are given clear messages that integration means becoming a part of the system by accepting and supporting existing structures and practices.

Secondly, this view is based on the assumption that reform is possible by working within existing sporting structures. Sport itself is not seen as the problem. It is assumed that with the appropriate alterations an integrated sporting system can be achieved. The results of efforts to create an integrated sporting system are that sporting structures and practices will remain basically the same, but the personnel involved in sport will give it a new and more "colorful" look. Once again this has a quite specific impact on intergroup race relations. When sport is seen as desirable and worth gaining access to, the women most likely to be recruited and retained are ones who will not overtly and explicitly challenge or question the structures and practices that exist within the system. This means that women of color face a very real double bind. If they name the racism that they encounter and challenge it, they risk being forced out of the system labelled as "trouble makers" with "attitude" problems. But being a "team" player and staying in the system is no easier. It means, for many women of color, having to remain silent in the face of oppression. Yet in so doing they risk being used by those in authority who can argue that the very presence of women of color in the system shows just how fair, just, and committed to equality sport really is.

Efforts to achieve integration through formal efforts to achieve equality of opportunity are riddled with problems. What is missing in this view is the recognition that sporting structures and practices are not ahistorical, neutral, and universal constructions that stand outside the relations of power and privilege that create and perpetuate racism as well as other forms of oppression. Sports have long histories of exclusion and oppression, and they have been developed and created to privilege the interests and needs of white, middle-class, heterosexual men.[4] Yet the popular images on sport mask these histories. For example, in our culture sport is often presented as one area that is free from racism. It is presented as an activity in which hard work and talent are the primary contributors for success because the bottom line in the sporting world is winning and putting the best team or individuals into any competitive situation. Evidence that is often cited to support these assertions is the fact that African-Americans males have begun to dominate certain sports (football and basketball in particular) and are overrepresented in others (baseball and track) and that this domination would not be possible in a racist sporting system. The descriptive data collected in the distributive research described earlier are used in defense of this assertion. Yet, all of this denies the ways in which sport can and does reproduce racism.[5] What is missing from these analyses is an examination of the ways in which power and privilege are linked to the creation and perpetuation of oppression in sport.

Some questions that need to be addressed if we are to move beyond descriptive distributive analyses of equality of opportunity in sport are:

-What does it mean for a sport to be integrated?
-Does equal representation mean integration?
-Does integration mean assimilation into existing sporting structures?
-Who benefits when integration is defined in ways that lead to assimilation?
-What is meant by equality?
-Is it possible to achieve equality without changing sporting structures and practices?
-What would anti-oppressive sporting structures and practices look like?
-What kinds of resistance might we face if we attempt to challenge

oppression and change sport?

-Where will this resistance come from and why?

-Who should be involved in the development of new sporting structures and practices?

These questions begin to suggest alternatives to distributive analyses of race in sport and to suggest that it is important to explore the ways in which notions of equality of opportunity can reproduce rather than challenge and change oppression in sport. Gaining access to sport is not enough. Understanding the conditions under which access is achieved and the consequences of gaining access to existing sporting structures is critical if we are to understand the complex ways in which individuals negotiate spaces within these structures. We need to understand who gets selected to gain access to the sporting world, the impact of their selection, and their abilities to challenge and confront oppression when they encounter it.

Arguments for equal opportunity that insist on the necessity of treating everyone the same way mask the fact that in reality "equal treatment" often means treating all people as if they were white, middle-class, heterosexual, and male. Thus, being integrated into sport under these conditions means being assimilated into a system in which one has to deny or down play the existence of any "differences" in the name of developing "human" values, which in reality are the values of those in power (white, middle-class, heterosexual men).

One of the reasons that this view of equality is so compelling in our culture is that it means that nothing really changes: Those in power remain the same, and the price of admission is the acceptance of the status quo in exchange for an opportunity to participate within the system. For those who are not white, middle class, heterosexual, or male this is an enormous price to pay. Playing under these conditions can mean that we are contributing to our own oppression. Yet alternatives that involve challenging the system may mean that one risks being denied an opportunity to play at all and risks all of the rewards that go along with this.

Alternative to Distributive Analyses:
Working Towards Antiracist Policies and Practices

Although I have argued for the necessity of moving beyond analyses of sport that have their basis in liberal democratic notions of equality of opportunity and humanism, I want to be clear that my arguments need not be seen as a retreat from strategies that are currently being used in an attempt to open up and equalize sport. What I am struggling with in the writing of this essay are the tensions that exist in trying to challenge oppression in sport. In the absence of alternatives, what can we do? Is it inconsistent to work for short-term changes that at least allow access to what is a very closed system while at the same time pushing for changes that move beyond access to challenge how we define and structure sport? I do not believe that it is. At least in the short term I think we need to be pushing for both. We need to be arguing for and working towards the recruitment and retention of women from different racial groups at all levels of sport and in a diverse set of roles. These efforts must be accompanied by a strong commitment to develop an understanding, both theoretically and practically, of the complex ways in which racism contours women's lives. This means that as white women we need to embark on antiracist work. That is, I mean that we need to examine the extent of our privilege and to understand the ways in which this privilege supports racist ideology and practices both inside and outside sport. I am in agreement with Birrell (1989), who suggests that

> If race is understood as a social construct, our analysis of racial relations and sport clearly must move beyond the treatment of race as a descriptive variable and address ideological questions about the production of race relations and the specific forms such relations take in particular times (p.218).

Birrell (1990) begins her own antiracist work by exploring the ways in which critical feminist sport scholars can learn from reading the work of women of color whose insights describe the complex ways in which power and privilege intersect in different ways in different women's lives. As Birrell (1990) suggests, "I contend that any analysis of sport, gender, and racial relations must begin with an appreciation of the issues and concerns as they are understood and articulated by the women themselves" (p. 187). She also warns against the dangers of appropriating these insights to further our own concerns and to further our own ends. She argues that

> We must be careful to find a way to connect these discourses so that we can preserve their separate insights and produce an even more powerful, critical and radical way of theorizing about the connections between race, class, and gender. At this time it seems wisest to take a lesson from the resistance of women of color to such assimilative tasks, regardless of how sensitively those tasks are conducted. We must work to familiarize ourselves with theories that use racial relations as their point of privileged access rather than risk

colonizing the experiences of people of color within our current theories. (Birrell, 1990, p. 199)

One way to begin to do this work is to rethink feminist work in the sociology of sport.

Beginning Antiracist Work: Rethinking Feminist Sport Sociology

My concerns and desires to rethink my feminist work stem from a feeling that, despite considerable amounts of feminist theorizing about oppression (at least about gender-based oppression) in sport, such theories seem to have had little or no impact on actual sporting practices.[6] Thinking critically about feminist sport sociology involves questioning the relationships that exist between theorizing about oppression and developing practices that allow us to work to challenge oppression in specific ways in specific locations in our (sporting?) lives. In order to do this I am going to begin by asking some questions about how feminist work can be and is being, used to challenge and change racist oppression in sport. I will then move to a brief discussion of the ways in which much of our feminist theorizing about sport makes it difficult, if not impossible, to challenge and change many of the oppressive formations that are constructed through, and constitutive of, sporting practices in our culture. I will conclude with an exploration of some strategies that might allow us to see the relationship between theory and practice as an integral and connected one. I will explore the possibilities that exist for the development of ways of thinking about and practicing feminisms that make explicit the idea that changing and challenging oppression is a continual struggle involving a commitment to explore, reexamine, and rethink our positions and practices.

Changing Practices in Sport: Challenges to Live
What We Think as Feminist Sport Sociologists

There is something of a paradox in discussing the relationships between theory and practice in feminist sport sociology when the very basis for feminist critiques of sport arose from women's experiences of oppression in the sporting world. In fact, it has been argued that because of our experiences as "others" in the culture and because of our experiences from the margins (hooks, 1984), we are uniquely placed to name, challenge, and interrupt the oppressive structures and forces that shape our lives (Collins, 1990; Haraway, 1988; Harding, 1986). This is also an argument that has been made by other feminist sport sociologists. For example, M. Ann Hall (1985) has argued for feminist research and scholarship that

...not only addresses the actual concrete conditions of women's experience in sport both past and present, but also recognizes that knowledge, to be useful, must contribute to the practical reconstruction of the sports world in which women's interests are no longer subordinated to men. (p. 33)

Although standpoint theory has been criticized by feminists (particularly women of color) because it has been constructed in ways that both falsely universalize women's experiences of oppression (Collins, 1990; hooks, 1984, 1989; Spelman, 1988), it is important to recognize that these criticisms are aimed at the ways in which we have used the experiences of a few to develop theories of oppression for the many, and not at questioning the importance or relevance of experiences and practices in our feminist thinking and acting. In fact, I would suggest that such criticisms have challenged us to think much more carefully about the relationships between thought and action. The fact that we have developed our theorizing in ways that have privileged the standpoints of white, middle-class, Christian-raised, non- disabled, heterosexual women illustrates to me that we need to rethink and reexamine the ways in which we understand the diverse and complex relationships between our experiences, thoughts, and actions.

Challenging and Changing Sporting Practices: Feminist Ideals or Real Possibilities?

My concerns about the relationships between our thinking and actions in feminist sociology of sport stem from the discomfort that I experience when I am asked two different, but related, questions. The first question is frequently posed in one of the following ways: Now that I see the racism that exists in sport what can I/we do to change this? Or I am very angry, what can I do to challenge racism and other forms of oppression in sport? The second question that I am asked is: How has feminist theorizing actually changed sport? My discomfort with these questions is directly related to my inability to answer them in any satisfactory ways. The problem I face is that I can only give broadly based answers to the first question and cite examples from a few research studies for the second. Both of these answers may be a place to begin, but I believe that it is also critical that we recognize that linking our theorizing to actions means thinking about the ways in which specific, local sporting practices can be challenged and changed as well as developing more broadly based strategies for working against the various oppressive formations that are constructed and reconstructed in and through sport.

In thinking about challenging and changing specific sporting practices and the impact that our work has had on athletes and coaches in the sporting world, we are forced to refocus our attention to both thinking about and acting upon our thinking rather than simply theorizing about potential actions. I suggest that the fact that few female athletes or coaches appear to embrace feminist ideas, struggles, and commitments needs to be understood as more than a theoretical problem. It is a very practical one. We need to be sensitive to the fact that in our attempts to name and understand our experiences of oppression in sport we have chosen to do so in ways that have separated theory and practice.

One needs only to look at what is taken as "theorizing" and its sources to see this separation. Unfortunately, most of the feminist theorizing about sport emanates from privileged white, female academics rather than from players and coaches who are involved in the daily sporting practices. What this separates theory from practice and creates a message that theory is not for coaches and athletes and that changing practices is not for theorists. This is not a problem that is unique to feminist sport sociologists. bell hooks (1984) makes a similar argument about the ways in which white, bourgeois feminists have ignored and excluded women of color from contributing to developing theory. Her arguments are ones that can easily be applied to much of our work. She argues that

> Given the class nature of feminist movement so far, as well as racial hierarchies, developing theory (the guiding set of beliefs and principles that become the basis for action) has been a task particularly subject to the hegemonic dominance of white academic women. This has led many women outside the privileged race/class group to see the focus on developing theory, even the very use of the term, as a concern that functions only to reinforce the power of the elite group. Such reactions reinforce the sexist/racist/classist notion that developing theory is the domain of the white intellectual. (hooks, 1984, p. 30)

She goes on to suggest that

> ...since bourgeois white women had defined feminism in such a way to make it appear that it had no real significance for black women, they could then conclude that black women need not contribute to developing theory. We were to provide the colorful life stories to document and validate the prevailing set of theoretical assumptions. (hooks, 1984, p. 31)

In order to work against this narrow, elitist, and oppressive view of theory I believe that we need to struggle to develop a view of theory and practice in which we see them in a *both/and* relation rather than an *either/ or* one (Collins, 1990). Developing such a view is one that does not privilege thinking over acting and work against the tendency to separate the acts of theorizing and practicing. The promise of such thinking, as Patricia Hill Collins suggests, is "by espousing a both/and orientation that views thought and action as part of the same process, possibilities for new relationships between thought and action emerge" (p. 29).

This is a challenge that we can and ought to embrace as feminists working against racism in sport. We need to take seriously the fact that few female athletes and coaches seem prepared to accept and claim identities as feminists. This does not necessarily mean that women are not challenging the racism, heterosexism, classism, and sexism that exist in sport through their daily practices; it may be that as academics we have been unwilling to see challenge as an integral and central part of creating theories or narratives that link thought and action. One way to embrace the challenges of developing both/and perspectives is to critically analyze our work as feminists and use this as a starting point for dialogues, discussions, and actions.

Critical Feminist Thinking in the Sociology of Sport

Although there are multiple forms of feminist work in the sociology of sport I am going to limit my discussions to critical relational feminist analyses of sport.[7] Before beginning my analysis I want to be clear that I am not antitheory. What I am arguing for is a different way of theorizing as feminists.[8] This essay is a first step for me. As a part of this I will examine our responses as feminists to racism in sport.

Racism in Sport: Critical Feminist Responses

You don't really want Black folks, you are just looking for yourself with a little color to it. (Bernice Johnson Reagon, cited in Spelman, 1988, p.114)

White feminist sport sociologists have been, and continue to be, reluctant to develop ways of thinking and acting that allow us to work against the racist formations that exist not only in sport but also in our analyses of the sporting world.[9] With few exceptions (see Birrell, 1989,1990; Lovell, 1991; Paraschak 1991) we have created theories that have presumed a certain commonality among all women's experiences of sexism. The problems with this kind of thinking are explained in the following statement by Spelman (1988), who argues that

...the "problem of difference"for feminist theory has never been a general one about how to weigh the importance of our differences. To put it that way hides two crucial facts: First, the description of what we have in common "as women" has almost always been a description of white, middle class women.

Second, the "difference" of this group of women—that is, their being white and middle class—has never had to be "brought into" feminist theory. To bring in "difference" is to bring in women who aren't white and middle class. (p. 4)

Because we have tended to produce analyses of "women's" experiences of oppression in sport that are rooted in this kind of falsely universal thinking, it is important that we recognize that these ways of knowing and thinking are themselves embedded in the production and perpetuation of racism. We cannot continue to lament the absence of writings and actions of women of color in sport without asking ourselves how we have created structures and practices within our intellectual communities that not only exclude women of color but also make it impossible for them to participate in creating the conditions that allow all of our voices and actions to be heard and visible.

Analyses of racism in sport are not solely the responsibility of women of color. As white women we must begin to understand how our privilege is constructed and developed in ways that bolster racism in our thinking and everyday actions in the sporting world. We cannot presume to speak for or about the experiences of women of color, nor can we define the standards and forms that these experiences must be understood. The problem is not how white women can understand the experiences of women who are "different" but how feminists can create practices and ways of theorizing that recognize our similarities and differences and do so by locating them and understanding them in terms of the complex ways in which oppression structures our lives.

What I am arguing for here is not going to be easy. But challenging oppression is hard work. It requires enormous amount of energy, passion, commitment, and determination. Recognizing this, understanding how each of us is involved in this struggle, is perhaps a way that we can begin or continue our efforts to challenge and change the various forms of oppression that shape both our own lives and those of others. Although I believe that there are signs that this is beginning to happen I also believe that we need to be cautious in how we proceed. It is not enough to read the works of a few prominent (and establishment-sanctioned) women of color[10] and appropriate their insights for our own use. We need to examine how we are reading and understanding both our own work and lives as well as those of other women. We need to locate ourselves in this process, to identify and interrogate the ways in which our thinking and actions are themselves embedded in a complex matrix of oppression and privilege.[11] If we can do this then it is possible to develop and/both perspectives about theory and action. It might be a way to develop alliances with the many women of color who are involved in the sporting world and provide a place to meet and share ideas and practices that will inform all of our lives. After all as Barbara Smith (1982) suggests, feminism is "the political theory and practice that struggles to free all women. Anything less than this vision of total freedom is not feminism, but merely female self-aggrandizement" (Trinh, 1989, p.86).

Learning From Antiracist Work: Recommendations for Practice
Part of my struggle in writing this essay has been to make the links between what we know about race relations in sport and feminist, womanist analyses of the ways in which antiracist work can be done to help challenge oppression in all women's lives. This struggle is an ongoing one. One of the parts of this struggle is to begin to try to translate what we are learning from our antiracist work into actual practices that might be implemented and developed in sport settings. It is possible to begin this work in women's sport, and in so doing we may be able to challenge and change dominant sporting practices and develop alternatives that are based on antiracist and anti-oppressive politics.[12]

The recommendations that I am going present do not are by no means exhaustive nor are they carved in stone. I prefer to think of that these ideas might provide a basis for discussion and debate and that each of these recommendations will be challenged and changed to meet the needs of different individuals in different sport settings. I will outline each of the recommendations and provide a brief description of my interpretation of their potential for change.

1. **We must work towards developing and implementing affirmative action programs to ensure the recruitment and retainment of women of color**. What I mean by the implementation of affirmative action programs is more than the hiring and recruiting of women of color into existing sport programs. My sense of affirmative action is one that has been informed by Patricia Williams (1991), who suggests that affirmative action is more than a hiring program but needs to be conceptualized in

ways that recognize that it is a "an act of vision, an act of social as well as professional responsibility" (p. 121). By this she means that affirmative action is an affirmation; the affirmative act of hiring - or hearing - blacks is a recognition of individuality that includes blacks as a social presence, that is profoundly linked to the fate of blacks and whites and women and men either as sub groups or as one group. (Williams, 1991, p. 121)

She goes on to suggest that in acting affirmatively one develops a different view of the world, one in which Justice is a continual balancing of competing visions, plural viewpoints, shifting histories, interests and allegiances. To acknowledge that level of complexity is to require, to seek and to value a multiplicity of knowledge systems, in pursuit of a more complete sense of the world in which we all live. (Williams, 1991, p. 121)

This view of affirmative action means that part of acting affirmatively means being prepared to embark on the necessary work to enable the development of a just, antiracist, and anti-oppressive system.

2. All individuals involved in women's sport programs, administrators, coaches, athletes, and trainers, must embark on antiracist work. This recommendation is linked to the first in that acting affirmatively means beginning to develop policies and practices that actively support and encourage the recognition of oppression and the commitment to challenge and change it. Working against oppression is not easy. Workshops, readings, and discussion groups can be used to help begin this process. It is important in doing this work that all the women (and men) involved in women's sport recognize that we have work to do and that we need to find ways of working that are not defensive, angry, or guilt based. This means that reward structures will need to be changed so that we are all held responsible for our actions. This means rethinking the value of sport in colleges and questioning the heavy emphasis on winning and competing at the expense of developing just practices and ways of being in and through sport. This does not necessarily mean that excellence cannot be achieved but that the processes by which we evaluate success and failure should be scrutinized and re-evaluated.

3. We must rethink power relationships and work towards developing alliances across our differences. An integral part of developing antiracist and anti-oppressive practices is the recognition that it is possible to develop alliances across our differences. This means that we need to rethink the nature of our power relationships and identify the ways in which the power invested in particular positions of privilege have and can be used to create and promote oppression. Lisa Albrecht and Rose Brewer (1990) argue that classic western patriarchal views of power are ones that see power in terms of domination and control, or power over. This seems to reflect traditional notions of power as authority in sport, where coaches have power over athletes and administrators have power over coaches. Reenvisioning power means rethinking how we relate individually and collectively. It means recognizing the diversity that exists between and among us and working out ways to build bridges across these differences in ways that respect them. Thus, power comes from our connections and our ways of acting as allies in the struggles to create anti-oppressive sporting structures and practices.

These recommendations are very broadly based. In my explanations of these I have outlined some of the ways in which these might affect on our practices. I see these recommendations as a beginning; a necessary first step, and I see them as related and interconnected. Thus, they co-exist, and embarking on this work means trying to achieve all these goals and more.

Working Towards Politics and Practices of Difference: Some Concluding Comments

My arguments for the development of theories of oppression that link thinking with practices to end oppression have been developed as a result of a number of different influences. They come from my experiences, as a teacher, and as a lesbian and feminist struggling to bring together my politics and practices in my daily life of reading and struggling with the diverse issues raised in feminist and womanist writing. Although these are and continue to be painful struggles for me they are also engaging and exciting, and they seem to promise ways of resolving the tensions between thinking critically and acting to change and challenge oppression in localized, specific incidents in our lives and in sport.

I believe that part of this struggle is the commitment to be critical and to continue to be so. I am reluctant to simply embrace new (and trendy) ways of thinking as solutions to our problems. I think they offer us possibilities for dialogue, and this is what I find challenging and exciting about my work. I am convinced by Iris Young (1990), who suggests that we should be working towards the development of a politics of difference. That is whatever the label, the concept of social relations that embody openness to unassimilated otherness with justice and appreciation needs to be developed. Radical politics, moreover, must develop discourse and institutions for bringing differently identified groups together without suppressing or subsuming the differences. (p. 320)

For feminist sport sociologists the time has come to develop politics of difference. I see this essay as one part of my attempts to begin to engage in this struggle. I hope that this will be an ongoing struggle that helps us to clarify what we mean by sport and the practices that constitute it. This means being open to new possibilities and being prepared to take the necessary risks to ensure that change occurs. It is impossible to say what these new antiracist, anti-oppressive sporting forms might look like. They may take many forms and will, it is hoped, develop in ways that celebrate our differences and reflect diverse cultural meanings and values. The promise in doing this work is that we can develop connections among women and develop an understanding of the ways in which our bodies and physical bodily practices are related to and reflect the different ways in which we are positioned and located in the world. The challenges we face are great but not impossible. Changing sport can be a way to challenge oppression, to realize the power that exists in sport to connect women, and to build alliances across our differences.

Summary
This essay argues for the development of antiracist policies and practices in sport. The essay focuses on an analysis of race relations in women's sport. The essay begins with an examination of dominant views of intergroup race relations in sport. In this section I argue that much of the work on race relations in sport presents simplistic and reductionist views of race and race relations. This work tends to be descriptive and focuses on identifying patterns of participation of different groups of individuals within sport. In documenting and identifying the distribution of groups within sport this research defines race relations in terms of opportunity and access to existing sporting systems. I conclude my discussion of this section with an analysis and critique of the assumptions underlying this descriptive, distributive research.

Having critiqued distributive research on race relations in sport I move on to outline some ways in which we might begin to develop antiracist polices and practices in both our work in the sociology of sport and our practices within the sporting world. In this section I argue for linking theory and practice in a both/and relationship and suggest that as feminists we need to begin by examining the ways in which we are located in the world and the power and privilege that are associated with our work and behaviors both as individuals and as members of different groups. As part of this process I suggest that we need to begin our antiracist work in earnest and develop and implement affirmative action programs in sport. I also argue that all individuals involved in sport must commit to recognizing and changing oppression in sport. This means developing educational programs to name oppression and creating structures that reward and support practices designed to eliminate oppression. I conclude by arguing for the development of a politics of difference whereby we can learn to work together across our differences in ways that show that we have a respect for and willingness to learn about and celebrate those differences.

Footnotes

[1] There are notable exceptions to this. For example, Susan Birrell's (1989; 1990) work argues very strongly that "critical scholars need to attend far more carefully to the sport" (p. 223). Other examples are Tessa Lovell's (1991) exploratory ethnographic study that examines the role of sport in the lives of Southern Asian and Afro/Caribbean women in Britain and the ways in which racism controus these experiences. And Vicky Paraschak's (1991) study of sport festivals and race relations in the Northwest Territories of Canada that focuses on the history of sport festivals in the North as a way of examining how race relations are contested and reproduced.

[2] I do not mean to suggest that we should not be working towards democratizing sport in ways that ensure access for all individuals from a wide range of racial and ethnic groups. This is important work but I see it as a short term solution to a difficult and complex problem. The problem as I see it is one of fighting simultaneously for access to sporting structures and practices that are oppressive, while at the same time struggling to change and challenge sport in fundamental ways to end oppression. What this might mean is that we are fighting for contradictory things. One fight is for access to and the other for the destruction of existing sporting practices and structures and the reformulation and reconceptualizing of sport.

[3] See Dewar (1991) for a more detailed discussion of distributive research in sport.

[4] See Jarvie (1991) and Birrell (1990) for more detailed accounts of the ways in which sport has been developed to serve and perpetuate the interests and needs of white, middle-class men.

[5] See Birrell (1989), Davis (1990) and Mathisen and Mathisen (1991) for

much more detailed accounts of the ways in which sport is used to reproduce racism.

[6] In the process of writing this paper this became clear to me in the following way: The proliferation of cases of the harassment of women reporters in professional football over the issue of access locker rooms has illustrated just how important it is to begin to address the ways in which specific practices can help us to understand the links between our theoretical understanding of oppression and actual experiences of this in sport.

[7] For discussion of the varieties of feminist work in the sociology of sport see Birrell (1988), Hall (1990). I am limiting my analysis to "critical" feminist perspectives because my own thinking and work grow out of this perspective and, as such, this analysis is one that is part of my personal political and intellectual struggles to develop new more inclusive ways of thinking and acting as a feminist.

[8] See hooks (1989), Collins (1990) and Nicholson (1990) for more detailed discussion of the importance of theory and different forms of theorizing in feminist work.

[9] I am deliberately focusing on racism in this example to help identify one problem that needs to be addressed in our work as critical feminists. In so doing I do not wish to suggest that our analyses of oppression can be isolated and seprated. Oppression takes multiple forms and work in multiple dimensions and our thinking and actions need to address this complexity. I am beginning with an example of racism as a way of illustrating the importance of developing different kinds of analyses of oppression in sport.

[10] Pat Hill Collins (1990) suggests that one way white feminists have appropriated the work of Black women is to "canonize a few Black women as spokespersons for the group and then refuse to listen to any but these select few" (xiii). She argues that "assuming that only a few exceptional Black women have been able to do theory homogenizes African-American women and silences the majority. In contrast, I maintain that theory and intellectual creativity are not the province of a select but instead emanate from a range of people"(xiii).

[11] I have been struck by the fact that we rarely, if ever, locate ourselves in our work. I know this is often difficult and runs counter to "academic" style but I believe that it is important that we identify as white women writing about women of color so that our standpoints are explicit and identifiable. It is not that I believe that as white women

we have nothing to say, quite to the contrary, but that what we say and how we say it needs to be viewed in terms of the kinds of privilege that goes along with being white, tenured, feminist sport sociologists. The question of the authority of certain voices, how we legitimate ideas, whose ideas we see as legitimate all need to be made part of the our efforts to develop theories and practices to end oppression.

[12] It is impossible to say what these alternative sporting forms might look like. An integral part of doing this work is to develop possibilities and to try them out. I also want to state that one very real possibility arising from this work is that it leads to the complete destruction of intercollegiate sport, as we now know it. It may not be possible or even desirable to try to "reform" existing structures and practices. In fact, the absence of many women of color from traditional forms of sport may be a form of resistance and these women may be putting their energies into developing alternatives that in our racist culture we do recognize or value as sport. However, since a reality that we are working with is that intercollegiate sport for women has developed in ways that promote traditional, Eurocentric, middle-class, male practices as "sport" the recommendations that I present will be aimed at challenging and changing these practices.

References

Albrecht, L., & Brewer, R. (Eds.). (1990). *Bridges of power: Women's multicultural alliances.* Santa Cruz, CA: New Society Publishers.

Berghorn, F.J., Yetman, N., & Hanna, W.C. (1988). Racial participation and integration in men's and women's intercollegiate basketball: Continuity and change, 1958-1985. *Sociology of Sport Journal, 5*(20), 107-124.

Birrell, S. (1988). Discourses on the gender/sport relationship: From women in sport to gender relations. In K. Pandolf (Ed.), *Exercise and sport science reviews,* (p. 16). New York: Macmillan.

Birrell, S. (1989). Racial relations theories and sport: Suggestions for a more critical analysis. *Sociology of Sport Journal, 6*(3), 212-227.

Birrell, S. (1990). Women of color, critical autobiography, and sport. In M. Messner & D.Sabo (Eds.), *Sport, men, and the gender order: Critical feminist perspectives,* (pp. 185-199). Champaign, IL: Human Kinetics.

Collins, P. H. (1990). *Black feminist thought: Knowledge, consciousness, and the politics of empowerment.* Boston: Unwin Hyman.

Davis, L. (1990). The articulation of difference: White preoccupation with the question of racially linked genetic differences among athletes. *Sociology of Sport Journal, 7*(2),179-187.

Dewar, A. (1991). Incorporation or resistance?: Towards an analysis of women's responses to sexual oppression in sport. *International Review for the Sociology of Sport, 26*, 15-25.

Hall, M. A. (1985). Knowledge and gender: Epistemological questions in the social analysis of sport. *Sociology of Sport Journal, 2*(1), 25-42.

Hall, M. A. (1990). How should we theorize gender in the context of sport? In M. Messner & D. Sabo. (Eds.), *Sport, men and the gender order: critical feminist perspectives*, (pp. 223-239). Champaign, IL: Human Kinetics.

Haraway, D. (1988). Situated knowledges: The science question in feminism and the privilege of partial perspective. *Feminist Studies, 14*(3), 575-599.

Harding, S. (1986). *The science question in feminism*. Ithaca, NY: Cornell University Press.

hooks, b. (1984). *Feminist theory from margin to center*. Boston: South End Press.

hooks, b. (1989). *Talking back: Thinking feminist, thinking black*. Boston: South End Press.

Jarvie, G. (Ed.). (1991). *Sport, racism and ethnicity*. London: The Falmer Press.

Lovell, T. (1991). Sport, racism and young women. In Grant Jarvie (Ed.), *Sport, racism and ethnicity*, (pp. 58-73). London: The Falmer Press.

Mathisen, J.A., & Mathisen, G.S. (1991). The rhetoric of racism in sport: Tom Brokaw revisited. *Sociology of Sport Journal, 8*(2), 168-177.

Nicholson, L. (Ed.). (1990). *Feminism/Postmodernism*. New York: Routledge & Kegan Paul.

Paraschak, V. (1991). Sport festivals and race relations in the Northwest Territories of Canada. In Grant Jarvie (Ed)., *Sport, racism and ethnicity*, (pp. 74-93). London: The Falmer Press.

Spelman, E.V. (1988). *Inessential woman*. Boston: Beacon Press.

Trinh, M.T. (1989). *Woman. native other: Writing postcolonality and feminism*. Bloomington, IN: Indiana University Press.

Williams, P. (1991). *The alchemy of race and rights: Diary of a law professor*. Cambridge, MA: Harvard University Press.

Young, I. (1990). The ideal of community and the politics of difference.

In Linda Nicholson (Ed.), *Feminism/Postmodernism* (pp.56-76). New York: Routledge & Kegan Paul.

Section Four:
Analyses of Racism and
Future Prospects for Change

Section Four

Analyses of Racism and Future Prospects for Change

Throughout these essays all of the contributors agree that sport is not immune from racism; in fact, its structure maintains and assures the continuation of oppressive processes. As we move into the twenty-first century, the proportion of racial and ethnic minorities, particularly African-American men and women, attending high schools and colleges will continue to grow. Turning to the near future, democratizing sports and ensuring opportunity for individuals from every racial and ethnic group, as Alison Dewar insisted, means to fight against oppressive sport practices, while at the same time challenging sport in the most fundamental ways to end oppression.

Carol Oglesby's (sport sociologist) essay, "Where is the White in the Rainbow Coalition?", challenges us to risk the chance to make a difference in racial matters. Targeting those in career positions in sports, Oglesby outlines strategies for antiracist activity by whites. The author differentiates prejudice from racism, discussing the psychological stages of racism. Positive in addressing real and potential projects in sports, the essay concludes with some promising ways to enhance our multiracial future.

Stanley Eitzen's (sociologist) essay focuses on the social injustice that has affected African-American women and men in sport. He believes that aversive racism in college sports is especially paradoxical because sport is based on achieved, not ascribed status, and because colleges espouse ideals that are progressive, not oppressive. Focusing on big-time revenue sports, on basketball and football for males, Eitzen discusses many important issues and presents information about the status and condition of African-Americans. Eitzen argues that we know what ought to be done to obtain social justice for racial minorities in big-time college sports. If we know what's wrong, then strategies can be devised to deal with problems faced by African-American athletes and to eliminate racism in sports.

Essay 9

Issues of Sport and Racism: Where Is the White in the Rainbow Coalition?

Carole Oglesby

Abstract: This essay focuses attention on racism as, initially, a creation of white people and a present and continuing problem that white people must resolve. Through examination of several types of model programs in sport and athletics, each individual is presented the possibility of dedicating a "tithe of time" to personally healing antiracist, color-affirming behaviors.

Introduction

In his presidential campaigns, Jesse Jackson coined the term "Rainbow Coalition" to signify a new majority (he hoped) composed of blacks, browns, reds, yellows, and whites, who would work together toward a bright tomorrow for all. The Rainbow Coalition was a shining promise that has not materialized. One of the problems seems to be the weakness of white support, generally, for systematic efforts to mitigate the problem of racism in American. "We are not racists" and "no problem here" are comments that stand in the place of hard-eyed commitment to end the problem, and this is true in sports and athletics as well as in any other aspect of American life.

This book is filled with facts documenting the existence of racism in sports and athletics. These facts range from exclusions of the past and present, stereotypes and myths that lead to stacking African-American players in positions with life-long career effects, disproportionate ratios of African-American players compared to coaches, to pay inequities. This list is long and will not be the central focus of this essay. The spotlight here is on the white person, especially the career educator-professional, involved in sport and athletics. We will look at the following questions: (a) What is the "face" of the racism practiced daily - what does it look like?; (b) What is white racial identity and why is the idea of the existence of a white racial identity resisted?; (c) What is the price paid for white racial identity today?; and (d) What are the steps we can take to change and enhance the future in our increasingly multiracial, multicultural society?

What Does Racism Look Like on the Gym Floor, Court, or Field?

White persons in a white-dominant society have had the privilege to determine if, when, and under what conditions we would encounter African-American people. In order to begin to comprehend the full meaning of racism in sport, we must remember that almost total segregation was the social rule until the early 1950s. Professional colleagues (coaches, administrators, officials) who are African-American and over age 45 probably first attended regional or national tournaments or AAHPERD conventions while staying in "colored hotels" and eating in "colored restaurants." Their first professional memberships may well have been in black coaching or teaching organizations. Black sport participation was limited to certain (far from ideal) facilities and leagues. The breaking of the color line in professional baseball by Jackie Robinson, Chuck Cooper in basketball, and Althea Gibson in tennis is an easily recalled personal, as well as collective, history for many of us. Like slavery before it, this segregation was rationalized and enforced by whites, on the basis of beliefs of racial inferiority, and we must acknowledge this reality.

Beliefs, practices, and policies, which directly or indirectly have racial implications and impacts, abound in our sporting past and have been eradicated slowly, unevenly, and only minimally. One of the principal obstacles to desirable change is the reluctance of the white athletic establishment to say straightforwardly, "We have a race challenge here, and we are prepared to work on it." Instead, we see the walls of denial. There is a deep misunderstanding of the power and institutionalized privilege vested in a white-dominant group. Precisely because one is a member of a dominant group, there is little awareness of group membership. "White people don't have to see themselves as white, we have the luxury of seeing ourselves as individuals. People who are oppressed by the system can never forget who they are" (Katz, 1978, p. a). To be exercising the privilege of whiteness is not necessarily to be hating blacks but "simply" assuming that white is the norm. For example, nobody in the NCAA leadership thought it strange that the early work on the (then) "Proposition 48" regulations was conducted by a commission of college presidents who were all white although the regulations themselves affected blacks. The policies and practices of society and its components need not be malicious to be racist.

We really need to be clear about the distinction between two important words: prejudice and racism. Jones (1972) subsumed the work of Allport and others to develop helpful definitions of these concepts: "Prejudice is the prior negative judgment of the members of a race, or religion, or the occupants of any other significant social role, held in disregard of facts that contradict it."(p. 171) "Racism is the transformation of race prejudice through the exercise of *power* against a racial group defined as inferior, by individuals and institutions with the intentional or unintentional support of the entire culture." (p. 172)

Prejudices are attitudes or expectations that members of one group hold about another. On an athletic team where racial conflict or alienation is prominent, the African-American and white group members may each reflect highly prejudicial expectations. By definition, however, the African-American group members are not *racist*. They cannot be. They do not have the institutionalized power to control or inflict damage on the white team members. For example, if some kind of grievance is brought by a black athlete against a white, as the grievance works its way through the system--NCAA, NAIA, or the college itself—the black athlete will find her- or himself in an ever "whiter" group as the proceedings go on. Whether in proceedings that are legal, political, scientific, medical, or economic, the African-American is practically always playing a game made up by (and of) white folks. Whites practically never face such a situation vis-a-vis African-Americans. The *NCAA News* ("Blacks underrepresented,"1989) banner-lined the underrepresentation of blacks in all athletic jobs, with only 6% of full-time athletic administrative positions held by blacks. (If numbers from the staffs at historically black colleges were removed, the figures would be worse). Smith (1991) stated that 92 to 95% of all physical education teaching, coaching, and sport leadership positions are filled by whites. The sense of being the "different/other" in the surrounding social systems brings feelings of powerlessness and alienation that white-dominant group members have not, yet now must, come to understand.

Although, understandably, we might wish to believe otherwise, our American collegiate sport system has functioned in accord with other elements of our racist society. By policy and practice, African-American colleges, teams, and individuals have been excluded, controlled, labeled, stereotyped, and ignored. In sport, we know from Yogi Berra, "It ain't over 'til it's over," and in regard to racism and sport, it ain't over!

One exclusion of the past was the absence of coverage on the printed page. Another was absence from most important fields of play. Grambling's great football teams never got the chance to test the mettle of a Notre Dame or an Army. A color line is still there, however, and we have got to see it. Exclusion today principally takes the form of economic closed doors. The great majority of African-American players are located in a few, public-school accessible sports, namely, football and basketball. Many other sports, like golf, swimming, and tennis have few performers of color because of the high costs of equipment, apparel, coaching or lessons, facility rental, medical care, travel to competitions and housing, geographic limitations, and the pressure of home responsibilities for child care or earnings to supplement the family income. Certainly for the growing black upper and middle classes, these are surmountable problems. For a larger segment of racial minority populations, however, without specific affirmative plans to change the status quo, the doors will not open. Another example of exclusion of the African-American athlete from the benefit of athletics is presented in the recently published report of the Women's Sport Foundation (1989):

> Consistent with patterns of racial and ethnic inequality elsewhere in American, it was mainly whites for whom athletic participation proved to be related to upward mobility after high school. With some exceptions, high school sport served as a reinforcer of white privilege, giving advantage to those already advantaged. (p. 4)

Our response to data like these typically has been to define the academic or employment unreadiness of African-American youth as an individual problem related to each students ability or effort. We have refused to see the complicity of our educational, social, and economic system in these results. This is cultural and institutional racism. It sits down to eat with us at every training table; it has a ringside seat on the bench and in the bleachers; it hinges on the lanyard of each coach and official. How have we acquired this unwelcome guest?

White racial identity. During the past 10 to 15 years, some exciting work has been ongoing to advance efforts to understand the roots and etiology of white racism. Particularly meaningful was Hardiman and Jackson's stage-theory approach to white racial identity (Young, 1979). By applying certain principles of the developmental psychology of Piaget, Maslow, Kohlberg, and others to the racial self-identity context, a pathway from initial socialization in a white-dominant framework to a fully actualized state was described. Each of us is able to assess our progress along this pathway.

Level one - White is superior; black is inferior. This individual is an open bigot, using whatever tactics are situationally available to isolate, avoid, and/or control African-Americans.

Level two - "I don't see color" stage. This individual, like the Level 1 person, believes that blackness is a stigma and a problem. Perceptions of what constitutes "good manners" or "patronizing tolerance" lead this individual to maintain silence on race. This individual believes that "some blacks" are able to succeed in life as they imitate white people.

Level three - Social activism beginner. This individual has experienced a conversion enabling clear perceptions of bigotry in relatives, friends, and the larger society. Inequities visited upon racial minority members become impossible to ignore. This individual may feel guilty about his or her own status as a white person and helpless about creating change. Such a conversion usually follows real-life experiences in close contact with racial minority members.

Level four - Immersion in black. This individual makes a deep commitment to self-education about African-American history and culture, attempts to surround one's self with African-American friends and colleagues, will probably feel an alienation from white culture, and may be strident in antiracist activism.

Level five - Transcendent integrationist. This individual, as Martin Luther King so eloquently described, evaluates the content of character and only notices the color of skin. This individual is fully informed about the strengths and vulnerabilities of black and white in this country and is committed to the value of diversity.

Unfortunately it is probable the case that few Level 5 people are, or ever have been, walking the earth. It can also be pointed out that most of these developed souls would probably be African-American rather than white. Level 5 orientation is fully informed about white *and* black society. It is well recognized that members of a socially subordinant group are forced to study, learn, and memorize the characteristics of the dominant group. The dominants, on the other hand, appear able to get along quite well with no first-hand knowledge of the subordinate group. Thus, whites have a longer path to Level 5, but it is not an impossible one.

As indicated earlier, our first step is to recognize and accept our white-dominant history and orientation. As Val Young (1979) put it, "No one handed our parents a form upon checking out of the maternity ward offering the option (a) yes, I would like my child to be socialized as a racist or (b) no, I prefer my child to skip that class." (p. 2)

Various studies have indicated that children from age four show negative attitudes toward black and a preference for being white (Young, 1979). Such findings were not necessarily a consequence of direct contact between the racial groups. Researchers concluded that "negative racial attitudes and feelings were a product of subtle communication from parents, peers, teachers, and television" (Young, 1979, p. 3). The white child grows up in America essentially believing that everyone is white and associating whiteness with goodness, respect, and positions of authority (Citronn, 1971).

The price we pay for white racial identity. Being aligned with institutionalized power is highly rewarding in many respects. The automatic positive connotations associated with whiteness are seductive to accept at face value and attempts to be overtly antiracist can result in feeling cast out by whites and blacks. It is the contention of this essay that the "benefits" of accepting racism in one's social milieu must be balanced against the price paid, knowingly or not, by the complicit white. Part of the price is related to external considerations of "marketability" in a multicultural, global village. Another part of the price is clarified when we examine the profound psychological damage incurred in the aftermath of lifetime dominance struggles.

The data are clear that today's minorities are tomorrow's numerical majority. Commentators are noting the way in which the 1990 census documented a dramatically changing racial mix in American society (Barringer, 1991; Vobejda, 1991). African-Americans, Hispanics, and Asians all form demographic cohorts that education, business, and political inst: utions are hurrying to court. White Americans who are unable to work, play, and be comfortable with diverse groups; who are resistant to yielding to a black superior or establishing an equitable relationship with a black co-worker will simply be left behind in the twenty-first century. Duda and Allison (1990) recently have described how it will be extremely difficult to function appropriately in applied sport psychology research and intervention work without sensitivity to relevant racial/ethnic differences in life experiences, perceptions, and needs.

These authors make their point even more powerfully when they assert that "restricting the study of the psychological aspects of sport and exercise to predominantly one group (mainstream) is in conflict with the nature of scientific inquiry" (p. 129). In truth, to ignore the research and educational situation of the racially diverse is not simply to pass over a peripheral issue in sport and athletics. It is a violation of core tenets of the scientific and educational process.

Increasingly, departmental curricula will not be judged acceptable by external reviewers without diversity issues being fully addressed. Even now our various professional certifications are beginning to include competencies in working with diverse groups. Each of us, trained before such requirements were in place, must view this as an area where in-service training and upgrading experiences are necessary. An old spiritual has a refrain about "the freedom train leavin'; better get on board." Surely it will be unaware whites left at the station this time if we do not bestir ourselves from complacency. Of even greater concern is the profound personal damage exacted when lengthy training and socialization in the fear and ignorance of racism create an insidious cruelty in the hearts of many white people. Media provide account of the reasons why we cannot simply discount white "racial problem":

American's racial and ethnic make-up is diversifying, and so is hatred in this country. A good deal of what is going on is genuine culture conflict, which then calls out the sort of underlying prejudice and racism that exists in society as a whole (Morganthau, 1992, p.30).

Hallie (1969) conducted an extensive study of cruelty as viewed in the medieval and modern worlds. In his section on slavery in the United States, he comments on the strange manner in which the practice of slavery led to a "savage, ignoble hatred of the Negro" (p. 106). He points out that not all slavery took the same form. In Spain, for example, slaves could marry in the church and remain together as a family, testify in court concerning cruelty by the master, and buy freedom upon earning a fixed sum. None of these options were allowed in America. We are heirs to a past with a particularly violent form of cruelty.

This scholarly analysis of cruelty reveals that it is not always practiced by a sadistic person, nor is it always in the form of dramatic torture. Hallie describes vividly how cruelty can be institutionalized in a faceless way and, in fact, be unintended. "A victimizer need not want to hurt a victim—he needs only to want something which requires him to hurt the victim" (p. 13). Particularly Hallie defines cruelty as holding a person prisoner; cruelty is controlling a person without allowing the freedom of humane existence.

Thus we are able to see the cruelty of the treatment of African-Americans in the sport system of today. To stack players is to control them, to restrict them from the opportunity to fill a position their talents might have earned. To employ hiring criteria that keep racial minority people from getting a selection also is a cruel act. The speed of enactment of the "Prop. 48-style" academic requirements, with so little examination of the ramifications for athletes, is a further recent example of institutional cruelty. This latter example appears to be a textbook case of "blaming the victim." As Young (1979) states, "The logical outcome of analyzing social problems in terms of the deficiencies of the victim is the development of programs aimed at correcting those deficiencies. The formula for action becomes extraordinarily simple: change the victim." (p. 15)

Despite differing vantage points and differing analysis techniques, Young and Hallie come to similar conclusions. The devastating aspect of institutionalized cruelty, with regard to the victimizers, is that ultimately it "veils our precious disgust with the destruction of human life" (Hallie, 1969, p. 103) and decent, ordinary people (even sometimes the victims) go along with these systematic abuses. We can see this loss of "our precious disgust" today in the white flight from the cities and the lack of involvement most professionals exhibit with the terrible conditions physical educators and coaches face in many urban school systems.

Oh yes, we may think these various situations are "a shame," but what are we specifically doing, individually or in our associations, to make things different? Tolerating cruelty to others, like performing cruel acts, ultimately dehumanizes the victimizer, and one's soul and heart are diminished beyond redeeming. This does not have to happen. There are examples before us of affirmative steps, small and large, that can be taken. As white professionals we need to commit ourselves to continual involvement for a portion of our working hours, in antiracist activity. We do this, not so much on behalf of African-American people, but on behalf of ourselves. "The opposite of cruelty is not kindness; it is freedom" (Hallie, 1969, p. 159).

Taking steps to enhance our multiracial future. There are three types of steps to be described here. Some of the proposed steps are large, and some are small. Many are related, not mutually exclusive of one another, and could be approached in clusters. In my own experience, however, it has proved valuable not to take on too much antiracist activity at one time. It has seemed most productive to make efforts a "tithe of time," which never stops yet never demands so much that one burns out. Efforts will be described that are *personal, research oriented*, and *programmatic*. These are samples of types of steps that can be taken. Many other examples abound, and it is too bad that credit cannot be extended to all.

Personal Efforts
The first step for the antiracist white person is the pursuit of an education in African-American studies. Most institutions, even night schools or continuing education classes, have at least one class (perhaps many more) that would provide a deeper awareness of African-American culture.

Some people reach out to racial minority acquaintances in the hope that "some of my best friends" can give a "quick read" on people of color. Certainly I am indebted to many Temple University colleagues and students who have taken me as far as they could. It is not fair for us as whites to place our whole burden of ignorance on our black friends. It is up to us to attend lectures, read books, go to conferences, take classes, and do volunteer projects in order to increase racial awareness.

It has been pointed out that one need not be born in the South, nor in the urban Northeast to develop racist attitudes. These can be learned in Wyoming, Minnesota, or any white suburb. Thus racism is particularly a white creation and a white problem to be solved. The term "white on white" racial awareness training has been coined (University of Massachusetts School of Education, I believe) to designate the focus for white efforts at self-education, social consciousness-raising, and commitment to life change with regard to racism.

Once educators learn something, they usually become invested in teaching it. As these self-education projects proceed, they may soon want to offer units or entire classes on these topics. "African-American in Sport" units or classes can multiply information available, and school projects focusing on the local community can unearth remarkable local figures who have never been recognized for their sport accomplishments.

More difficult, more volatile, will be efforts to present experiential classes or units focusing on racial dynamics, in school physical education classes and on sport teams. Such classes are very valuable, but specialized training in the conduct and handling of this type of psychological education is necessary for some (if not all) of the staff. It seems likely that only by proceeding through intellectual matters into the areas of one's emotions and past personal history will emerge the identity we might designate as the *Color Affirming White*, the CAWs with a cause! This is a white individual who is committed to building an equitable, racially diverse network of relationships. We need CAWs in physical education and athletics.

Research Efforts

For those of us whose careers entail scholarly work to advance the body of knowledge of sport and exercise science, a "tithe of time" devoted to race-related inquiry would be helpful. Several authors (Duda & Allison, 1990; Lapchick, 1984; Women's Sports Foundation, 1989) have commented on the paucity of such efforts in the past.

It probably needs to be pointed out that comparing subjects from different race groups on an infinite variety of dependent variables is but the simplest form of any race-related study. That is the predominant form of race-related research in our field to date. These are many other types of investigations that might valuably be undertaken.

Content analyses. A number of studies could investigate differential descriptors utilized in print-based assessments of athletes, coaches, and administrators of different races. Content analyses of visual materials could also be conducted. Scientific work on subjects from different racial groups could also be content-analyzed regarding types of variables utilized, complexity of approach, or degree of funding available.

Demographic assessment. During the 1970s and early 1980s, studies (Alexander, 1978; Barclay, 1979) assessed the percentages of racial minority collegiate student-athletes, coaches, and athletic department personnel. Edwards (1983) and Lapchick (1984) have reported similar types of data for males. This effort needs to be maintained continually at national, regional, and local levels for all athletes and personnel. This is our clearest and most direct way to gauge the effectiveness of our efforts (a) to diversify the types of sports experiences of racial minority people, and (b) to diversify the racial makeup of sports leadership.

Qualitative/Descriptive work. The efforts of racial minority people to achieve, to excel, to overcome have created a cohort of unforgettable people and stories that essentially has gone unrecognized. No questionnaire or inventory could capture the essence and the depth of these stories. Masses of undergraduate and graduate students could be sent out into the field to collect interviews and/or case studies of local, regional, and national racial minority figures in every sport. Every day that goes by without such major, systematic efforts means irreparable losses as death erases the story of people whose lives have never made the printed record book.

Experimental studies. A content area of exercise and sport studies might be formulated as "Race/sport relations." This content area would focus on a historically constructed pattern of power relations between the races. Researchers in this specialization would attempt to study the interactive effects of racial identity (including white racial identity) and all manner of sport-related variables. For example, we could research the possibility that a program to enhance racial identity would affect on the cohesion of a racially diverse sport team. Studies of the interactive effects of sport and racial identity seem important, through unpursued, in our multiracial society.

Outcome research. Lastly, as we begin to design and implement programs aimed at enhancing racial understanding, equality, and identity, it will be important to monitor the effectiveness of such programs and constantly improve them. Ongoing outcome research is necessary to accomplish the goals of such efforts. Consistent funding for such research must come from the institutions of sport at the professional, elite amateur, collegiate, secondary, and youth sport levels.

The research efforts described here could be conducted by qualified scholars whatever their racial background. It seems, however, highly desirable (perhaps necessary initially) for white scholars to team with racial minority students and/or colleagues in the conduct of such studies. It has been my experience that, without such collaboration, unrecognized racist assumptions are built into instruments, measurement procedures, and interpretations.

Programmatic Efforts

The type of antiracist effort that probably makes the greatest impact is one in which a *program* is created, supported within an ongoing organizational base, and continued into the future beyond the energies of those who initially instigated it. The institutionalized form of racism in our society will only be fully eradicated when we have installed enough *anti*racist institutionalized programs to neutralize the historical toxicity of ordinary social life.

Three sample programs can be described that exemplify the point. The NCAA, for example, has a funded program for racial minority graduate students in sports administration. A pool of "qualified candidates" for many new sport administration positions is being created. Additionally, a vita bank for female and racial minority candidates has been created and is available for use as positions open up. Unfortunately, this bank has been the source for very few "winning" job candidates. This is expectable as managers tend to use their "old sources" for position candidates rather than consult an unfamiliar computer list. Eventually this bank can work for minority candidates, and we need to encourage people to enter the bank while not sitting back to let that source get them a job.

The USOC, under the leadership of Harvey Schiller, has also instituted an important racial minority leadership recruitment and training program. Four 1-year positions were created by Schiller. The racial minority person who is selected for the position serves on rotation in three to four areas of USOC staff responsibility, so each receives excellent training in Olympic Committee management. There is a commitment from the USOC actually to place this individual in a continuing position, within the Olympic movement, before the year's tenure is completed.

A third, quite different, program is a low-income-focused swim program that has been running at Temple University for many years. The Tiger-Sharks were created by Malachi Cunningham and aided by Charles Lumkin, a Temple University faculty member who had been a collegiate All-American in swimming. Both knew that few elite swimmers were African-American and that the problem was opportunity and little else. Their program was specifically designed to attract and hold inner-city low-income youth. The products of this program are now reaching Olympic levels, and there is yet another delicious irony for the leadership to savor. The success and accessibility of the program has led to an avalanche of requests from suburban parents to allow their children to join the Tiger-Sharks. The Sharks have an affirmative action program that allows a few suburban youths each year to join, without overwhelming in numbers those for whom the program was created (C. Lumkin, personal communication, October, 1991).

The last "program" to be discussed is a sequential effort demonstrating one solution to the pressing challenge of "holding" at-risk youth in school and providing other life-enhancing activities at transition points where these young people might otherwise be lost. This effort begins, from a chronological standpoint, with the National Youth Sport Program (NYSP), a 20- year-old NCAA-funded summer activity for 10- to 16- year-olds held at Temple University, and ends with the "T/D (Talented and Diverse) Program," an admission-and-retention activity aimed at racial minority students in physical education at Temple University. Between these two are three other programs aimed at middle and high school students.

In describing these action programs in sequence, it must be made explicit that they were not designed at one time in some brilliant master stroke (would that were true). Rather, each was put together by dedicated people for differing and important reasons, and only recently has the possible sequential power been recognized. The efficacy of these program efforts is supported by formal outcome research, buy by only the testimony of the participants and those volunteers who continue to find the time to contribute and to attempt to find the financial support that would make so much more possible.

The NYSP is funded by the NCAA and the Athletic Department at Temple. It has an almost entirely African-American staff, and many of the leaders are former "campers" who have moved on to successful professional lives. The total program is much more than sport instruction. It features nutrition education, sex and drug education, self-concept and esteem enhancement, as well as personalized instruction and guidance. With its tradition of esteemed standing in the black community surrounding Temple, it has become a "backbone" to which other affirmative efforts are attached.

A separate, but related, effort has been the creation of a new program at Ben Franklin High School located within a mile of Temple. With the leadership and driving energy of Dr. Cassandra Jones, an Academy for Fitness, Health Promotion, and Sport Education (hereinafter the Academy) was instituted in 1989. This became the latest entry in a town-gown initiative in the city entitled Philadelphia High Schools Academies, Inc. The Academy is an enriched, secondary school major that is provided to Ben Franklin and advised and supported by an advisory council of Philadelphia sport educators and outstanding business leaders in the local sport and fitness industry. A class of 25 students, drawn from across the city and rigorously screened by Dr. Jones, is added each year. The results will be graduating seniors who are prize candidates for admission to health, physical education, and/or sport management programs across the country. The first graduates should come forward in 1993.

Associated with the development of the Academy, the Physical Education Department at Temple has approved a T/D program aimed at recruitment and retention of candidates who offer nontraditional proof of their potential as students in the programs of the Department. Aware of the fact that many racial minority students have outstanding grades and scores on standardized tests and, thus, are heavily recruited by virtually all institutions, we were also interested in another type of student.

Many of us have observed that some students, who do not show potential through traditional prediction schemes, have been among our most successful graduates. We determined to hold a certain number of positions in our freshman and transfer classes for students who proceed through a rigorous screening with high credentials that may not be consistent with the individual's test scores. The T/D students will receive a variety of enriched support services, when necessary, as they proceed through the academic system. The standards of performance will not be altered for the T/D students, however, study guides and emotional support will be more prominent. Talented and Diverse entry will be at both the undergraduate and graduate levels and will not be limited only to racial minorities.

In addition to the NYSP, the Academy, and the T/D program is what has been called the "Summer Bridge Program." In Summer Bridge, selected students in the Academy are given the opportunity to study at Temple University during the summer as well as be employed as counselors for the NYSP program. The Academy students take classes weekly with university professors from the Physical Education Department and work as 'older', experienced peers in the NYSP, which has campers 8 to 14 years old. Financial support comes from the students themselves, the NYSP, the Academy, and Temple departmental budget lines.

A last example of a program for at-risk youth that builds on NYSP is the "Sports Unlimited Program" for girls at Wanamaker Junior High School, also near the Temple campus. Through the authors' involvement with the original "Sports Unlimited," a national project of Girls' Clubs of America, and initiatives of the Girls' Coalition (a volunteer, community-based advocacy group in Philadelphia), a program was created for inner-city girls who were not involved in sports and were viewed as at-risk for teen pregnancy. Permission was gained to utilize the format and some materials of the Girls' Club program, and cooperation was built with the physical education departments at Temple and Wanamaker School in the school district of Philadelphia. A program featuring a kaleidoscope of sport experiences, a group selection of a sport to emphasize, and a six-week immersion in that sport has been offered for two years. The design of the program leads the girls to enter the NYSP program during the summer with a view that the intensity of that experience will support the maintenance of an active life-style for girls who are identified by their teachers as uninvolved in such activities.

The full impact of these various programs is difficult to gauge because all except the NYSP are quite recent. The concept seems important, however, that a child might be initially encouraged in health and exercise through NYSP; moved to programs beyond those for highly skilled athletes only in junior high; encouraged to consider careers in health, fitness, and/ or sport in high school; and admitted, retained, and supported at a college of choice nearby. It seems that we might profitably view some racial minority youth as needing such affirmative efforts to hold and attract them in school and sport systems that may seem foreign and less exciting than street life.

The antiracist steps described in this last section must be undertaken with the recognition that progress may be slow and that one may well receive little or no recognition for one's efforts. We do these things for our own satisfaction and education, not for the applause or approval of black or white colleagues and friends. We *can* make a difference, and the firming of the resolve to make a difference in racial matters is a very important step on the path to personal empowerment.

Summary

This essay begins with a description of racism as it has expressed itself in American athletics. The focus is on racism as a white creation, a white problem and on the negative effects of racism on white racial identity.

It is recommended that each white person make a commitment to a regular "tithe of time and service" in order to become a more "color-affirming" person. The steps a person might take include personal educative efforts, conduct of research, presentation of workshops or classes, and support of programmatic experiences in schools and communities.

References

Alexander, A. (1978). *Status of minority women in the AIAW*. Unpublished master's thesis. Philadelphia: Temple University.

Arendt, H. (1963). *Eichmann in Jerusalem: A report on the banality of evil.* New York: Viking Press.

Asante, M. (1980). *Afrocentricity: The theory of social change.* Buffalo, NY: Amulefi.

Barclay, V.M. (1979). *Status of black women in sports among selected institutions of higher education.* Unpublished master's thesis. Iowa City, IA: University of Iowa.

Barringer, F. (1991, March 11). Census shows profound change in racial makeup of nation; shift toward minorities since 1980 is sharpest for the 20th century. *New York Times, 140,* p. A1(N), A1(L).

Blacks underrepresented in all athletics jobs, Survey shows. (1989, October 10). *NCAA News, 25* (35), 1.

Brittan, A., & Maynard, M. (1984). *Sexism, racism, and oppression.* Oxford, UK: Blackwell.

Carmichael, S., & Hamilton, C. (1967). *Black power: The politics of liberation in America.* New York: Vintage Books.

Case, B., Greer, H., & Brown, J. (1987). Academic clustering in athletics: Myth or reality? *Arena Review, 11*(2), 48-56.

Cash, W. (1941). *The mind of the South.* New York: A.A. Knopf.

Citronn, A. (1971). *The rightness of whiteness.* Detroit: PACT.

Cleaver, E. (1968). *Soul on ice.* New York: Dell.

Cogdell, R., & Wilson, S. (1980). *Black communication in white society.* Saratoga, CA: Century Twenty-One.

Douglass, F. (1962). *Life and times of Frederick Douglass: Written by himself.* New York: Collier Books.

Dubois, W. (1965, Original 1903). Souls of black folk. In J. Franklin (Ed.), *Classics.* New York: Avon.

Duda, J., & Allison, M. (1990). Cross cultural analysis in exercise and sport psychology. *Journal of Sport & Exercise Psychology, 12,* 114-131.

Edwards, H. (1983, August). Educating black athletes. *The Atlantic Monthly,* pp. 31-38.

Freire, P. (1970). *Pedagogy of the oppressed.* New York: Seabury Press.

Fromkin, H., & Sherwood, J. (1976). *Intergroup and minority relations: An experiential handbook.* LaJolla, CA: University Associates.

Grier, N., & Cobbs, P. (1968). *Black rage.* New York: Bantam.

Gurin, P., & Epps, E. (1975). *Black consciousness, identity, and achievement: a study of students in historically black colleges.* New York: Wiley.

Hallie, P. (1969). *The paradox of cruelty.* Middletown, CT: Wesleyan University Press.

Jones, L. (1972). *Black psychology.* New York: Harper & Row.

Katz, J. (1978). *White awareness: Handbook of anti-racism training.* Norman: University of Oklahoma Press.

Koch, J., & Vanderhill, C. (1988). Is there discrimination in the "blackman's game"? *Social Science Quarterly, 69,* 83-94.

Lapchick, R. (1984). *Broken promises.* New York: St. Martin's Press.

Leonard, W., Pine, J., & Rice, C. (1988). Performance characteristics of white, black, and Hispanic major league baseball players: 1955-1984. *Journal of Sport and Social Issues, 12,* 31-43.

Logan, R. (1957). *The Negro in the United States: A brief history.* New Jersey: D. Van Nostrand.

Matthew, J. (1988, June 1). Mentor program brings student, faculty, together. *Black Issues in Higher Education,* pp. 11-16.

Morganthau, T. (1992, May). Rethinking race and crime in America: National affairs. *Newsweek.* New York: Newsweek, CXIX: 20, p. 28-30.

Myrdal, G. (1944). *An American dilemma: The Negro problem and modern democracy.* New York: Harper & Brothers.

Poussaint, A., & Comer, J. (1974). *Black child care: How to bring up a healthy black child in America: A guide to emotional and psychological development.* New York: Simon and Schuster.

Sarbin, T. (1969). The culture of poverty, social identity, and cognitive outcomes. In V.L. Allen (Ed.), *Psychological factors in poverty.* Chicago: Markham.

Smith, Y. (1991, March). Issues and strategies for working with multi-cultural athletes. *Journal of Physical Education, Recreation, and Dance, 62,* 39-44.

Vobejda, B. (1991, June 12). Asians, Hispanics giving nation more diversity. (Census Report). *The Washington Post,* Vol. 114, p. A3.

Wilcox, R. (1971). *The psychological consequences of being a black American: A source book of research by black psychologists.* New York: Wiley.

Women's Sport Foundation. (1989). *The Women's Sport Foundation report: Minorities in sport.* New York: Author.

Young, V. (1979). *Towards an increased understanding of whiteness in relation to white racism.* Unpublished paper, University of Massachusetts, Department of Psychological Education, Amherst.

Essay 10

Racism in College Sports: Prospects for the Year 2000

D. Stanley Eitzen

Abstract: This essay summarizes where we are in race relations as a society and in big-time college athletics; where we are headed in the near future; and what changes should be instituted to improve race relations in college sport. Examined first are the two contexts in which male African-American athletes participate—the interracial climates of U. S. society and of big-time college sports. Second, this essay examines the trends occurring in society, in universities, and in college sports, in order to assess the near future for African-American athletes. The final section asks and answers: What ought to be done to accomplish social justice for racial minorities in big-time college sports?

Introduction

The United States has never lived up to its promise of social justice for all. The essays in this volume show vividly that social justice for African-Americans has fallen short, way short, in the college sports world. This is especially ironic because (a) sport is one arena where achievement, not ascribed status, should be the fundamental criterion for participation and reward; and (b) colleges and universities claim to hold progressive ideals, leading by example and by persuasive argument, one would hope, to accomplish a climate of positive race relations in higher education and in society.

The Contemporary Context for African-Americans in Big-Time College Sports

The Societal Context

The evidence is clear and consistent that African-Americans are disadvantaged in the United States (information for this section is taken from Rainie, 1991; Eitzen & Baca Zinn, 1991, pp. 286-296). A few examples make this point:

--The median wealth for African-American families is one tenth that of white families.

--The unemployment rate for African-Americans is twice that for whites.

--Overall, African-Americans earn an average of just 59 cents for every dollar earned by whites. This is explained in part by the lower educational level of African-Americans, but when controlling for education, whites still make more. For example, well-educated young African-Americans earn only about 85% of what their white counterparts earn.

--African-Americans experience discrimination in jobs (getting them, keeping them, and advancing within them).

--Thirty percent of African-Americans live in racial isolation in segregated neighborhoods. Housing is where researchers find the most persistent open discrimination.

--About one-third of African-Americans attend public schools that are "intensely segregated," that is, 90% or more black.

--About one-third of African-Americans live below the government's official poverty line. From two to three million poor African-Americans are locked in an underclass of extreme deprivation.

Although some African-Americans are economically successful, many are not. The accrued disadvantages stemming from discrimination lead to poorer life chances for most. For example:

--Whites live about ten years longer than do African-Americans; black babies are nearly twice as likely as white babies to die within the first year; 22% of the African-American population is without health insurance compared to 14% of the white population.

--One out of four black men between ages 20 and 29 is under the jurisdiction of the criminal justice system (in prison, on parole, or on probation), which is higher than the proportion of African-American men this age in college.

--Sixty-one percent of African-American children are born out of wedlock (up from 23.6% in 1965). This is a consequence, according to William J. Wilson (1987), of wage discrimination and joblessness. That is, black fathers who are employed are more likely to marry than are those who are unemployed. Similarly, men with higher incomes are more likely to be married than are men with lower incomes.

--Urban, poor, African-American neighborhoods are often saturated with crime, drugs, and dysfunctional schools.

The societal context is characterized by growing racial polarization. Race relations are growing hotter rather than cooler. Racially motivated attacks on individuals and organizations have increased in the past decade. The membership of the Ku Klux Klan and other white supremacist groups is on the rise. Racial tensions are often caused by deteriorating economic conditions--lack of jobs, housing, and other resources--that lead to minority scapegoating on the part of whites. They are also fueled by the new patterns of immigration that are changing the racial composition of society.

Bigotry is not confined to white working-class or poor settings. Racist acts are becoming widespread on college campuses (Williams, 1992). Instances at MIT; University of Michigan; University of California-Berkeley; and on other campuses reveal an extensive problem of intolerance in settings where tolerance is essential to the pursuit of knowledge.

Contemporary racial division has been exacerbated by reactionary government policies. Conservative economic strategies during the Reagan and Bush years accelerated the economic decline of racial minorities. These strategies involved severe cutbacks in social programs as well as the appointment of judges to the federal courts and the Supreme Court who favored the dismantling of civil rights legislation, especially affirmative action and other protections against discrimination for minorities.

Big-Time College Sport

Many economically, socially, and educationally disadvantaged African-American males are recruited from this environment to play football and basketball in big-time university athletic programs. These programs are big-business operations (the following is taken from Eitzen & Sage, in press, ch. 6). Some have budgets exceeding $20 million (the average for an athletic program in the 106 football schools in Division IA is $12.5 million). In 1990 the schools in the bowl games divided $57 million. The annual incomes for some of the coaches (from salaries, bonuses, perks, endorsements, shoe contracts, and television and radio programs) approach $1 million. The NCAA's 1990-91 budget was $160.6 million. CBS agreed to pay the NCAA $1 billion over seven years ($143 million annually) for the television rights to the NCAA men's basketball tournament. Syracuse has a basketball arena that seats 50,000, and the University of Michigan's football stadium seats 105,000, which it sells out. The University of Florida rents skyboxes at its football games for $30,000 a year, with a minimum five-year lease. Each year, supporters of university athletic programs donate about $400 million.

These examples show that big-time college sport is a large-scale commercial entertainment enterprise. The success of programs at individual schools (and of coaches) depends on winning, interesting the media, and attracting spectators. This requires getting the best athletes and extracting the most from them. In many cases, this search for talent has led to abuses, such as illegal recruiting practices, alteration of transcripts, physical and psychological abuse of athletes, and exploitation of athletes (for a summary, see Sperber, 1990). William F. Reed (1990) of *Sports Illustrated* has characterized college basketball (and, the description fits football as well), in these harsh, but accurate, terms:

> Every fan knows that underneath its shiny veneer of color, fun and excitement, college basketball is a sewer full of rats. Lift the manhole cover on the street of gold, and the odor will knock you down. Look at this season [1990]: The programs at North Carolina State, Florida, Illinois, Missouri, and Nevada-Las Vegas--to cite only the most prominent examples--are up to their backboards in scandal.

> The misdeeds allegedly committed by college basketball programs today are the same stuff that has plagued the game for decades--buying players, cheating in academics, shaving points, etc. And the NCAA is powerless to stop it. Make a statement by coming down hard on a Kentucky or a Maryland, and what happens? Nothing, really. The filth merely oozes from another crack. (p.66)

These programs want winners, and if the past serves as a guide, we have not cared how they won. As John Underwood (1981) has characterized the situation:

> We've told them that it doesn't matter how clean they keep their programs. It doesn't matter what percentage of their athletes graduate or take a useful place in society. It doesn't even matter how well the coaches teach their sports. All that matters are the flashing scoreboard lights. (p.81)

Young men are recruited into this setting. Some athletes are recruited even though their high school records and test scores show they have little hope of educational success in college. At Tulane University, for example, in 1985 entering freshmen had average SAT scores of 1132, whereas, the scores for athletes in football and men's basketball averaged 648 (Select Committee, 1986, p. 5), which was 52 points *below* the requirement of 700 later instituted by the NCAA in Proposition 48.

In the words of syndicated columnist George Will (1986):

The worst scandal does not involve cash or convertibles. It involves slipping academically unqualified young men in the back doors of academic institutions, insulating them from academic expectations, wringing them dry of their athletic-commercial useful-ness, then slinging them out the back door even less suited to society than they were when they entered. They are less suited because they spent four years acquiring the idea that they are exempt from normal standards. (p. 84)

Some athletes, perhaps, are not in college for an education, viewing college, rather, only as a necessary avenue to the professional sport level (an unrealistic goal to all but very few). Those who want an education find that they have signed a contract that makes them an employee (not in the eyes of the NCAA, but an employee nonetheless), and the demands of sport come first. Achieving an education is incidental to the overriding objective of big-time sports (there are exceptions such as Notre Dame and Duke, but as exceptions they prove the rule). Since a primary concern of some coaches is the eligibility of their athletes, rather than the education of their athletes, the athletes are enrolled in phantom courses (correspon-dence or residence courses that give credit for no work or attendance) or in easy courses with professors sympathetic to the athletic department.

The research by Peter and Patricia Adler (1985; 1991) shows how the athletic experience actually tends to extinguish educational goals of the athletes. Adler and Adler found that most athletes entered the university feeling idealistic about their impending academic performance; that is, they were optimistic about graduating, and they considered ambitious majors. This idealism lasted until about the end of the first year when it was replaced by disappointment and a growing cynicism as the athletes realized how difficult keeping up with their schoolwork would be. The athletic role came to dominate all facets of their existence. Coaches made huge demands on the time and commitment of their athletes. The athletes received greater positive reinforcement from their athletic performance than from their academic performance. They were isolated increasingly from the student body. They were segregated in an athletic dormitory. They were isolated culturally by their racial and socioeconomic differences from the rest of the students. They were even isolated from other students by their physical size, which some found intimidating. They interacted primarily with other athletes, and these peers tended to demean academics. In their first year they were given courses with sympathetic professors, but this changed as athletes moved through the university curriculum. The academic expectations escalated, and the athletes were unprepared. The resulting academic failure or, at best, mediocre academic performance led to embarrassment and despair. The typical response, according to the Adlers, was role distancing: "To be safe, it was better not to try than to try and not succeed" (1985, p. 247). This attitude, and the resulting behaviors, were reinforced by the peer subculture.

The noneducation and miseducation of college athletes is especially acute for African-Americans. Every study that has compared black athletes to their white counterparts has found black athletes less prepared for college and more likely to fulfill this prophecy in college: African-American athletes tend to enter college as marginal students and to leave the same way. Harry Edwards (1984) has argued that the black "dumb jock" is a social creation: " 'Dumb jocks' are not born; they are systematically created" (p. 8).

This social construction results from several factors. First, black student-athletes must contend with two negative labels: the dumb athlete caricature and the dumb black stereotype. This double negative tends to result in a self-fulfilling prophecy as teachers, fellow students, and the athletes themselves assume low academic performance. Moreover, many African-Americans are ill-prepared for college because of their socioeconomic background, inadequate schools, and the special treatment often given athletic stars in junior high school and high school. This special treatment continues in college with professors who inflate grades, surrogate test takers, and coaches who intercede for student-athletes with the police when necessary. Thus, there is "little wonder that so many black scholarship student-athletes manage to go through four years of college enrollment virtually unscathed by education" (Edwards, 1984, p. 9).

African-Americans (athletes or not) on mostly white campuses typically constitute only four or five percent of the student body. Thus, they are frequently alienated by the actual or perceived racism they experience and by their social isolation.

A major unintended consequence of this situation in which black athletes find themselves is that their individual adaptations--denigrating education, opting for easy courses and majors, not making progress toward a degree, emphasizing the athlete role, and eventually dropping out of education without a degree--reinforce the very racial stereotypes an integrated education is meant to negate. Thus, unwittingly, the universities with big-time programs that recruit marginal students and do not educate them offer "proof" for the argument that African-Americans are genetically inferior to whites in intellectual potential.

In sum, African-Americans are disadvantaged in the United States. To use a sports metaphor, for them the playing field is not level: To succeed, they must advance *uphill*. For a few African-American males, a way to advance is through athletic accomplishment, which will, at a minimum, provide a college education. The college scholarship, however, is no guarantee of a college education. Only about 20% of African-American males who play in big-time college programs graduate. Some of these young men are responsible for not graduating. They may have sought the easy way that did not lead to graduation. However, many of the 80% of African-American athletes who do not graduate have been victims. They have been exploited by universities that used their athletic skills for economic gain but did not help to develop the intellectual skills of these students in their employ.

Anticipating the Year 2000

Societal Trends Affecting Race Relations in the 1990s
There are three major trends that will shape race relations in the near future. The first is the dramatic change in the racial composition of the United States. From 1980 to 1990 while the white population grew by 6%, the number of African-Americans grew by 13.2%, Hispanics by 53%, and Asians by 107.8% (the proportions for the racial minorities are actually understated because approximately 5 million people--mostly poor and racial minorities--were missed in the 1990 Census) (Barringer, 1991). From 1990 to 2000 the racial composition of the United States will become more racially diverse--from 20% nonwhite in 1990 to nearly one-third in 2000. The growing racial minority presence will add tensions in society. The growth will occur mostly in urban areas, straining already exhausted budgets. The urban, minority underclass will continue to grow. In cities and regions experiencing economic hard times, the presence of growing racial minorities will be a source of turmoil between whites and the

minorities and among the minorities themselves, as individuals compete for a shrinking number of jobs.

The tensions among these groups increase when there is a perception that the economy is not expanding to include oneself and one's group. This leads to the second important trend: The unequal distribution of wealth (and income) in society is becoming even more disparate. From 1977 to 1988 average incomes in 1991 dollars rose 122% after taxes for the top 1% of households (the top 20% rose by 34%) but fell 10% for the bottom fifth, and 3% for the second-poorest fifth (Rich, 1991). The gaps between both the rich and poor and the rich and the middle class are wider now than at any time since World War II (Sklar, 1991). Ironically, the resentment fostered by this situation is not aimed at the benefactors--the rich--but toward the poor who are viewed, typically, as wanting government entitlements for doing nothing. These feelings lead to combustible race relations because racial minorities are disproportionately in the poor category.

The third trend that does not augur well for race relations in the near future is the transformation of the economy. There are four interrelated forces that are fundamentally changing the economy: new technologies based on microelectronics, globalization, capital flight, and the shift from manufacturing to services (Eitzen & Baca Zinn, 1989). As a result, the nature of work is shifting, and this has had, and will continue to have, devastating effects on minority communities across the United States. The employment status of minorities has fallen (employment rates, occupational standing, and wage rates), especially in areas of industrial decline. In effect, African-Americans have fewer job opportunities, and what is available for minority skilled and semiskilled workers tends to have lower pay and fewer, if any, benefits compared to manufacturing jobs. Again, this increases racial acrimony as whites and blacks, affected by automation and competition from overseas, compete for fewer and fewer good jobs.

Trends in Universities and Athletics Affecting Race Relations

One disturbing trend is that fewer African-Americans are attending colleges and universities. This is the result of three factors: ever higher tuition rates (increasing 6 to 12% a year), combined with the lower federal contributions to scholarships (a legacy of the Reagan administration), and the relatively low economic status of African-American families. Rising tuition also squeezes middle-class families (white and black) making college more difficult for their children to obtain. The result may be student bodies composed more and more of the children of the elite, with the shrinking number of blacks on campus more isolated than ever.

There are two countervailing trends on college campuses regarding race relations. On the one hand, there appears to be a growing commitment on the part of many university administrators and boards of regents toward greater racial diversity in student bodies and faculties. Thus, there is extra effort to recruit minority students (not just athletes) and minority faculty members. At the same time, there is a backlash on the part of some within and outside the academic communities against what they consider racial favoritism (in scholarships and hiring), racial enclaves (e. g., "African-American Studies," "Asian Studies") and what they see as the erosion of Western values through the adding of multiculturalism to the curriculum. Both of these efforts have heightened and will continue to heighten, racial tensions on college campuses.

A potentially favorable trend in universities is the changing of the professorate. During the 1990s about one-third of professors (overwhelmingly white and male) will be retiring, a trend that will accelerate after 2000. These powerful individuals (senior full professors, for the most part) will be replaced by much younger and more diverse (in terms of race, gender, and world-view) assistant professors.

On the athletic side, there seems to be no pause in the quest by universities with big-time programs for success on the field and for profit from sport. When Richard Lapchick, Director of the Center for the Study of Sport in Society, was asked the cause of the illness in college athletics, he replied:

> Beyond any question in my mind, the root of the problem is money. Only thirty or forty athletic departments in the country make a profit. But the rainbow that is out there is so extraordinary... what that thirty or forty *do* make... that the others want to chase it (cited in Marchese, 1990, p. 2).

A second trend is that the NCAA has begun, tentatively, to consider efforts to reform the wrongs in college sport. Throughout its history the NCAA has been relatively powerless to control the scandals of big-time intercollegiate sport or to run sport in congruence with the goals of higher education. The fundamental reason for this was that athletic directors at the member schools cast the votes for their schools, meaning that the rules were determined by the athletic establishment rather than by the academic establishment. This began to change in 1984 when a commission of university presidents was formed by the NCAA to help in the reform and redirection of intercollegiate athletics.

The Presidents Commission had little impact on the rules of the NCAA until the 1991 convention. At that time, the major agenda items were the commission's; members of the commission lobbied actively for their proposals, and a number of presidents (about 100 more than usual) attended to cast votes for their institutions. Many observers felt that the passage of their reform package signaled a turning point. That's the good news. The bad news is that the proposals of the commission did *not* address many of the key issues. Instead, they concentrated on cost containment. Scholarships were reduced by 10% (reducing the number of athletes on scholarship by 1,500 nationwide), and coaching staffs were reduced (limiting, by the way, the number of jobs for black coaches). To their credit, rules were passed by the NCAA members, to help student-athletes: (a) All Division I schools must make counseling and tutoring services available to all recruited athletes; (b) all athletic dormitories are to be eliminated by August 1996; and (c) in-season practice time must be limited to a maximum of 4 hours a day and 20 hours a week. Although these rule changes were in the right direction, that is, in the direction of bringing the "student" back into the student-athlete role, they were mild and timid moves at best. The convention did not address the issue of freshman eligibility. It did not confront the scheduling of games at odd times for the convenience of television but at the expense of athletes' missing class time. A proposal was defeated that would have required Division I schools to graduate 50% of their scholarship athletes. A proposal to require athletes to post minimum gradepoint averages each year was also defeated. Thus, it appears that although the presidents seem to be taking more of a role in the NCAA, the resulting rule changes have been cosmetic, not really addressing the ills of big-time college sports. Clearly, the commercial nature of sport, and the problems related to this, have not been questioned by the presidents.

Reforming College Sport to Eliminate Racism

Contemporary trends in society suggest that racism will intensify in the near term. Big-time college sport will occur in that environment adding to the racism as it exploits African-American athletes for profit, often discarding them without an education. When this occurs, the stereotype that African-Americans have physical but not intellectual gifts is rein-forced. This section addresses what ought to be done by the NCAA, the schools, the coaches, and the athletes to correct this situation. I will not attempt to address how big-time sport itself should be reformed (for suggestions to reform the system see Eitzen & Sage, in press, ch. 6, and Lapchick & Slaughter, 1989, sec. 4). The discussion is limited specifically to racism and the general issues regarding exploitation and miseducation of African-American athletes in big-time programs. Although the following recommendations are made specifically for African-American athletes, they often apply to all college athletes (I am indebted to Lapchick & Slaughter, 1989, for many of these recommendations).

Problem: African-American athletes are sometimes ill-prepared for college academics.

1. Athletes should not be admitted into college unless there is evidence of their potential to graduate. In short, if the academic potential of recruits is doubtful, then they should not be recruited. If the recruits have potential, they must be provided with the academic assistance (tutors and remedial courses) to get them to their appropriate academic level quickly.
2. The demands of Proposition 48 should be strengthened. At current levels, the limits are so low that recruits can be admitted with SAT scores 300-400 points below the student average. This places them at high risk educationally.
3. Middle schools and high schools must prepare their potentially college-bound athletes for college.
4. Athletes at all educational levels, as well as their parents, and leaders from their communities must be counseled to realize that (a) a college education is the most significant step they can take for success in American society; and (b) the odds of a professional career in sport are very long and even if attained, that career will last but a few years.

Problem: African-American athletes often come from economically disadvantaged backgrounds.

5. Athletes must be provided with a monthly stipend ($300 or so) for incidentals, clothing, and entertainment. This will provide some justice by paying the athletes a portion of the money they generate for their universities. Moreover, it will permit students from poor families a chance to fit in with their more privileged classmates.
6. Athletes must be provided two trips home during each school year. Moreover, the parents of athletes should be provided with two trips to the university each year. These actions will accomplish three goals: (a)

provide the athletes with a form of financial aid that they have earned; (b) promote better ties between the athletes and their communities; and (c) promote family bonding.

Problem: African-American athletes who are admitted have low graduation rates.

7. Freshmen must be ineligible for athletic competition so that they can concentrate on the adjustment to the social and intellectual demands of college.

8. The institution must provide adequate study time, counseling, and tutoring. The object of these aids is not eligibility for sports participation but satisfactory progress toward a degree.

9. The time demands of sport on the athletes in-season and off-season must be reasonable. Thus (a) practice time must be limited; (b) the number of games in a season must be limited; and (c) the number of class days missed because of sport must be limited. The NCAA has begun to place some restrictions on excessive time demands.

10. The athlete's academic progress must be closely monitored by the school's (not just the athletic department's) academic advisors.

11. Athletes must retain their scholarships, including housing, meals, and books for up to two years, if needed, after their athletic eligibility is completed. This recognizes the necessity of at least five years for graduation in most cases. At present, many schools eliminate educational assistance to athletes who have used up their eligibility, which makes it especially difficult for the economically disadvantaged to continue.

12. Coaches should be evaluated in part by the graduation rate of their athletes. This form of institutional control of coaches will, of course, increase the efforts of coaches to recruit athletes with academic potential and for them to see that those whom they do recruit make progress towards a degree.

Problem: African-American athletes are isolated in athletic ghettos, and there is often racial segregation within them.

13. Athletic dormitories and separate eating facilities for athletes must be eliminated. (Athletic dormitories will be eliminated by NCAA action, by 1996.).

14. Athletes should be encouraged to become involved in social, organizational, and academic activities within the school context. At a minimum, this means that coaches should not impose restrictions on the nonathletic campus activities of their athletes, which is often the case.

15. Housing arrangements, meals, and road trip accommodations must be integrated. This can easily be accomplished through random assignments.

16. Positional segregation by race (stacking) must be eliminated. Racial stacking promotes racial stereotypes (e. g., whites are "naturally" more intelligent and better leaders whereas blacks are "naturally" more gifted physically). Moreover, it tends to make competition for starting positions intraracial. This is a difficult proposal to implement because the procedures are often subtle. However, at a minimum coaches should declare their acceptance of open competition for each position, and the results of this competition should be monitored by the administration.

Problem: There are not enough African-Americans in leadership positions in athletic departments.

17. African-Americans must be considered seriously for positions of athletic director and head coach. As this is written, only two Division I football schools have an African-American as athletic director. Moreover, not one of these schools has an African-American head football coach.

18. African-Americans must be considered seriously for positions of assistant athletic director, trainer, and sports information director, positions where they are rarely found.

19. Black assistant coaches must be given more responsibilities beyond the typical ones of recruiting black athletes and serving as a liaison between the black athletes and the white coaches.

Problem: Some coaches are racist and dehumanizing.

20. Players must have a mechanism by which they can report the racist and dehumanizing acts of coaches and others in the athletic department to the administration without fear of reprisal.

21. The university and athletic department administration must take strong and immediate action to eliminate discriminatory and dehumanizing practices.

Problem: Racial stereotypes are sometimes promoted unwittingly by the members of the athletic department.

22. Athletic department personnel must be educated about the subtleties of racism, including the negative use of language. In particular, the sports information director must be sensitized to the negative and sometimes subtle ways that minorities are often portrayed in press guides and press releases, and in the media.

There are three fundamental requirements if these recommendations are to be implemented. First, the NCAA must expand its recent reforms, focusing on the explicit goal of promoting educational and humane values in college athletics. All other goals, including making money, are secondary to meeting the educational needs of student-athletes. Put another way, the operating principle must be that the health and education of student-athletes are infinitely more important than television ratings, corporate sponsorships, and profits. If the NCAA does not prove capable of this, and there is reason to suspect that it is not (see Sperber, 1991), then the member universities through their presidents must form an organization that will.

Second, university presidents must make a commitment to their athletes as students. They must take responsibility for the educational and moral integrity of their institutions. They must establish mechanisms to monitor their athletic programs, devise rules to insure compliance with educational goals, and budget the necessary monies to implement them.

Finally, money must be raised by the NCAA and distributed to the schools equitably to fund the expensive items in these recommendations. This is not as difficult as it seems. Richard Lapchick has proposed an "Academic Superfund" that would tap the various profit centers in sport:

One of my suggestions was that for every player who makes it to the pros, the NBA and the NFL would donate the equivalent of a full four-year scholarship to the Superfund. The money would then be used for those players who don't make it to the pros, to continue their educations in a fifth or sixth year.

Given that 50 players a year enter the NBA and 150 the NFL, and given an average of $10,000 a year for tuition costs, the total comes to about $8 million a year. That sounds like a lot of money, but consider that the telesports are worth $1.675 billion a year.

I also proposed a one percent federal tax on ticket sales for all sporting events. Even on a $30 ticket, the tax would cost only 30 cents; yet, that 1% would raise $33 million a year, because we sell $3.3 billion in tickets.

I've also written to NCAA Executive Director Dick Schultz, suggesting that 10 percent of the increase in the NCAA's television revenues...just of the $83 million *increase*...go into the Superfund. That's another $8.3 million.

The total amount in this new Superfund would be something like $50 million a year (Lapchick, cited in Marchese, 1990, p. 4).

To conclude, despite the impediments to achieve social justice in college sport, the situation can be improved mightily. We know what's wrong. That's the easy part. We must acknowledge the problems and demand that sport be cleaned up. The NCAA has allowed social injustice to occur and is now only beginning to reform. But these efforts, so far, are weak. That organization or one like it must oversee university sport to insure that educational values prevail. The administrators at each university along with faculties, students, and the public must insist on the same. At present, these groups demand excellence on the fields and in the arenas. This type of tunnel vision is at the heart of the problem because it has led to abuses, compromises, and hypocritical behaviors that are contrary to educational goals. Most important, it has allowed athletes, most often African-American athletes, to be used by these schools for their athletic skills and then discarded without diplomas. That is not only embarrassing but also immoral. Since educational institutions exist to serve their students, it is obvious that big-time college sport must be restructured to focus on the educational outcomes of athletes. To do otherwise makes a mockery of the educational mission of universities.

Summary

African-American athletes in big-time college athletic programs are part of two contexts, both of which disadvantage them. The first context is the interracial climate of U. S. society. On every dimension related to health, housing, work, income/wealth, and education, African-Americans when compared to whites are disadvantaged. Conservative economic strategies have cut back social programs that might help reduce the problems of the disadvantaged. Moreover, racial tensions are increasing. Bigotry, even on college campuses, is real. This situation will not ease in the near term as politicians focus on the needs of the middle-class, the economy remains weak, and racial/ethnic minorities increase their proportion of the population.

African-American athletes recruited to big-time college programs are also part of a corporate/entertainment world. They are hired (for room, board, books, and tuition) to perform on the athletic fields and in the arenas to generate monies, media interest, and public relations for universities. They are recruited for their athletic talents but not necessarily for their intellectual abilities. Since African-American athletes come disproportionately from economically, socially, and educationally disadvantaged backgrounds, the situation is loaded against them. From the perspective of many coaches and athletic administrations, these young men are athletes first and only incidentally students. As a result, many of these athletes who are marginal students retain their athletic eligibility by being "taken care of" through phantom courses, "friendly" professors, surrogate test takers, and the like. This means, of course, that many African-Americans will not graduate, even though they have played for four years. In effect, they have been used by the universities.

The NCAA has begun to take tentative steps to reform the wrongs in college sport. But these weak steps are not enough. The universities through the NCAA (or other organization) need to be bold in their initiatives. As they consider reforms to eliminate racism, the following broad changes are essential: (a) Athletes admitted to universities must be prepared for college-level academics; (b) Athletes should receive fair compensation for their work, which will especially help athletes from economically disadvantaged backgrounds; (c) Athletes must be provided with whatever it takes for them to achieve educational goals; (d) Racial/ethnic minorities must be integrated into all athletic and university activities; (e) The staff of athletic departments must be integrated at all levels; and (f) Athletic departments must be monitored carefully to determine that procedures are fair and nonracist, and to ensure that educational goals have the first priority.

References

Adler, P., & Adler, P.A. (1985). From idealism to pragmatic detachment: The academic performance of college athletes. *Sociology of Education, 58,* 241-250.

Adler, P.A., & Adler, P. (1991). *Backboards and blackboards: College athletes and role engulfment.* New York: Columbia University Press.

Barringer, F. (1991, March 11). Census shows profound change in racial makeup of the nation. *New York Times,* pp. A1, A12.

Edwards, H. (1984). The black "dumb jock": An American sports tragedy." *The College Review Board, 131,* 8-11.

Eitzen, D.S., & Baca Zinn, M. (1989). *The reshaping of America; Social consequences of the changing economy.* Englewood Cliffs, NJ: Prentice-Hall.

Eitzen, D.S., & Baca Zinn, M. (1991). *In conflict and order: Understanding society* (5th ed.). Boston: Allyn and Bacon.

Eitzen, D.S., & Sage, G. H. (In press). *Sociology of North American sport* (5th ed.). Dubuque, IA: Wm. C. Brown.

Lapchick, R.E., & Slaughter, J.B. (1989). *The rules of the game: Ethics in college sport.* New York: Macmillan.

Marchese, T. (1990). After the cheers: Is higher education serving its student-athletes? An interview with Richard E. Lapchick. *AAHE Bulletin, 42,* 1-10.

Rainie, H. (1991, July 22). Black & white. *U. S. News & World Report,* pp. 18-21.

Reed, W. F. (1990, March 26). Absolutely incredible! *Sports Illustrated,* p. 66.

Rich, S. (1991). Rich got richer, poor got poorer during the 1980s. *The Washington Post,* reported in the Fort Collins *Coloradoan* (July 24), A4.

Select Committee on Intercollegiate Athletics. (1986, March). Report. Tulane University.

Sklar, H. (1991). The truly greedy III. *Zeta Magazine, 4,* p. 10-12.

Sperber, M. (1990). *College sports, inc.* New York: Henry Holt.

Sperber, M. (1991). Why the NCAA can't reform college athletics. *Academe, 77,* 13-20.

Underwood, J. (1981, February 23). A game plan for America. *Sports Illustrated,* p. 81.

Will, G. (1986, September 15). Our schools for scandal. *Newsweek,* p. 84.

Williams, M.L. (January 1, 1992). Racial and ethnic relations in American higher education. *Vital Speeches of the Day, 58,* pp. 174-177.

Wilson, W. J. (1987). *The truly disadvantaged.* Chicago: University of Chicago Press.

Epilogue

Looking Towards the 21st Century: Lessons From the Past

Dana Brooks and Ronald Althouse

In 1903, W.E.B. DuBois wrote one of the landmarks in African-American literature, *The Souls of Black Folk*. He was able to articulate two major issues facing the "Negro" community during the twentieth century: (1) the color line and (2) double consciousness. This double identity refers to the fact that American "Negroes" were longing to attain a level of self-consciousness.

Internal conflict, according to DuBois, existed between being "Negro" and being American. Today, the African-American is still challenged to maintain his or her African heritage and yet be a part of the larger American society.

Nearly a century after W.E.B. DuBois wrote his book and 40 years after *Brown v. the Board of Education of Topeka* (1954) African-Americans are still having to address the issue of color line and self-identity. George Sage recognized these continuing problems and writing in his introduction to this text said, "It is too bad that a book with such a focus is necessary because it is an account of human practices that have heaped injustice upon injustice on African-Americans" (p. 1).

It is within the context of racism and the search for self-identity among the African-American population that we would like to summarize the major concepts and arguments presented in the previous essays in this text.

The first essay provided an historical analysis of racism in college athletics. David Wiggins pointed out that sport participation and discrimination of African-American athletes from the beginning have presented a study in sharp contract, a point-counterpoint process. For example, the signing of Jackie Robinson in 1945 to play for the Dodgers was the beginning of the end for many all-black sporting organizations. Similarly, desegregation resulting from the civil rights movement reduced the impact of the black revolt and black power movement during the late 1960s. Over the past century, the dominant themes of discrimination, Social Darwinism, inferiority or superiority of African-American athletes, Proposition 48 and 42, and a concern over the graduation rate of African-American athletes surfaced.

In "African-American Predominance in Collegiate Sport," Othello Harris focuses primarily on the factors leading to the influx of African-Americans into college sport after World War II. The black militancy movement and subsequent changes in college sport participation increased the predominance of African-Americans in Division I college sport during the of 1970s and 1980s. The author focused on racist stereotypes, superspades, stacking, NCAA reform, and strategies to increase academic preparation of African-American student-athletes. Harris insists that unless significant reform takes place in the NCAA, the patterns of oppression and racism will continue into the twenty-first century.

In recommending certain college athletic reforms, the Knight Commission Report insists that intercollegiate athletics have been, and should be, a key aspect of college life. Proposing the "one-plus-three" model to project reforms in college athletics in the twenty-first century, the Commission targeted three critical areas: (a) college presidents need to take control over athletics and athletic policy; (b) academic integrity, placing a strong emphasis on increasing student-athlete graduation rates; (c) financial integrity, reducing the amount of financial support that foundations and booster clubs can provide the university. While these are pivotal issues awaiting action by the NCAA to provide legislation to enact the Commission's recommendations as noted by Anderson and South (Essay 3), nowhere in the Knight Commission Report does it address the issues of racism in college athletics.

The NCAA maintains that its regulations equalize athletic competition. Although this may be the stated purpose of these regulations, some of the NCAA rules have had a racially discriminating effect (McCormick and

Meiners, 1988). Anderson and South (Essay Three) present data supporting racial differences in collegiate recruiting, retention, and graduation rates. They provide an excellent overview of Proposition 48 consequences. Notably, data revealed that a significant portion of African-American athletes has been declared academically ineligible because they failed to meet minimum SAT or ACT scores and/or they did not achieve a grade of "C" or better in 11 designated high school courses. As a result, Proposition 48 became the focus of heated opposition from African-American civil rights leaders, coaches, and administrators.

The historically black college voiced objection to this bylaw citing that it was discriminatory and would have a negative impact on their athletic program. Many of these colleges did not have the financial base to provide support to those student athletes who did not meet Proposition 48 guidelines.

New NCAA proposed standards (Proposal No. 16) for 1996 include: raising the initial eligibility overall GPA and corresponding minimum SAT score (e.g. GPAs above 2.50 must have a minimum SAT of 700 or ACT of 17; GPAs of 2.0 must have a minimum SAT of 900 or ACT of 21). In addition, an increase from 11 to 13 core courses will be required. Members of the historically black colleges objected to this new legislation because of perceived racial bias within standardized tests. Supporters of Proposal No. 16 suggest the new standard will challenge high school student athletes to meet these new standards.

It becomes apparent that the NCAA community should have learned a very important lesson from this struggle to enforce similar bylaws. It is important that predominantly white institutions and historically black institutions begin to build bridges and work more closely together prior to submitting regulations to be voted on by the NCAA body.

In the twenty-first century, it is reasonable to expect there will be continued demand by the American public to improve the graduation rates of all college student athletes, especially minority athletes. We can expect to see stricter entrance requirements and better monitoring of the athletes' academic progress. Providing the student athletes with financial support and academic support systems will begin to address the concern that many of us have about the perceived economic and academic exploitation of our African-American athletes.

Racial imbalance in coaching and managerial positions (Essay 4) by Brooks and Althouse challenged NCAA member institutions to evaluate those factors that have contributed to the paucity of African-American male and female head coaches. The authors were able to identify the following factors leading to this condition: (a) overt discrimination by athletic directors, (b) exclusion of African-Americans from central playing positions (i.e., pitcher, catcher, quarterback) during their college careers, (c) differential available professional pathways (institutional prestige was associated with initial coaching employment), and (d) African-American coaches not having access to existing head coaching/ recruiting network structures (there are no Division I-A African-American head football coaches).

During the twentieth century, a good deal of literature in the area of racism in sport focused on the relationship between athletic playing position and racial discrimination; African-American athletes were underrepresented (stacked) in noncentral positions (e.g. wide receiver). This is important to note because a high percentage of college coaches were recruited from central positions. Positional segregation (stacking) was related to future career mobility opportunities.

Discussion turned away from these traditional arguments and began to identify and describe African-American coaching career avenues: (a) talent avenue, (b) personal attribute, (c) internal mobility, and (d) coaching mobility network. None of these avenues could totally explain the career path followed by African-American head coaches. Since 1986, there has been an increase in the number of Division I head basketball coaches. However, coaching career patterns were unique to each individual. Structural barriers and persistent discrimination patterns, old-boy network patterns, and media publicity affected coaching career patterns.

Recently, Smith and Ewing (1992) have advocated more diversity in coaching at the high school and college level. They argued that men and women minorities should be encouraged to pursue coaching careers while they are still in high school. Brooks and Althouse support this position but recognize that the number of African-American head and assistant coaches will not increase unless we are able to increase high school and college graduation rates of ethnic minorities. In the twenty-first century the African-American athlete will continue to strive for access to college. The college system treatment of the African-American athlete must be humane, and the educational skills learned must be rewarded. The changes in policies governing college athletics and access to education via sport may serve to gain a measure of equality for African-Americans. Once African-American athletes are recruited to play college athletics, measures must be taken to eliminate racism and racial isolation on campus. The NCAA member institution and specifically college presidents and athletic directors must take a proactive stance for social justice in college athletics. A climate of diversity and inclusiveness must be established and maintained for all minorities (males and females).

Robert Sellers' essay, "Black Student-Athletes: Reaping the Benefits or Recovering from the Exploitation," asked the important question, "Does participation in college athletics provide African-American athletes with the opportunity for social mobility, or does it exploit their physical skills?" Sellers argues that the quality of the African-American athlete's postathletic careers is influenced by their college experiences. Existing data were used to compare the experiences of African-Americans with those of white students. He concluded that African-American student-athletes experienced college life similar to that of white student-athletes. Notable exceptions were that (a) African-American student-athletes experienced more racial isolation than did white student-athletes and (b) the NCAA reform movement (Proposition 48 and Proposition 42) had a greater impact on the African-American student-athletes than on white athletes. According to Sellers, the NCAA is making slow progress addressing the real problems influencing the relatively poor academic performance of student-athletes, particularly of the African-American student athlete.

At the public school level, initiatives must begin to focus on and correct the discrepancies in the educational preparation between white and African-American students. Sellers advocates strengthening the public school system, especially those schools located in urban areas.

In the twenty-first century it will become critical for NCAA member institutions to make academic support systems available for all student-athletes. Establishing developmental programs (e.g., communication skills, time management) aimed at enhancing the retention and graduation rates of minorities and economically disadvantaged student-athletes should become a priority on college campuses.

Likewise, the tie between the family and the African-American student-athlete must be strengthened. The African-American family assumes an active support role in encouraging its children to develop career goals and to attend and graduate from college.

Sellers was able to summarize clearly the African-American college athlete experience when he said, "the quality of black student-athletes' lives after sports is directly influenced by the quality of their experiences in college..." (p.163).

Essay 6 by Doris Corbett and William Johnson, and Essay 7 by Tina Sloan Green reached similar conclusions: The road for the women to gain equality in sport has been long and arduous. With the passage of Title IX in 1972 there has been a dramatic increase in the number of women participating in high school and college sport. However, as early as 1974, Houzer noted a discernible decline in the participation rate of African-American females in sport. The decline in participation rates for African-American females was linked to social factors, reward structures, and lack of professional preparation for coaching positions. As identified by Corbett and Johnson, specific barriers facing African-American female athletes were limited financial support, lack of administrative support, and discrimination in team selection and hiring practices.

Breaking down these barriers is difficult, but not impossible. Relatively few research data are available on the female athlete and the development and application of specific gender-based sociological theory. Therefore, it was not surprising to note that the analysis of the role performed by the American athlete in American sport was focused primarily on the African-American male athlete.

Leonard (1988) argued that the experiences of African-American women in sport differ from those of white women. According to Leonard, African-American women have been systematically excluded from sport participation because (a) they have been disproportionately located at the lower end of the economic level and, therefore, have been unable to afford such sports as golf and tennis; (b) overt racial discrimination prevented African-American women from gaining access to the sports participated in by white women, and (c) the cultural image of femininity has been defined by white men. The essay written by Corbett and Johnson tends to support many of the statements made by Leonard. For example, Corbett and Johnson's analysis of the historical differences between African-American and white females provided a clear understanding of the perceptions that American society has about the African-American female: She is often portrayed as a tough woman and a strong matriarch.

Tina Sloan Green concludes that as we move toward the twenty-first century African-American females will find it necessary to create jobs in the black community. The purpose of these jobs is to hold clinics and camps necessary to develop the skills of African-American female coaches and administrators. This is a reasonable alternative that should provide the African-American female with the opportunity to develop network structures, and should also develop a potential recruiting pool from which to draw future coaches and administrators.

It was surprising to note that very little research was available on the African-American female, and the majority of work utilizing African-American females as subjects has been unpublished analyses. If we are going to address issues of racism and sexism in college athletics, it becomes imperative that scholars begin to conduct research in this area. Too often research in the area of racism in college athletics has meant a focus on African-American males.

The Gender and Race Intersections in College Athletics section concludes with Alison Dewar's Essay 8 on "Intergroup Race Relations: Success or failure?" Birrell (1989) was one of the first researchers to call for a more critical analysis of race relations theories and participation. Dewar's essay met this challenge and appeared to have broken new ground in race relations theory development. The essay focused on racism, sexism, and classism as forms of domination and oppression. Throughout this essay the author forced the reader to question how these forms of oppression affect race relations.

During the twentieth century, the majority of research in race relations and sport participation centered on access and participation rates of African-Americans on various sport teams. This model did provide some insights into the problem of racism in sport; however, as Dewar points out, this is not enough. Her vision for change and better racial understanding includes (a) developing and implementing affirmative action programs to ensure the recruitment and retainment of women of color, (b) requiring all individuals involved in women's sport programs, administrators, coaches, athletes, and trainers, to embark on antiracist work; and (c) rethinking power relationships and working towards developing alliances across our differences.

Currently under the NCAA structure, the programs identified by Alison Dewar do not exist. The concerns that she raises may be contested by those currently in power (white males). The implementation of these recommendations may result in a loss of power, prestige, control, and domination. If this model is to succeed in the 21st century new alliances need to be established between the various oppressed groups in American society who are willing to work toward the goal of enhanced race relations.

The last two essays (9 and 10) written by Carole Oglesby and Stanley Eitzen, project us to the year 2000 and cause us to think critically about racism and race relations in the next century.

Oglesby chose to present her discussion of racism as seen through the eyes of a white educator-professional. Similar to Alison Dewar, Carol Oglesby was a strong advocate for antiracist activity. The point was made that white individuals need to be more aware of and sensitive to the African-American culture (as well as to all other minority cultures) and its contributions to American society.

We were struck by the statement, "...racism as a white creation , a white problem ..." (p. 265). The challenge here is for the white community to reassess its own belief system and become a catalyst for changing racial attitudes and racism in general and to establish action programs to remediate racism. Several of the more noteworthy programs include the National Youth Sport Program and the T/D program aimed at the recruiting and retention of nontraditional students. According to Oglesby, white professionals must bear some of the responsibility for racism, and they must continue to be involved in antiracist activity.

Stanley Eitzen concludes by addressing the basic question, does social justice among racial minorities in big time sports exist? Unfortunately, the immediate answer to the question is "no." The African-American does experience inequality in employment, job discrimination, income level, infant mortality, crime rate, and drug usage. Many of these inequities can be attributed to recent government policy.

Eitzen identified those major societal trends that he perceives will have a significant impact on race relations in the 1990's: (a) change in racial composition of the United States, (b) the unequal distribution of wealth in our society, and (c) transformation of the economy. Together, the trends will manifest themselves and result in higher levels of racism in society and college sport. If the scenario is accurate, it will be very important for all to begin engaging in antiracist activities immediately.

Eitzen concludes his essay by identifying social injustice issues existing in college sport and by offering recommendations to correct these situations. Many of the issues or problems described by Eitzen, such as concern for academic entry skills; the high percentage of African-Americans who are economically disadvantaged; the low college graduation rates of student athletes in general; African-Americans' feeling a sense of isolation and alienation, lack of African-Americans in leadership positions, stereotyping racist attitudes on the part of coaches, players, and administrators, have been discussed throughout this text. We have been able to identify the issues that have resulted in social injustice in college athletics. The challenge now is to bring about change and social justice.

A vision for change must begin with college administrators, coaches, players, and faculty being committed to reform. It appears that we are witnessing the early stages of a process of transformation within the NCAA. It will be interesting to chart the course of these proposed social justice initiatives currently being undertaken by the NCAA. History may credit the African-American community with triggering the demand for this transformation to occur.

NCAA: Change Agent

The NCAA can and should be a significant agent to bring about reform and begin to establish policy based on equality. We were especially interested in knowing the position of the NCAA on social justice and sport. Similarly, we wanted a measure of how the NCAA was going to provide leadership to alleviate these injustices.

The NCAA did recognize the need to address racism, discrimination, sexism, and the lack of minorities in leadership positions. Richard Schultz (personal communication, October 19, 1991), executive director of the NCAA, first addressed the issue of making sure that women and ethnic minorities were gaining access to all phases of the Association. At the 1988 NCAA convention, the director's commitment to social justice led to the formation of the NCAA Council Subcommittee to Review Minority Opportunities in Intercollegiate Athletics and more recently (January, 1991) to the Minority Opportunities and Interest Committee. Schultz believes one of the main functions of this latter committee is to review with the NCAA council and other NCAA committees issues that affect minority participation in college sport. He readily concedes that minorities are underrepresented in coaching and other managerial positions. It was noted that some measure of improvement has been made in the number of minority head basketball coaches. It is interesting to note that the NCAA is establishing ties with pre-college ethnic minorities to assist them with adjusting to college participation. The NCAA's "Choices" program and the National Youth Sport Program represent two outstanding programs aimed at providing minority students access to colleges.

A Special Subcommittee to Review Minority Opportunities in Intercollegiate Athletics was established on September 24, 1987 (NCAA Council Subcommittee, 1991). The major charge of this committee was to address coaching, athletic administration, and officiating. The committee investigated these issues and made policy recommendations to address them.

From 1987 to 1990, this Subcommittee met throughout the United

States with such groups as (a) the Black Coaches Association, (b) Big Ten Conference Advising Committee, (c) NCAA Committee on Women's Athletics, and (d) National Association of Basketball Coaches. The purpose of these meetings was to establish linkages and to identify common issues and concerns.

The Subcommittee successfully implemented the NCAA Ethnic Minority Enhancement Program (establishing postgraduate scholarships, internships, and the Ethnic Minority Vita Bank), and a position to serve as primary administrator for the Enhancement Program, and conducted a survey summarizing minority participation rates in NCAA leadership positions.

The Subcommittee concluded its agenda by recommending to the NCAA that a permanent committee, the Minority Opportunities and Interest Committee, be established to further resolve the issues identified by this Subcommittee ("Minority Opportunities Committee," 1991).

The NCAA Minority Opportunities and Interest Committee (1991) moved quickly to establish long-range action goals and strategies. The elements of the five-year plan were as follows: (a) affirmative action and minority enhancement issues, (b) continued research opportunities, (c) identification of programs that may educate individuals regarding multicultural diversity, (d) promotion of levels, and (e) elicitation of support of minority enhancement from the private and public sectors ("NCAA Council," 1991).

The authors met with the NCAA Minority Opportunities and Interest Committee during one of their regularly scheduled meetings (September 23-24, 1991) in Ocean City, Maryland. The committee was asked to address the following questions: (a) What were the factors/conditions that led to the formation of this committee?; (b) What are the current and near term goals and objectives of this committee?; (c) How was membership selected for this committee?; (d) What issues are central to this committee?; and (e) Will the committee develop specific guidelines to address the issues identified by this committee?

As a result of this meeting the authors were able to gain some important insights into the structure and function of the NCAA. Likewise we gained a better understanding of the role of the NCAA in addressing the many issues presented in this text.

Members of the NCAA Minority Opportunities and Interest Committee represent faculty, coaches, and administrators. They have a wealth of experience and have demonstrated a commitment to social justice.

The Committee members were able to identify a series of issues ranging from lack of African-Americans in head coaching positions to a concern for the low graduation rates of student-athletes. These concerns were articulated in the form of current and near-term goals formulated by the Committee.

The Committee would like to set a national agenda and encourage minority participation in all NCAA-sponsored activities. Legislation and policies encouraging minority participation will be initiated by this Committee and forwarded to the NCAA voting members for approval. In addition to this function, the Committee perceives itself performing a clearinghouse function, receiving and disseminating information about job openings, discrimination complaints, graduation rates, and other social-justice-oriented information and data.

The Committee perceived itself as a major advocate to correct social injustices in college athletics. However, Committee members did voice concern that in five years this Committee might be seen as a racism committee with a narrow focus.

Addressing racism is one of the many issues that this Committee has been charged to identify and about which to offer recommended solutions. Throughout our discussion with committee members it became very apparent that they had an excellent understanding of issues facing minorities within the NCAA. Members were eminently aware of the need to establish racial awareness and diversity programs for all ethnic minority coaches and administrators.

Members on the Committee representing historically black colleges and universities made it very clear that social justice issues were also being addressed on their campuses. The enrollment at historically black colleges is escalating. Some attribute this increase to the rise of racism in America and specifically to racial attacks on African-Americans on predominantly white campuses.

Too often when investigating and reporting data on graduation rates, discrimination, hiring practices, and other social justice issues we fail to include data relative to historically black colleges and universities. These colleges and universities tend to have marginal status within the NCAA structure. It is hoped that by next century the status of these institutions will improve; the historically black colleges and universities should share in all the advantages of being members of the NCAA.

References

Birrell, S. (1989). Racial relations theories and sport: Suggestions for a more critical analysis. *Sociology of Sport Journal, 6*, 212-227.

DuBois, W.E.B., (1903). *The souls of black folk.* Greenwich, CT: Fawcett Publications, Inc.

Leonard, W. (1988). *A sociological perspective of sport* (3rd ed.). New York: MacMillan.

McCormick, R.E., & Meiners, R. (1988). Sacred cows, competition and racial discrimination. *New Perspectives, 19*(1), 47-52.

Minority opportunities committee moves ahead with long range plan.(1991, September 30). *NCAA News,* p. 2.

NCAA council subcommittee to review minority opportunities in intercollegiate athletics: Final report (1991). Opryland Hotel, Nashville, Tennessee.

Smith, Y., & Ewing, M. (1992 Winter). Diversity in coaching. *NASPE News, 32*, pp. 1, 8-9.

Subject Index